The Semiotics of Clowns and Clowning

ADVANCES IN SEMIOTICS

Semiotics has complemented linguistics by expanding its scope beyond the phoneme and the sentence to include texts and discourse, and their rhetorical, performative, and ideological functions. It has brought into focus the multimodality of human communication. *Advances in Semiotics* publishes original works in the field demonstrating robust scholarship, intellectual creativity, and clarity of exposition. These works apply semiotic approaches to linguistics and nonverbal productions, social institutions and discourses, embodied cognition and communication, and the new virtual realities that have been ushered in by the Internet. It also is inclusive of publications in relevant domains such as socio-semiotics, evolutionary semiotics, game theory, cultural and literary studies, human-computer interactions, and the challenging new dimensions of human networking afforded by social websites.

Series Editor: Paul Bouissac is Professor Emeritus at the University of Toronto (Victoria College), Canada. He is a world-renowned figure in semiotics and a pioneer of circus studies. He runs the SemiotiX Bulletin (www.semioticon.com/semiotix), which has a global readership.

Titles in the Series:

A Buddhist Theory of Semiotics, Fabio Rambelli
A Semiotics of Smiling, Marc Mehu
Introduction to Peircean Visual Semiotics, Tony Jappy
Semiotics of Drink and Drinking, Paul Manning
Semiotics of Happiness, Ashley Frawley
Semiotics of Religion, Robert Yelle
The Language of War Monuments, David Machin and Gill Abousnnouga
The Semiotics of Che Guevara, Maria-Carolina Cambre
The Visual Language of Comics, Neil Cohn

The Semiotics of Clowns and Clowning

Rituals of Transgression and the Theory of Laughter

PAUL BOUISSAC

Bloomsbury Academic
An imprint of Bloomsbury Publishing Plc

B L O O M S B U R Y
LONDON · NEW DELHI · NEW YORK · SYDNEY

Bloomsbury Academic

An imprint of Bloomsbury Publishing Plc

50 Bedford Square   1385 Broadway
London   New York
WC1B 3DP   NY 10018
UK   USA

www.bloomsbury.com

BLOOMSBURY and the Diana logo are trademarks of Bloomsbury Publishing Plc

First published 2015

British Library Cataloguing-in-Publication Data
A catalogue record for this book is available from the British Library.

ISBN: HB: 978-1-4725-2173-6
PB: 978-1-4725-3278-7
ePDF: 978-1-4725-3111-7
ePub: 978-1-4725-2508-6

Library of Congress Cataloging-in-Publication Data
Bouissac, Paul.
The semiotics of clowns and clowing : rituals of transgression and
the theory of laughter / Paul Bouissac.
pages cm. – (Bloomsbury advances in semiotics)
Includes bibliographical references and index.
ISBN 978-1-4725-3278-7 (paperback) – ISBN 978-1-4725-2173-6 (hardback) –
ISBN 978-1-4725-3111-7 (epdf) 1. Semiotics. 2. Performing arts–Semiotics.
3. Clowns–Semiotics. 4. Wit and humor. 5. Visual communication.
6. Modality (Linguistics) 7. Multimedia communications. I. Title.
PN1590.S26B68 2015
791.3'3014–dc23
2014037436

Series: Bloomsbury Advances in Semiotics

Typeset by Integra Software Services Pvt. Ltd.
Printed and bound in India

This book is dedicated to the memory of
Charlie Cairoli (1910–1980) and Pépète (Alfred) Pauwels (1912–1989),
who embodied for me the legendary vis comica *and*
often made me irresistibly laugh.

Contents

Introduction

July 2013. Zirkus Charles Knie has set up its red-and-white big top in Frankfurt-am-Main. For more than three weeks, it will present its program there twice a day. One of the best and most successful circuses in Europe, its management makes sure that new acts and staging are introduced periodically. After 10 years of experiencing its shows, I am still high with anticipation as my plane lands in the crowded airport of this German metropolis. This is a very hot summer. Fortunately the circus is set up in the midst of a park. As I get close to the lot, I can see in the distance horses and elephants slowly moving around in their large, shadowed enclosures. This time, however, I don't have a date with them; I am here to meet the clowns. André Broger and Cesar Dias are part of the 2013 program. I saw them perform in April, made some notes then, and decided to come back and devote more attention to their acts. They are creative young artists who embody the immemorial tradition of clowning without playing out the purely nostalgic style of previous centuries. In brief, they are relevant to their audience. Last time, I witnessed their consistent success with both young and mature spectators. This is an unmistakable indication that they create deep meaning in the minds of their public through their apparently ludicrous behavior. But what kind of meaning do these multimodal signs produce? Trying to answer this question will be the object of this book.

Clowns are a part of the cultural landscape of most countries in the world. Some belong to old local traditions and their religious or secular institutions; others ride the waves of the global market in the form of commercial icons or mass media entertainers. However, their universalism remains ambiguous: on the one hand, clowns address fundamental properties of the mind—laughing is a defining feature of humans—but, on the other hand, jokes and gags are context-sensitive not only because they exploit the resources of particular languages but also because they refer to the gestures, artifacts, norms, and values characteristic of their immediate material and social environment. The first time I saw a clown of the Moscow Circus being offered a cucumber because he was complaining of being too sick to work, I was puzzled when I noticed that the Russian audience was laughing heartily. I struggled with trying to find anthropological or psychoanalytical interpretations for this gag until a Russian friend told me that, in his country, cucumbers are supposed to cure hangovers. In documenting and discussing clown performances from a comparative perspective, this book will endeavor to meet the challenge of explaining both their global appeal and local relevance.

The ten chapters in this volume are grounded in several decades of ethnographic fieldwork in circuses and other theaters in Europe, Asia, and the Americas. My main goal was to record in detail the appearances and actions of clowns, and to explore the interface between the performers and their audiences. It required countless hours of observation from the point of view of an attentive spectator mindful of the reactions of the public of which I was a part. This situation, though, was somewhat anomalous because the only variable was the public, which changed from performance to performance, while I was, for a significant period of time in each case, the constant observer of clown acts that hardly varied from day to day. As part of a circus or a theatrical troupe, performers must meet the terms of their contracts by representing short comedies and interludes that fit in the overall structure of the advertised program. Their jokes and gags survive the passing of time from year to year as long as they make their audience laugh. It is to uncover the reasons for such merriment, as well as occasional failures, that I have undertaken the research on which this book is grounded. Getting a hint of the "why" requires indeed that utmost attention be paid to the "what," "when," and "how." In this quest, I have greatly benefitted from perusing the recent literature on clowns—in particular McManus (2003) and Davison (2013), which fortunately appeared while I was in the midst of writing this book.

The whole enterprise is based on qualitative methods, which are discussed as we progress through the text. Suffice it to say for the time being that when I observe clown performances, the focus of my attention is the dramatic patterns unfolding before my eyes. The characteristics of the dramatis personae are exhaustively documented through notations and photographs or pencil sketches. I have avoided above the term "actors" to refer to clowns, because clowns are known as fixed characters, while movie and theater actors and actresses constantly switch roles without ever totally losing their civil identities. We know each of the latter both as a kaleidoscope of recognizable avatars and as a person whose story life is monitored and publicized by the media. In Japan, for instance, the Kabuki actors impersonate a variety of characters but are known otherwise as individuals who are members of traditional performing families. In the West, cosmeticians who work for the film industry have to adapt a period hairdo, for instance, to the iconic profile of actors of either sex who insist on preserving a consistent personal image despite interpreting historical dramas set in Roman or medieval times.

By contrast, clowns are generally known only through their performing names and visual made-up identities. We will amply discuss this remarkable characteristic in the course of this book, but let me point out at the outset that the iconography of clowns since the eighteenth century—a time when some of them started acquiring a kind of celebrity status—always portrays them with their facial makeup and typical costumes. They are what they are in the circus ring or on the theater stage, and this identity exhausts, so to speak, their existence in the public eye and imagination. Clowns in civilian clothes, shown without their makeup in a family portrait, for instance, would be a shocking anomaly that would damage their appeal by tainting their performing identities. The attractiveness of actors and actresses of all ages is always foregrounded more or less subtlety in the media. But sexual themes can be represented in clowning only in the mode of parody, as we will show in Chapter 7.

My research on clowns also included some interviews, which were usually conducted on circus lots between shows over a period of time. On rare occasions, I had lengthy discussions with artists outside their circus environment. These dialogues, though, were always bearing upon the technical aspects of their art rather than on biographical details. Although my prime concern is the production of meaning at the time and in the context of the observed performances, some amount of historical background information is indeed necessary in order to take the measure of the resilience of traditional scenarios and the subtle changes they often undergo during a remembered lifetime. Such variations, of course, must be taken into consideration, as they reveal the hidden dynamics of circus clown acts with respect to their sociocultural evolution and the way they are received by their public.

As I sip an espresso in the small patio under the awning of the circus coffee stand, a man approaches with a smile. It takes me a few seconds to recognize André. It is the first time I have seen him without his makeup and stage costume. The contrast with the goofy, good-natured character of the ring is striking. He is pleased to hear that I appreciate his acts and that I will return to Frankfurt during the next weekend to have some photographs made for my book. He seems happy to discover that this is not just another journalistic interview. My goal is to establish social rapport and to explain what kind of books I write. He quickly mentions that, in his home in Switzerland, he keeps a collection of several hundred books on the circus. I have seen his acts many times and have recorded every detail in writing. They are original creations. For me, a clown act is a work of art that deserves to be viewed like a masterpiece in an art museum. It has been crafted to unfold in time and hold the spectators' attention until they succumb to laughter or feel immersed in merriment. We briefly discuss his interlude with the bathtub and the shark, three minutes packed with surprises, drama, and emotions. He laughs when I say that the first time I saw it, I was convinced the bathtub was full of water. I had indeed to wait for the next performance to discover that this illusion was the result of his perfect miming. André will join another circus next year. His contract specifies that he must provide five new interludes. He is currently working on some ideas. The hard part, though, is to find the right end, a visual punch line so to speak. We will stay in touch. I hope to get a glimpse of this creative process. But he warns me that he might only succeed at the last minute, as he finds his best ideas under stress.

Our conversation was winding up. As I was shaking hands with André, whose young daughter had joined us to let him know lunch was ready, I noticed that a handsome, shy-looking young man was waiting not too far away. Cesar Dias introduced himself. He had come with Adrian, a flying trapeze artiste from Mexico, who would serve as an interpreter. Cesar is Portuguese and is not very proficient in other languages. But he is an outstanding clown who brings down the house at every performance, without uttering a word except for an occasional "hehehehe," the global visual lingo of Twitter and other Internet chats. I have admired his skillful art for some time. He is a rising star in the circus world. Once again it is hard to immediately relate his bare face to his clown persona. Not that he wears heavy makeup in the ring: light patches of vermillion high on his cheeks; thin, dark lines circling his eyes; black-rimmed, thick glasses; and a single waxed lock of hair that would reach his nose if it were not curling up at its end. His fine natural features and his smiling eyes are far from conveying the geek look he has constructed for his performing identity. The glasses, which he definitely does not need for his sight, function both as a mask and as a prop. This is something we will discover when his acts are described and discussed. The first contact is warm and spontaneous. In spite of the generation gap, we both come from southern European cultures. The resources of nonverbal communication and a few words of English soon make the services of the interpreter superfluous. We have friends and friends of friends in common in the global village of the circus. I feel free to tell Cesar that his act reminds me a lot of George Carl's. Nothing could have made him happier. The late George Carl was his inspiration, and he worships his memory. Carl's act was minimalist. He was doing practically nothing in the ring, and whatever he was attempting to achieve failed in spite of the simplicity of the goal. But this vacuity was delivered with a compelling rhythm. This leads us to remark how timing is essential in such performances. Take the timing out and nothing is left of the act. Cesar agrees. Does he count the measures when he performs? No, but once he enters the ring, the ticking is within him. We debate in which seat the photographer should be located next weekend during the act. Cesar will remember and will periodically glance at us. Now, he has to get ready for *the afternoon show. We know we will meet again. Later, during the trapeze act, I discover what a fantastic flyer Adrian Ramos is.*

This snapshot of the ethnographer at work shows that gathering data on clown performances is far from being a dispassionate, purely methodical enterprise. While the focus of my interest is individual performances and the way in which they produce meaning for their audience, an empathetic understanding of the artists themselves can yield an enlightening access to the creative process of humor. Reliable information on the particular tradition from which a clown draws his or her inspiration is an important part of the bigger picture this book endeavors to capture. It will become obvious as we progress through this volume that clown acts are not semantically isolated events. They emerge from a dense entanglement of precedents and traditions. They are rife with intertextuality through visual allusions and references to opera, theater, and cinema, as well as to broader cultural events permeating popular culture. They also relate to each other to form a virtual network that extends beyond the realm of the circus to encompass past and modern folklore and the old myths that manage to survive in them despite being driven toward extinction by more potent new narratives. Each clown act has indeed a tacit history and even a remote archaeology that can be tentatively deciphered through comparative analyses.

Despite the heat and the jetlag, speaking at length with André and Cesar has energized me, and I decide not to miss the afternoon show. I need to prepare the photo session planned for the next weekend. My instructions to the photographer must be precise, because the images he will capture cannot be simple, random illustrations but will constitute an essential part of the argument I will develop later in the book. Now the time has come to focus on André's three-minute interlude. I straighten myself in my seat in observation readiness as the circus hands bring a prop to the center of the ring. It looks like a regular household bathtub. Soon, the spotlight draws everybody's eyes to the clown walking down an aisle amid the public. He has donned a burgundy bathrobe and put a blue shower cap over his hair. As he approaches the bathtub, his facial expression shows ravishment in anticipation of a pleasurable bath (Figure 1). With a slight hint of embarrassment because the spectators might assume he is naked under his gown—the staging indicates indeed that this is a private bathtub—he disrobes and reveals that he actually wears old-fashioned swimming trunks covering his body from the mid-thighs to the neck. The music is cheerful, and his behavior suggests that he is going to dive in the bathtub as if it were the sea (Figures 2 and 3). We are now transported to a beach scene. He tests the water with his foot and happily settles in the bathtub. Only his upper body is now visible as he uses a long-handled brush to reach his back. We seem to be safely again in a homey bathroom (Figure 4). But, quite unexpectedly, his face changes to signal extreme worry. He anxiously looks toward the water. The cheerful music has stopped, and the sinister leitmotiv of the film Jaws brutally flips the mood of the scene to the horror side (Figure 5). The fin and face of an inflatable shark briefly emerges from the bathtub, and a battle ensues during which both the man and the shark appear to fight under the water. Three seconds of silence and immobility … Only the motionless feet of André protrude from the bathtub (Figure 6). But his right hand, forming the V of victory, soon emerges, and he rises from the tub holding the skin of the deflated plastic shark (Figures 7 and 8). The clown's face exudes triumph, and martial music briefly concludes the interlude as the next circus act is being ushered in. This was at least the fourth time I had watched this short but very effective visual narrative. Each time, I was caught by its dynamic even though I knew how it would end. I could sense the many layers of meaning that a semiotic reflection would unearth: the act's absurdist, even surrealist quality, while conveying a deep human universality; how tragedy lurks in the trivial; how fighting back is the only response; that monsters are often merely the inflated toys of our imagination. Each time, I had noticed how the audience was captivated and gratified by these three minutes of a skillfully crafted blend of action and emotions, loaded with symbolic values. I will ask the photographer to record André's successive facial expressions, through which the story is told better than it could be in any verbal language.

FIGURE 1 *Clown André is going to take a bath.*

Photo credit Zbigniew Roguszka.

FIGURE 2 *Well, he seems a bit overdressed for a bath. Is he going to dive into the bathtub?*

Photo credit Zbigniew Roguszka.

FIGURE 3 *No! But is it not a strange way to dip into the water? Is it a swimming pool or the sea?*

Photo credit Zbigniew Roguszka.

The cursory sketching out of a clown act is a task relatively easy to complete, but it is only the first step toward a full account of the information densely packed and patterned within the boundaries of a micro-narrative such as André's heroic adventure in a bathtub. A reliable multimodal analysis demands many successive viewings. Because a clown act essentially repeats

FIGURE 4 *Now André can enjoy a nice bath.*
Photo credit Zbigniew Roguszka.

FIGURE 5 *What is that thing moving around under the water? A shark!*
Photo credit Zbigniew Roguszka.

itself day after day with minimal variations, such an observation is analogous to the contemplation of a work of art in a museum that one visits more than one time in order to appreciate it in its actual dimensions and from varying angles. Naturally, the capacity to produce a first accurate summary of a clown act requires a previous observation of the show during which the events still

FIGURE 6 *The fight does not seem to turn to André's advantage.*
Photo credit Zbigniew Roguszka.

FIGURE 7 *But it did. Victory!*
Photo credit Zbigniew Roguszka.

possess for the naïve spectator their novelty value. As I mentioned to André during our afternoon conversation, the first time I saw this act in 2012, I was so overwhelmed by its semiotic dynamics that it led me to believe I had actually perceived water being splashed in the tub—or at least I was not sure whether or not there was water in the tub. In our perception of fast-happening events,

FIGURE 8 *Here is what is left of the shark.*
Photo credit Zbigniew Roguszka.

we cannot consciously process all the information available, and our brain tends to fill in the gaps with information consistent with the context but not necessarily present. The circus in general, and magicians in particular, exploit this capacity of the brain to anticipate and construct perceived scenes and actions on the fly, so to speak. It is an adaptive behavior, but it also can lead to pitfalls such as creating illusions with dramatic consequences. However, this behavior generates pleasure when we experience a spectacle in which we read a surplus of meaning by spontaneously restructuring and enriching the available information. For instance, the slapping that forms an important part of some clown acts does not come from actual hits on the face of the victim but from the clapping of the victim's own hands synchronously with the slapping gesture of his partner. Nevertheless, what we see and hear is a noisy slap on the cheek.

Engaging in an in-depth description of a clown act involves the uncovering of the multiple strands of sensorial information whose combination and structuration aim at creating a coherent, albeit often surprising, experience in the minds of the spectators. We will address these issues in greater detail in the chapters of this book when we undertake an extensive analysis of several acts by André and other clowns.

Obviously not everybody in an audience experiences a clown act in exactly the same way. André often performs his bathtub interlude for over a thousand spectators, whose ages may range from 5 to 90. Not quite the same information is picked up by all of them even though all are exposed to the same set and André underlines the most significant moments of the narrative by holding brief pauses, showing the appropriate emotions in relation to typical situations (pleasure, uncertainty, terror, triumph). Most spectators understand that all this is a represented fiction and switch to the suspension-of-disbelief mode, paying attention only to the relevant aspects of the narrative. As André reported during our conversation, though, some children seated in the front row occasionally shout, "There is no water!" They obviously take what they see at face value because they have not yet internalized the pragmatic rules implied in watching a performance. As they cognitively mature, they will come to understand the difference between a real-life situation and events represented according to appropriate cultural conventions.

Moreover, the cue of looming danger evoking a shark is signaled by the musical motif of a popular film that may not be familiar to all. However, it has sound qualities of its own, if only by contrast with the previous tune that it follows after a brief instance of tense silence marked by André's change of facial expression, indicating that something must be amiss. This musical score was used in *Jaws* precisely because of its intrinsically dramatic emotional value. The fact that it may now signify "shark" in this context is accidental. In spite of the diversity of the spectators' cognitive and affective responses, the act itself offers robust semiotic constraints that form the common denominator of all possible interpretations. One may appreciate the skill of André as a mime or enjoy the creativity of this mock epic. Unexpected turns of events, wrapped within a narrative structure, are what keep the audience focused and involved until the comic relief is provided by the visual outcome of the action: triumph over adversity.

In addition to reflexively documenting a representative number of clown acts and discussing their cultural relevance, this book endeavors to explain why clowns create the mirth and laughter sustaining their very existence both as working artists and as symbolic types. It also will address the reasons for which, at times, clowns are feared by some people. However, on the whole, circuses and other popular entertainment industries consistently feature them to attract spectators. In addition, clowns sometimes are called upon to engage in social and therapeutic works, and even to articulate public protests and stimulate insubordination, if not insurgency. These psychological and political dimensions of humor cannot be considered totally separated from the comic power that clowns display in the ludic context of the circus. We will discover, in the course of this book, many instances of transgressive behavior verging on cultural subversion when clowns apparently ignore the tacit rules of social games to indulge in symbolic actions that amount to toying with these norms as if they were mere arbitrary, dispensable conventions. This behavior is performed, though, in a ritualistic manner and within a marked space meant to keep the antics of these outcasts from spreading beyond the borders of the circus world.

Accounting for the deeply human experience of humor remains an age-old challenge for philosophers and psychologists. Rather than trying to confront this challenging issue with abstract arguments or empirical protocols, this volume grounds its theoretical efforts in the attentive experience of the multimodal, dialogic discourse of actual clown performances and their exhaustive descriptions, which have been methodically elaborated during the past few decades. It will show that more happens in the circus ring than meets the eye. Clown acts are not only entertaining spectacles; they are also for most spectators a transformative experience.

Ultimately, this book will contend that all the circus clown acts that have been performed in European circuses over approximately the past 200 years belong to a single grand narrative. I will show that all instances of professional clowning as they are observed in circus rings relate to a powerful mythical discourse that can account for the meanings they create in the minds of their spectators. Particular clown acts implement only fractal parts of the overall narrative every time they are performed, but each narrative, however brief it may be, reflects the whole story in a dramatic nutshell. This narrative can be heuristically considered as an epic in which two protagonists confront each other through multiple episodes. The two protagonists appear under a great variety of guises and are endowed with individual performing personalities and characters, but they are all avatars of their respective types. Clown acts also come in solo versions in which an individual works his or her way through a trying ordeal to reach eventual public recognition. These acts can be said to be transcultural only in a relative sense, because it seems that they can be observed in their stereotypical forms primarily within the confines of European cultures. Nevertheless, this European cultural tradition is generated by a more fundamental dynamic structure that can be traced back to a much broader cultural area—even perhaps as a universal kernel at the heart of all cultures. This will be suggested by examples selectively taken from the Indian and Javanese clowning traditions.

Most research done so far on the topic of clowns has been of a historical nature, bearing on the civil identities and life stories of clowns and the reporting of the places in which they were performing, with a concern for the characteristics that contributed to distinguishing each from the others. Documentary efforts have focused on individual artists and have relied heavily on anecdotes that could be gleaned from circus lore and occasional biographies or autobiographies. But the traces left by the numerous clowns who performed in the nomadic circuses that crisscrossed Europe and the Americas from the eighteenth century on are extremely elusive. Those who performed for a certain length of time in stable circuses located in major urban centers have often been memorialized not only in the popular press but also in the literary works of authors who fostered a deep interest in the circus and its heroes. Before the cinema used clowns in the plots of films, painters represented and interpreted their striking presence through pictorial art. Some clowns, indeed, attained the status of celebrities in capital cities such as London, Paris, Berlin, Moscow, and Washington during the nineteenth and twentieth centuries. But this is only the tip of the iceberg. Circus clowns formed a massive population of entertainers well distributed over whole continents. However, except in major cities, they remained under the radar of highbrow culture, so to speak. Considered a lower form of popular, unsophisticated entertainment, they were hardly mentioned in literature. This is why it is extremely difficult to identify the modern clown's cultural lineages with any reasonable certainty.

This book will first take a comprehensive view of clown acts and focus on what they all share in common rather than their artistic differences. Together we will look for narrative patterns and the kind of transformations they achieve through their dramatic unfolding. In addition to considering the idiosyncratic combinations of signs each individual artist uses in order to create his or her persona, we will make an inventory of all the features and properties among which individual choices are made. Some significant contrasting clusters will thus appear and will offer a clue to the consistency of the compositions determining the typical roles transcending the individuality of the performers. In this tradition, each clown strives to be original and makes choices that will establish his or her distinctive identity. But the resulting selection must conform to the semiotic constraints of the stereotype of the role chosen in the first place. These choices bear upon the name, the facial makeup, the costume and demeanor, the way of speaking, and a unique "signature" within each of these semiotic domains. This is why the first step in this volume will focus on the face of the clown.

Chapter 1 explores the range of makeup through which artists are identified as clowns. These colorful patterns transform their natural faces according to some specific cultural codes that can be made explicit through systematic comparison. Clowns create role categories and define semiotic values through the marked oppositions they maintain across their great variety. They transform and filter the expressive movements of the facial muscles in a way consistent with the narrative functions of the characters they portray. This chapter provides a basis for the semiotic understanding of the clown acts we will analyze in the course of this volume.

Chapter 2 complements the first chapter by examining the clowns' bodies as they appear in the ring. It focuses on their demeanors and costumes, which are consistent with their facial makeup. The obvious contrasts characterizing the faces are reinforced by the kind of garments clowns don to perform.

Shapes, colors, styles, and degrees of adjustment to their natural trunk and limbs contribute to defining the clowns' performing identities. Even more than their makeup, the costumes are culture-sensitive and must be assessed with respect to the norms and fashions prevailing in the social context of their time.

Chapter 3 presents and discusses the various props clowns use in their acts. Some are regular artifacts that come from their cultural environment, such as tables and chairs, pails and plates, boxes and ladders. Some others resemble domestic artifacts but are constructed in ways that betray their apparent functionality—for instance, chairs that collapse under the weight of the body or musical instruments that are filled with water or foam. Idiosyncratic objects are also crafted by clowns, often through tinkering, combining two different functions in innovative manners. Among these, strange violins and guitars have a prominent place. The objects we trust in our daily lives are endowed by clowns with unexpected dysfunctions or, on the contrary, super functions that transcend their trivial appearance. This chapter also reviews the use of animals in clown acts. These are exclusively domestic animals, typically farm animals over which clowns assert their control with various degrees of success or failure. This paradigm includes mainly cows, pigs, donkeys, mules, and geese. Dogs and horses provide the possibility of developing more sophisticated training and take part in comedies in which clowns are the butt of the apparent wit of their animal partners. This chapter examines in detail two such interactive acts in which four-legged "actors" steal the show at the expense of seemingly helpless clowns.

Chapter 4 discusses gags that form the main substance of clown acts. It raises the issue of the nature of gags and the ways in which they are constructed. These short, often instant events can be construed as micro-narratives embedded within precise social contexts. Indeed, they produce mirth and laughter only when they occur in a dialogic structure. The observations and analyses presented and discussed in the first three chapters provide the necessary background for the understanding of even the crudest slapstick. A collapsing chair is in itself neither comic nor tragic. It depends on who is the victim and what kind of situation frames such an event. Some acts are described in detail and analyzed in view of their cultural context.

Chapter 5 comprehensively addresses a corpus of traditional scenarios that clown pairs or trios perform in the circus ring. Here I show that all these narratives are represented as multimodal discourse using the lexicon that has been introduced in the first four chapters: makeup, costume, props, and gags. The general picture emerging from this chapter evokes the symbolic breaking of the rules that govern our civil society. Clowns toy with these rules by playfully inverting them or simply ignoring them. They foreground the tension between nature and culture, the world of instincts, and their free expression on the one hand, and the universe of norms, codes, and constraints on the other.

Chapter 6 explores the general pattern that can be identified in most clown acts. In many respects, these narratives mirror the trickster stories found in many cultures. Their ambiguous heroes are both reviled and admired because of their cunning and audacity. They play tricks, which elicit laughter, but their outsider status makes them immune to the rigors of the law and situates them in the liminal fringe from which culture itself originated. This chapter raises the vexing question of the origins of European traditional clowns in the framework of cultural evolution and examines their possible relation to ancient northern religions.

Chapter 7 focuses on gender play and sexual politics. In themselves, clowns are in general asexual, almost genderless. However, they foster a tradition of gross sexual jokes that are nowadays played down in circuses promoting their shows as family entertainment. But in circus events aimed at adults, this potential comes to the fore. The sexual themes, though, are often implicitly present in the form of gestural allusions and stereotypical mimicking. There are also a fair number of acts involving cross-dressing. This chapter reviews some examples and draws general conclusions about the relevance of sex to clowning, because this theme permeates more or less subtly many of the narratives performed in the ring or on stage.

Chapter 8 considers the theme of death in clown acts, both in solo performance and team acts. It may sound paradoxical that death can be a topic for comedy rather than exclusively for tragedy. But clowns toy extensively with death in acts involving mock funerals, murders, ghosts, decapitation, and the like. Several acts involving this theme are analyzed in this chapter. We also consider the fact that literary and visual arts have often associated sadness and death with the representation of clowns since the early nineteenth century.

Chapter 9 is devoted to an issue recurring again and again in the previous chapters: the role of clowns as ritual transgressors of the rules and norms of civil society. This chapter goes a step further by showing that clowns straddle the red line separating the profane from the sacred. Some of their acts spell out the unmentionable and deconstruct the very basis of our cultural scaffoldings. Clowns even undermine the ground upon which our language and our society rest by revealing their fragility. They bluntly demonstrate the vacuity of the fear attached to the breaking of taboos. Nature is indifferent to these violations. But clowns pay a price for this; they are symbolically treated as scapegoats and cannot shake off their tainted status, because "clown" remains nowadays a term of abuse.

Chapter 10 examines the role of clowns in modern society beyond the circus ring and the stage. Indeed, the past 5 decades have witnessed the emergence of a phenomenon that could be described as the civil institution of clowning, through democratization and gentrification of the profession. Circus schools and clown colleges have flourished all over the world, and as a consequence the population of clowns has greatly increased. In many respects, clowning has emancipated itself from the traditional constraints of the circus and the stage. Clowning has become a multifaceted social activity largely independent from the circus trade and tradition. This chapter reviews the many functions these amateurs serve in society. It also discusses the role of the clown icon in political protests and critical movements.

The concluding chapter addresses the tantalizing issue of the nature of humor and the causes of mirth and laughter, which I often experienced myself during my fieldwork in circuses and which can be readily observed if attention is shifted to the audience while clown acts are unfolding in the ring. Causing laughter is the lifeline of performing clowns. Failing to do so spells for them unemployment. The final chapter ends with a cognitive hypothesis that could explain laughter, in neurophysiological terms, as the result of an overload of unexpected information. Merriment would then be the result of a different process involving the stimulation of the reward centers of the brain as an outcome of the audience identification with the games of losers and winners clowns play and replay in their ritualistic comedies.

The research for this book straddles four decades. It was conducted in circuses rather than libraries, although a fair amount of information comes from archives holding little-known material. Grateful acknowledgment is made here of a grant from the J. S. Guggenheim Foundation (1974–1975), which allowed me to spend a full year in Paris exploring the archives of Juliette and Marthe Vesque, then held at the Musée des arts et traditions populaires. These two dedicated artists have indeed recorded in writing and through exquisitely colored drawings countless circus acts they observed between the last decade of the nineteenth century and the mid-twentieth century. Many clown acts have thus been documented that otherwise would have left only some anecdotal and journalistic traces. A 2-year Killam Fellowship (1990–1992) was also crucial for this research. Finally, Victoria University at the University of Toronto has provided a grant allowing me to commission original illustrations for this work. These institutions will find here my grateful acknowledgment of their support.

I must thank my colleague, Professor David Blostein, for his line drawings, which illustrate the points made in the first two chapters of this volume. Rendering vivid colors in shades of gray was a real challenge. My thanks also go to my friend Zbigniew Roguszka, who took the photographs during some of the performances documented in this book. The task of a circus photographer is not easy, even if he has the full cooperation of circus management and artists. Terry Lau, from Beehive Graphic in Toronto, has prepared the plates. Last but not least, my gratitude goes to my partner, Professor Stephen Riggins, who has completed the copyediting of the manuscript and has provided me with continuous critical feedback during the writing of this book.

I cannot fail to state in concluding this introduction how pleasant and constructive it has been to work with Gurdeep Mattu, publisher at Bloomsbury Academic, and Andrew Wardell, his editorial assistant.

1

The Faces of the Clown

Appearance and identity

The face of the clown is a colorful configuration immediately recognized wherever it is encountered. This ubiquitous icon is found in paintings, children's books, toys, advertisements, and, expectedly, circus posters and banners. It ultimately refers to comic performers, but the image has taken a semiotic life of its own. This generic pattern of contrasting colors appears in countless different versions in which the human face is variously transformed according to a few basic principles that selectively change its natural colors and features while ambiguously preserving the humanoid character of the new combinations. What results is an altered human face that verges on the alien and the uncanny. Young children are usually frightened at first when they are exposed to real clowns, until they learn that this peculiar face means play in the culture in which they live. Later on, they will take these live masks for granted, although the film and television industry will occasionally revive the terrifying horror inherent in the face of the joker. But, in general, the representations of the clown face are meant to convey a sense of informality, freedom, and merriment. This, however, is not universal. Indeed, the irrational fear of clowns is an acknowledged psychopathology called "coulrophobia," a neologism of uncertain etymology. In this chapter, as we examine the great variety of makeup patterns observed among circus clowns, we will keep in mind that drastically and permanently altering the natural semiotics of the face is not a trivial exercise. Toying with the relation between appearance and identity can jeopardize the very foundation of the social contract, mainly if the encounter with clowns occurs outside expected contexts such as the circus ring or the stage, which include safeguards for their containment.

In the Guardian of September 16, 2013, columnist Laura Barton commented on coulrophobia following news that had appeared in the

Northampton Herald & Post: "A spooky clown has been scaring Northampton residents in full costume and makeup." Concerned people were reporting to the police that they were being visited by such an individual who made some nonsensical propositions. A few months later, clowns popped up in Norfolk County at unexpected places in towns and sometimes chased frightened pedestrians. Following a number of alarmed calls, the police advised people to stay away from these individuals who probably tried to shock passers-by but were not hurting anybody. Inspector Carl Edwards reassured the population that nobody had suffered injuries in these encounters, adding that merely dressing as a clown is not illegal in England." A blog published in the Le Monde of November 29 echoes the local British news under the hyped title "Les clowns inquiétants se multiplient en Grande-Bretagne" [Scary clowns multiply in Great Britain]. The blog features a color picture of a clown peering through a vent on ground level. His entire face is painted in bright white, with black highbrows drawn on his forehead, red lips, and a round, red nose. His wide-open eyes are circled with black makeup. The face is framed by a wig of reddish hair. It is expressionless, ghostlike, and out of place. It is a close replication of the face of the monster clown in the horror film IT (1990) based on Stephen King's novel (1986). Anybody familiar with professional circus clowns can immediately recognize that this makeup is the work of someone who has interpreted the use of colors and patterns in a manner markedly at odds with the conventional rules constraining the facial transformations of the performers we will document in this book. This is what probably makes such an apparition so unsettling, despite the fact that it evokes a clown face in the mind of the general population. Be they hoaxes or copycat deviant behaviors, these social phenomena are relevant to the object of this book inasmuch as they point to the disruptive potential of playing with the relationship between appearance and identity.

A professional clown is identified through the modified pattern and features of his or her face. This is to be expected. It is indeed the way in which humans recognize each other. In complex, modern societies individuals are required to carry an official document that authenticates their identity by matching a name with a face, sometimes also with fingerprints if not a DNA profile. Any mismatch indicates deviance and possibly criminal intentions. Pseudonyms have a special legal status, but aliases suggest deception. Civil society expects from its members a consistent and permanent identity kit. However, the face of the clown is an anomalous case, an exception to this rule because it is an artifact that creates a split identity that escapes social control to some extent. It is neither a mask lacking expressive mobility nor a cosmetic modification designed to beautify the appearance of a person as a kind of live "photo shop." By contrast, the face of the clown is made up with vivid, artificial colors and augmented by prostheses that create an appearance markedly different from the natural face of the individual who inhabits the performing identity. Indeed, a clown face usually includes additions such as a fake nose, false eyebrows, wigs, and other contrivances. It is sometimes surprising to discover how very small modifications can restructure a facial pattern to the extent that the underlying natural configuration becomes hardly recognizable. For instance, the minimal mask of a red bulbous nose often suffices to achieve such a drastic transformation.

The modified face of a clown is associated with a stage name that rarely coincides with the actual civil name of the performer, thus creating a new, artificial identity. For example, we find Chicky, Coco the clown, Grock, Pipo, Popov, Rhum, and Zippo, to name only a few illustrious artists. When the real name is used as the stage name, the effect is to suggest two distinct identities, as namesakes do. As I pointed out in the Introduction to this volume, clowns are essentially different from movie and theater actors to the extent that the latter never disconnect their civil from their performing identity. Actors and actresses interpret a variety of fictional or historical characters while remaining within the range of expressivity of their natural face and demeanor. This is not the case for clowns, who instantly switch from one identity to the other and usually exist during all their artistic life exclusively under their contrived appearances and fancy names in the public's eyes and imagination.

The purpose of this chapter is to document in detail the facial transformations that can be observed in past and contemporary clowns. It will endeavor to explore the many configurations that achieve these transformations and to uncover the biological constraints and cultural factors that account for the resulting semiotic effects.

The making of a face

Before considering the variety and details of the clown face, let us take a look at the human face and the organization and functions of its parts. This framework forms the basis upon which any makeup is selectively built, in order to construct a different semiotic order while preserving the fundamentals of human face-to-face communication. Ask anybody to quickly draw a face, and you will be presented with a circle or an ellipse showing two dots for the eyes in the upper part, a central vertical stroke for the nose, and a short line or an arc for the mouth. Smiley icons often skip the nose but are nevertheless irresistibly interpreted as credible representations of an expressive face. The biological and social face, though, is far more complex.

In humans and other primates, the face is the sensitive area through which visual interactions take place with the immediate environment, both physical and social. The scientific investigation of the underlying tangle of nerves and muscles that control the flow of facial actions and expressions goes back to the nineteenth century in the context of the fledgling discipline of psychology (e.g., Duchenne 1876). In the following century, advances in neuropsychology, evolutionary biology, and human ethology stimulated further scrutinizing of the dynamics of the human face in the framework of semiotics and nonverbal communication research (e.g., Izard 1971; Ekman 1973, 1979, 1982; Ekman et al. 1972; Fridlund 1994). Although a great deal of knowledge has accrued to date concerning the understanding of the face, many problems remain to be solved with regard to the brain circuitries and neurochemical functions that keep modifying the surface landscape of the face as we think, feel, speak, and interact visually and orally with others (e.g., Bruce et al. 1992; Singer 2006; Adolphs 2008; Schillbach et al. 2008). The difficulty of coming to grips with this complexity is compounded by the fact that the face packs into its relatively small surface many other biological functions, such as breathing, smelling, hearing, seeing, eating and drinking, and eliminating mucus and other secretions. All these biological imperatives, including the communicative ones, are bound to constrain each other and create interferences. From a biological point of view, the face must be understood as an adaptive compromise entailing unavoidable constraints and liabilities.

From a semiotic perspective—that is, the investigation of its meaning-making potential—the human face has been equated with a display board upon which interacting individuals can read and interpret each other's moods and intentions. There are ongoing debates about whether the configurations of features that can be perceived on the face are primarily expressive or manipulative (e.g., Fridlund 1994; Niedenthal et al. 2010). Do our emotions transpire like deep underwater turbulences, creating ripples on the surface of a lake? Or do we attempt to influence others' behaviors by playing out a range of appropriate moods? Are there ways of telling a "true" emotion from a fake one? No issue raises more controversies than the study of the smile, both within particular cultures and from a comparative point of view. How can we tell that a smile is genuine? Are there signs that reliably indicate that it is contrived? Ultimately, scientific studies of the face in interaction lead to the problem of the ratio of hardwired, universal dynamic patterns to the variations and constraints that appear to be culture-specific. These questions must be kept in mind when we consider the modifications clowns make to their natural face when, in the privacy of their secluded dressing room, they selectively add colors and patterns to the surface of their skin, to emerge in the circus ring under another identity.

Understanding the biological logic and cultural value of these changes requires that we distinguish at least three semiotic layers, so to speak, in the complex dynamic configuration of the human face and its role in communication. These distinctions, though, are artificial and purely heuristic, because the three hypothetical dimensions are always combined in actual interactions. All particular holistic patterns result from the contractions of muscles and the dilatation or constriction of blood vessels and sphincters. Genuine surprise, fear, arousal, anger, anxiety, and pleasure, for instance, are distinct configurations belonging to the natural repertory of the face and occur in spontaneous interactions. Cultures add two layers to this basic resource. First, children are encouraged or compelled to manage these natural reflexes according to social norms. They may be trained to hide their emotions in conformity with the ethos of their class, caste, or group; or, on the contrary, they may be rewarded for being spontaneous and open to others. Stereotypical examples include the British stiffening of the upper lip in adversity, the smile of the Japanese in embarrassing situations, and the manual and facial exuberance of the Italians. (The cultural management of the dynamic of the face is naturally more subtle and complex than these crude illustrations may suggest.) Secondly, cultures introduce permanent modifications regarding the differential treatment of hair according to age and gender; the preservation of skin integrity or its scarification and piercing; the addition of various elements such as the dying of hair, the reddening of lips, and other kinds of makeup; and the hanging of earrings, insertion of nose rings, and so on. The sociocultural habits and artifacts constrain to some lesser or greater extent the natural dynamic of the bare face, which remains our ultimate semiotic resource in interacting meaningfully with each other. Clowns of any kind add a fourth layer of colors and patterns to this complex base, thus both selectively suppressing some of the face's communicative resources and enhancing others in the context of public performances that imply that these artificial faces must be clearly perceived from a greater distance than the relative closeness of face-to-face interactions.

Kinds and scales of facial transformations in clowns

The face of the clown is a live mask. It is a mask inasmuch as its makeup hides the identity of the person who has applied it to his or her face. It is alive because, in contrast to a solid mask, it allows the production of all the meaningful muscular contractions that characterize the semiotics of the human face. However, the makeup significantly modifies the natural features to the extent that the communicative potential of the face is constrained in certain aspects. Some elements of the face are enhanced; others are played down. Also, artificial parts are often added. These changes bear upon the shape and colors of the face and have an impact on both the psychological determination of the character that can be inferred from the makeup and the range of communicative behavior it makes selectively possible or impossible. While this is true of the whole range of documented versions of clown makeup, a close examination reveals that the many variations of makeup used by traditional European circus clowns form two distinct clusters, each one exhibiting a remarkable, specific, formal consistency in spite of the great diversity found among performers. We will now present these two paradigms, mindful of the fact that each clown's makeup, whichever category it belongs to, bears the unique mark of the individual artist who wears it—very often for his or her whole life as a performer. Thanks to the makeup, the performing identity of a clown persists, indeed, over a long period of time without showing signs of obvious aging. For these reasons the clown is perceived as standing both out of time and out of space, to the extent that an outcast is always out of place, in the margin of the socio-spatial categories that assign statuses and functions to slots in the virtual grid of the social order.

But the clown does not permanently wear the makeup defining its identity in the circus ring or on stage. The colors are washed off after the performance, and individual artists can then reclaim their civil image in the context of their particular familial and socioeconomic condition. The makeup, however, is almost as permanent as the natural face of the artist, because it is created by following a set of instructions, an algorithm that generates, day after day, the same consistent appearance. The clown implements a recipe that has been handed over to him or her by tradition and that has been interpreted with variations whose purpose is to brand the artist as one of a kind within the generic role's appearance. The unique persona of a clown starts with its makeup. The comparative observation of a large number of examples shows that there is a system behind each of the two clusters that can be identified. Since the mid-nineteenth century, these two clusters have broadly been known in the technical language of the circus as the *whiteface* clowns and the *augustes*, and they are primarily based on the type of makeup they wear and the kind of behavior that characterizes them. However, this distinction is not as rigorous as it may sound, because historical iconography and contemporary examples provide evidence of blurred boundaries. Innovations and deliberate breaking of the rules indeed occur now and then in the individual choices of makeup patterns, and new cultural stereotypes coexist with traditional ones.

We will examine and discuss some examples of the latter in the last part of this chapter. There are nevertheless an overwhelming number of clown faces that comply with the basic principles generating the *whiteface* and the *auguste* genres. It is difficult to determine the status of these principles, as there is no written list of the laws from which newcomers could seek guidance. There are only precedents, which offer this implicit imperative: imitate but not totally. Doing so would be copying, a deviant behavior akin to plagiarism. The birth of a clown in any of the two categories mentioned above starts with this double injunction. Of course, before the Internet era, no individual had access to the full array of makeup that formed the complete paradigm of each genre. Models had to be picked within the extended family tradition or among the other artists with whom the aspiring clown was acquainted. Plagiarism was always possible, albeit not welcome, in a world that from time immemorial remained at the margin of civil society. Only nowadays can an original makeup be patented. There are several cases, though, of inherited makeup patterns and names, when a son succeeded his father and performed in the same category. Examples of this continuity nowadays include the whiteface Pipo and the auguste Charlie Cairoli. The latter has often been mistaken for his deceased father.

Or a well-known clown can have an understudy replace him for a period of time when he cannot take part in person in a show for which he is under contract. This is known to be the case for Barry Lubin, whose creation the original clown Grandma is at times impersonated by another artist who has been trained appropriately. This provides an interesting example— probably not the only one—of the fundamental split that exists between a clown persona and the human person who embodies it. Hypothetically, clowns could also rent out their face, costume, demeanor, and identity as a franchised brand.

Rather than assuming a normative, transcendent system, a kind of generative grammar or langue in the Saussurian sense that would account for all instances of makeup complying with either paradigm, let us adopt a pragmatic approach that will lead to an interpretation compatible with the tenets of cultural evolution. With masks and makeup, we are indeed in the presence of cultural artifacts that have changed over time and keep evolving even if their trajectories include periods of apparent stasis. As we will discover when we peruse the data provided by about two centuries of professional clowning, all cultural artifacts do not evolve at the same pace, and the meanings of those that are physically the most stable constantly shift as the socioeconomic context changes. As we proceed in this volume, we will encounter numerous examples of the semiotic fluidity and versatility of clowns, and we will see that innovations are subject to the laws of evolution because success with audiences determines whether or not a variation in makeup survives and is further imitated.

The crafting of a clown's makeup

Let us follow the step-by-step process in the crafting of an auguste makeup. Photographer Fernand Rausser was allowed, in 1975, to record the successive stages of the facial transformation of Swiss artist Eugen Altenburger

(1928–2013) into the clown Chicky. Outside the circus, Mr. Altenburger was characterized by one of his booking agents as a dignified, modest, self-effacing gentleman. He was coming through as someone "who might be mistaken for a retired bank-manager or lawyer rather than a high-spirited clown [...] [He] would appear at the poolside bespectacled and retiring, in a neat linen suit, every bit the typical English gentleman, ready for his habitual afternoon tea" (Stacey 2013: 30).

Now, let us peek through the little window of the caravan where Eugen Altenburger has just sat down in front of a small vanity mirror as he gets ready for a performance. We can see in the mirror the bare face of the artist that the photographer has captured before Altenburger started to apply his makeup. It is a rather square face whose seriousness is underlined by dark-rimmed glasses. The expression is serene, with the hint of a closed-lip smile. The lower lip is fleshy and sensuous. The hair and eyebrows are fair. The eyes reveal a contemplative mood with a dash of irony (Figure 1.1).

FIGURE 1.1 *The man behind the clown.*
Artwork by David Blostein.

Taking off his glasses, he first puts vermilion red on his eyelids, eyebrows, and temples, smearing the color over his skin in the areas around his eyes and drawing two symmetrical red lines from the bridge of his nose to the corners of his mouth. Then he applies the same color on his chin to form a circle just below his lower lip (Figure 1.2).

FIGURE 1.2 *First stage of the transformation: selective reddening of the facial background and painting of a red circle on the chin.*
Artwork by David Blostein.

Having reached for another jar, he now whitens his entire lower lip and paints the center of his upper and lower eyelids in bright white so that, from a distance, these patches will appear to greatly enlarge the white of his eyes (the sclera) around the center of his ocular orbits (Figure 1.3).

A third jar contains a light peach-colored paste, which he carefully transfers to his cheeks with his fingers to add a lighter touch on both sides of his face, thus enhancing by contrast the red vermilion with which he started coloring his face. Dragging his fingers down, he makes these lighter circular patches end up as narrow curves toward the tip of the chin (Figure 1.4).

FIGURE 1.3 *Second move: adding patches of white to enhance the signaling properties of the upper teeth and the sclera.*

Artwork by David Blostein.

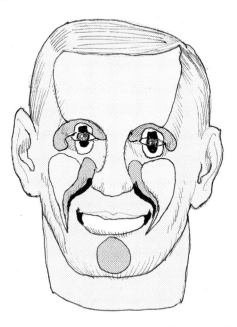

FIGURE 1.4 *Third move: black is used to artificially enlarge the pupils as the face will be perceived from a distance by the audience.*

Artwork by David Blostein.

The next move consists of using a delicate brush to add black to this facial composition: first in the center of both his whitened upper and lower eyelids in order to create the appearance of larger irises and pupils, then as a single line parallel to the red vermilion strokes that go from his nose to the corners of his mouth (Figure 1.5).

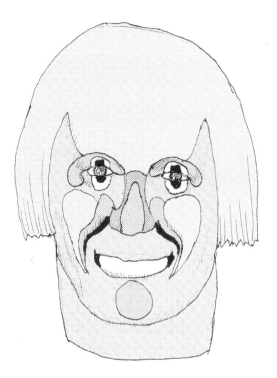

FIGURE 1.5 *Fourth move: augmenting and rounding the upper face to complete the neotenic configuration.*
Artwork by David Blostein.

Then he fixes a red bulbous artificial nose on the tip of his natural nose after having added some red of the same hue to the area around the edge of the addition in order to make sure that this artifact blends well with its background (Figure 1.6).

The last move is the addition of a wig showing a round, bald skull that enlarges his forehead and has only strings of reddish-yellow hair hanging from both sides. This wig restructures the form of his face by creating a rounder face whose center is the red nose. At the end, a light coat of talcum powder applied with a special brush slightly tones down the bright colors and will prevent unpleasant reflections when the clown moves around under the

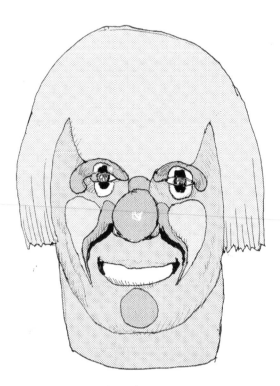

FIGURE 1.6 *Fifth move: adding the red nose.*
Artwork by David Blostein.

spotlights. Chicky will put a small black hat on before entering the ring, a hat that will often fall off or fly away during the act (Figure 1.7).

From the above reconstruction, based on the evidence provided by the six photographs by Fernand Rausser (1975: 134–135), it is obvious that the crafting of a clown's makeup is the result of an ordered series of instructions—in other words, an algorithm. Like a musician playing a tune, the clown replicates exactly, day after day, the same series of moves. Every stage offers a possibility of variations within a chromatic and morphological range defining the limits of the genre, whether the makeup creates an auguste or a whiteface clown. After discussing the semiotic significance of the successive steps performed by Eugen Altenburger to craft the facial identity of the auguste Chicky, we will examine some of the numerous variations that can be found in this makeup paradigm. But let us focus first on the effects achieved by the design.

The roundness of the face and the location of the eyes and nose approximately in the midline across its center are typical features of the heads of human babies. This effect is created by the addition of the wig, which increases the volume of the upper part of the face. Moreover, the erasing of eyebrows and the replacement of the long, vertical nasal appendage with

FIGURE 1.7 *Final transformation: capping the skull with a round hat.*
Artwork by David Blostein.

a smaller, roundish artificial nose complete the transformation of the artist's adult face into a stereotypical infantile pattern that has thus been magnified. Of course, nobody would confuse Chicky's face with the head of a human baby. However, our brains seem to spontaneously process patterns of facial features in a somewhat crude manner—for example, the tendency to read faces into any material including two aligned dots that approximately reproduce the relative position of eyes. On this level, we can tell an adult from a baby face and react accordingly. The latter interpretation usually triggers a positive, protective attitude, whereas the former is potentially aggressive and dominant and invites caution mainly if it is not a familiar face. Individual face recognition is performed through a second analytical stage by other neural circuitries that process fine-grained visual information. It is this secondary competence that allows us to distinguish one clown from another just as we readily distinguish the individuals we encounter.

Another noteworthy transformation achieved by the Chicky's makeup is the white arc painted in the area of the mouth. Because it resembles a display of upper teeth, it conveys the image of an open-mouth smile—a friendly and submissive social signal similar in many respects to the smiley icon we use in our email messages to express positive social contact and happiness. All these features are generally implemented with various degrees of intensity in the typical makeup of the auguste genre of clowns. When natural eyebrows are enhanced instead of being played down, the clown can direct highly visible eyebrow "flashes" toward the audience, thus signaling friendly feelings and prompting positive responses in return from the spectators, mainly when the clown appears to be the victim of an aggressive, authoritarian whiteface partner.

The face of dominance

Let us now turn our attention to Bruno Stutz, the whiteface clown of the duo known as The Chickys, an act that successfully toured with practically all major European circuses between 1950 and 2004 (Figure 1.8).

FIGURE 1.8 *The Chickys as they appeared on the program of National Swiss Circus Knie in 1974 (from the author's collection).*

First, as the generic term "whiteface" indicates, the whole face, including the neck, is covered with white makeup. Then the lips and nostrils are outlined with a thin red line. The ears are also colored in the same red. After this, a crayon of black is used to delicately draw around the eyes to endow them with perfect visual definition. Finally, two black eyebrows are painted well above the natural eyebrows, which have been hidden by the white makeup. The left artificial eyebrow is a curve following the form of the natural one, but continues vertically down the temple and the upper cheek. The right artificial eyebrow is a curve that runs from the temple to the bridge of the nose and then goes straight up to the middle of the forehead. Bruno Stutz's eyebrow design is a paradigmatic implementation of the basic algorithm, which includes two instructions: (1) do not make the black curve coincide with the curve of the natural eyebrows, and (2) make a dissymmetrical design. In view of the set of examples documented, only the first principle is imperative. Symmetry is indeed found in some special cases, but well above the natural eyebrows. Some other features of eyebrow design are optional. A 1932 photograph of Jean-Marie Cairoli shows the arrogant effect produced by symmetrical eyebrows located higher than the natural ones (Figure 1.9).

In most whiteface makeup, though, a vertical element is found in the center of the forehead, above the nose, but does not seem to be compulsory. Whiteface clowns distinguish each other by the design of their eyebrows, which they tellingly call their "signature." Many of them display a

FIGURE 1.9 *Whiteface Jean-Marie Cairoli (1879–1956) sported symmetrical eyebrows. He is shown here in 1927 with his two auguste partners: his son Carletto (the future Charlie Cairoli) and Porto (from the archives of Charlie Cairoli Jr.).*

single drawn eyebrow that includes a vertical stroke, thus emphasizing the dissymmetry of a facial expression that is typical of anger. This unnatural feature underlines the cultural artificiality of the makeup all the more, because the natural color of the flesh in any hue on a live face is drastically negated by the uniform white, also emblematic of death and representing ghosts in many cultures. The communicative functions of the natural white parts of the natural human face are neutralized by the fact that they cannot easily be perceived against a background that itself has become white. In addition, the whiteface clown traditionally wears a white conical hat that expands toward the top the oblong morphology of the face. He does not wear a bulbous red nose, but sports his usually long, aggressive, natural adult nose. His face embodies, in a somewhat caricatured manner, social dominance and cultural authority (Figure 1.10).

FIGURE 1.10 *A representative selection of whiteface eyebrows.*
Artwork by David Blostein.

FIGURE 1.11 *Charlie Cairoli with whiteface Paul Freedman, ca. 1950 (from the archives of Charlie Cairoli Jr.).*

The contrast between the two main kinds of makeup, the whiteface and the auguste, could not be more striking (Figure 1.11). It involves the use of white to redundantly define their respective characters and dramatic functions without ambiguity. This opposition is grounded in a deeply rooted system of signaling that can be observed in other species and provides semiotic resources for meaning-making processes in cultures. The use of white in opposition to any other color has indeed evolved to serve as the basis for digital coding based on the principle of all or nothing rather than the quantitative more or less that is typical of analogical communication. At the other end of the spectrum, black can also serve a similar function, notably by opposition to white in a figure-to-ground relationship of which writing and printing are good examples. Either is used to signify death in some cultures—traditionally black in Europe and white in Asia. But white achieves a better contrast in opposition to the whole chromatic gamut of the spectrum, whereas black creates fewer contrasts. These color codes are played out in the makeup of clowns but, as we saw above, their treatment is strikingly different in the two kinds of makeup.

In the auguste, the patches of white coincide with and expand the signal-producing white of the face: the sclera and the teeth. In the whiteface, the signaling potential of the naturally white areas of the face is neutralized because the contrast with the surrounding skin is greatly reduced, mainly when the made-up face is seen from a distance, as is the case in circus performances. Conversely, it is obvious that the artificial enlargement of the white areas on the auguste's face gives enhanced visibility to these signaling devices even if the spectators are located far from the ring. But what is the significance of such white signals, and why does it matter in the case of the auguste?

Many studies have shown that in face-to-face interactions utmost attention is spontaneously paid by the interacting subjects to the mouth and the eyes: whether upper or lower teeth are displayed and whether the direction of the gaze is clearly perceivable or not provides information relevant to the nature of the interaction. Whereas the showing of the lower teeth, accompanied by the clenching of the jaws, signals hostility and aggression, the baring of the upper teeth is a sign of friendliness and submission. It is noticeable in the photograph of Chicky that the lower lip is painted in white, forming an arc whose extremities are pointing up, thus creating an image that coincides with the pattern of an upper teeth display, meaning friendliness and submission. This mood is frozen on the auguste face, and he could hardly produce the opposite attitude because the makeup would filter it out. Closed eyelids, on the other hand, represent a denial of truthful communication and preclude the possibility of assessing the direction of the gaze. Wide-open eyes combined with the smile that includes the baring of the upper teeth create a generic pattern implying innocence, positive feelings, playfulness, and submission.

Looking now at the whiteface, we cannot fail to notice immediately the black marks designed above his eyes. It is not by chance that these artificial patterns are located above the natural eyebrows. With these hairy patches on the higher part of the ocular orbit, humans are indeed endowed with a unique greeting system—the eyebrow flash. It is caused by a spontaneous muscular contraction occurring when we encounter someone we know and like. Although the muscle can be contracted voluntarily, the ensuing movement is not as quick as the spontaneous one that flares on our face without our being aware of it. This signal lasts only a few milliseconds. But raising the eyebrows and holding them high for a while occurs when we are surprised and displeased. When raised eyebrows are combined with a frown, a vertical ridge appears in the central part of the forehead above the bridge of the nose. It often forms a dissymmetrical pattern, with one of the eyebrows being raised higher than the other. This is an authoritarian, repressive facial gesture that accompanies hostile feelings. It is aimed at the other member of the interacting dyad to convey intimidation and domination. It is the opposite of the begging attitude in which eyebrows are raised, eyes are wide open, and the head is slightly tilted backward or sideways. As we saw above, the makeup of the whiteface clown foregrounds one or two raised eyebrows, which are displayed upon the area of the forehead that, in contrast to the lower part where the eyebrows are located, cannot easily be moved by muscular control. Not only is the authoritarian expression of the whiteface frozen like a mask on the clown's face, but the complete whitening of his natural eyebrows also prevents him from producing visible signs of friendliness and spontaneous positive feelings toward others that would in any case be filtered out by his mask if they happened to occur.

Now, coming back to examine the makeup of the auguste Chicky, we notice that his natural eyebrows have been almost entirely erased and blended within the reddish portion. The strong chromatic contrast that the eyebrows create on the adult human face has been reduced to a minimum, to the point that the face resembles a baby's. Only a close-up can reveal the presence of normal eyebrows behind the makeup, but their quasi-absence, at least when the face is seen from a distance, deprives this august of the possibility of producing aggressive facial gestures of the kind inscribed on the mask of the whiteface. It also prevents the clown Chicky from sending eyebrow flashes, which, as we saw earlier, are an utterly friendly sign. However, the visual erasing of the eyebrows represents only one version of the auguste makeup. As we will discuss later, the other version, in comparison, emphasizes the natural eyebrows either by darkening them or by sticking false, black eyebrows on top of them. This allows the auguste to flash expressive signs toward the audience, which are all the more visible because white patches are usually added in the regions around the eyes as we noted earlier. Both the downplaying and the underlining of the natural eyebrows are in striking opposition to the treatment of the eyebrows in the makeup of the whiteface clown. The semiotic system underlying these two categories of makeup exploits one of the most effective resources of the human face to express attitudes and emotions in a way that largely escapes deliberate manipulation in real-life, face-to-face interactions.

Have these contrasting patterns become a part of European popular culture by design or by chance? It is difficult to answer this question because, in the case of the circus, we are confronted with a fringe of popular culture that remained undocumented for a long time before it caught the attention of historians and anthropologists. We can trace the makeup of clowns back through the past 300 years, mainly because Joseph Grimaldi acquired a celebrity status in England at the end of the eighteenth century and was portrayed in many color prints. The advent of photography helped create better archives, but for a long time it was in the form of sepia or black-and-white documents that lack the essential information provided by color. When contemporary technology allowed for the reproduction of precise chromatic imaging, the different kinds of contrasting masks had already stabilized in the forms described above. But they were not created suddenly; they progressively emerged through variations of existing patterns and seem to have reached some systematic coherence and complementarity that became the norm for about a century. As we proceed toward the end of this chapter, we will see that the formal duality embodied in the two kinds of makeup now tends to lose its canonical rigor to the point that, increasingly, the duo formed by the whiteface and the auguste is mostly perpetuated by the conjugated forces of cultural inertia and nostalgia. But the fact is that this biologically and socially meaningful opposition in the made-up faces of the two antagonists who perform traditional clown acts remains relevant for audiences in a large cultural area coextensive to Europe. The contrasting forms of makeup, though, remain totally puzzling for North American audiences, which are familiar with another kind of clown makeup that will be described and discussed later in this chapter.

Interpreting the face of a clown

The two juxtaposed versions of the makeup of clowns that have been described in the previous sections have in common that they radically distance themselves from the normal, average appearance of the faces of the civil population, even if we factor in the occasional extravagances of fashionable cosmetics, hairstyles, and hats. However, they mark their difference in opposite directions. This is most obvious when a clown act involves a whiteface, an auguste, and the ringmaster, who stands as an icon of formal normality between the two partners. Keeping in mind, of course, that in both cases the makeup is a carefully crafted artifact, the whiteface exhibits evidence of overgrooming to the extent of appearing almost inhuman, while the auguste displays signs of undergrooming to the point of looking grossly unkempt and definitely unrefined. The significance of these two masks is assessed by the audience in the context of the clowns' character and demeanor. The whiteface is articulate, moves graciously, and is elegantly dressed. In contrast, the garb of the auguste is gaudy and ill fitting, his behavior is awkward, and his way of speaking is unpolished as well as impolite. They form a semiotic couple in which the signs that define one are inverted in the other.

The thin outline of the lips of the whiteface lends elegance and distinction to his way of speaking, because it makes visible the articulation of the words he utters. But the heavy coat of grease paint around the mouth of the auguste emphasizes the animal function of this natural orifice and freezes a naïve, permanent smile, evoking denseness instead of wit—although it is generally the case that, at the end, the auguste often outsmarts the whiteface, as we will see when we document the actual performances that can be observed. The range of his expressions is indeed limited by the impossibility of subtly calibrating his reactions as a situation develops, but a rich repertory of gestures largely makes up for the restricted range of his facial expressions, and musical instruments are often called upon to lend him an eloquent voice.

The two types of clown makeup that define the performing dyad known as the whiteface and the auguste reached a state of cultural stability some 150 years ago and have kept generating countless versions through creative variations. This is a historical phenomenon whose cultural significance will be amply discussed in this book. Let us now consider the makeup of clowns before this dissimilar couple emerged as a staple of circus shows. We will later examine the current state of affairs, which is characterized by a fading out of this relatively recent tradition and the evolution of clown makeup toward more subtle, more humane transformations of the face, a semiotic shift holding, as I will show later, profound ideological implications.

Let us first take a look at the prototypical clown of modernity, Joseph Grimaldi (1778–1837), who offers a striking example of transformative makeup (Figure 1.12).

He was a British actor, dancer, and acrobat of Italian descent. The legacy of the Commedia dell'Arte and other traveling actors and acrobats indeed provided an abundance of performers, who entertained popular audiences at the famous theaters of Sadler's Wells, Drury Lane, and Covent Garden in London, as in other British and European cities. Joseph Grimaldi reached celebrity status in England during the Regency period, and snapshots of his most popular scenes were represented in numerous color prints. His civil identity, though, was not obliterated by his performing persona, because the character of *Clown* that he played in pantomimes was only one of his many roles. A painted portrait by John Cawse represents him in 1807, at the age of twenty-nine, posing barefaced in the fashionable attire of the time. *Clown* was a character in pantomimes, which Grimaldi elevated to the generic sense it has today, thanks to the influence of English performers in France and Europe in general in the nineteenth century. Grimaldi as *Clown* was known as "Joe," a name that has also become a generic term like "clown" in Britain and America. Contrary to most other comic performers, Joseph Grimaldi has

FIGURE 1.12 *Joseph Grimaldi (1778–1837) in the role of Clown.*
Artwork by David Blostein.

left significant records of his life and works, both in visual and written forms. These documents have been published and discussed in the exhaustive biography published by Andrew McConnell Stott (2009).

Joseph Grimaldi's makeup as *Clown* is quite striking: his entire face is whitened; his large lips are painted in red, apparently vermillion; two large red triangles are drawn on his cheeks; and his eyebrows are heavily darkened. He wears diverse forms of black or reddish wigs cropped down the center of his skull. The Mohawk style. The artificiality of the symmetrical triangular patterns restructures his whole face by superimposing on his natural features clear-cut geometrical figures that stand out on the whitened background of his skin. His eyes are surrounded by some more lightly colored makeup, with the effect that their visibility and expressivity are enhanced. The prints that have preserved Grimaldi's makeup as *Clown* are close-ups, but we must assess this performing face in the context of premises such as Sadler's Wells, Drury Lane, and Covent Garden: the stage was quite distant from the audience and the gas lighting was much less bright than today's spotlights.

In view of the interpretations proposed so far in this chapter, the heavy, dark underlining of the eyebrows and the bright-red coloring of the lips in Joseph Grimaldi's makeup indicate that his face was very communicative from a distance, all the more so because his skin was whitened, including his prominent nose, which thus blended into the background. This latter feature was crucial, as it helped project the friendly roundness of his face and allowed the audience to focus their attention on the expressive triangle formed by his eyes and mouth. The red patterns on his cheeks had curved sides that framed his eyes and mouth along natural lines, foregrounding the ocular orbits and the muscular ridges created by smiles and laughter. These added triangular patches evoked the redness of excitement and inebriation. At the same time, the geometrical makeup made the actor's natural face unrecognizable, as if it were a mask but a mask that would preserve all the main expressive functions of the human face. It had the advantages of a mask that hides the identity of the perpetrator of transgressive actions, but without the inconvenience of precluding the possibility of expressing attitudes and emotions toward a large audience. In fact, this makeup was a semiotic device crafted to produce redundant signs grounded in the biological repertory of human visual interactions.

We can now see how the legacy of *Clown* in the following centuries exploited this potential and generated a rich family of chromatic designs that can be construed as visual themes and variations, enabling comic performers to both protect their identity through the relative anonymity of a mask and express their individuality by branding themselves, so to speak, in order to compete in the crowded market of popular entertainment. Their performing persona exemplified various degrees of stupidity, greediness, disrespect, and amorality. Understandably, artists who impersonated *Clown* in the Grimaldi tradition would strive to distance themselves from the character they were playing in public. For instance, the makeup of the Victorian clown James Frowde (1831–1899) displayed on his whitened cheeks the same curved triangular patterns of red that were used by Joseph Grimaldi, although they appear to form smaller marks in its iconography (Bratton and Featherstone 2006: 129). Similar red geometrical patterns appear on the whitened face of the colored drawing of an acrobatic clown represented on a Victorian Christmas card originally published around 1885. Although the painter may have indulged in artistic license, the design obviously conforms to the contemporary expectations of what an English clown makeup should look like: clear-cut geometrical red patches superimposed on a uniformly whitened face. This design tends to distort so much the natural features of a human face that it truly acts as a mask that brings marked discontinuities to a natural morphology characterized by curved volumes and chromatic blending (Kervinio 2005; Lutz 1979). In particular, it interferes with the biologically meaningful signals produced by the eyebrows, the eyes, and the mouth. It is the prototype of a productive paradigm of makeup among British and North American clowns that, as mentioned above, are often called by the generic "Joes" in reference to Joseph Grimaldi.

The modern face of the clown

The role of the traditional auguste as a rebel victimized by the dominant whiteface came to prominence in some geopolitical areas in the context of the socialist revolutions at the beginning of the twentieth century and triggered a shift in the style of clown makeup in reaction to the stereotypes then reigning in the rest of capitalist Europe. Indeed, the exploitation of underclasses by elitist masters was played out quite blatantly in the comic mode by a couple of performers, such as Footit and Chocolat, who reached fame in the Parisian circuses of the late nineteenth and early twentieth century (1886–1910). We will return to this emblematic couple later in the book, but let us mention now that Footit was a whiteface endowed with a domineering, even cruel personality, while the auguste Chocolat was a good-natured man of African ancestry, who, as such, could dispense with heavy makeup. This was at the time of the French colonial expansion. The ridiculous antics of a naïve black man under a white master, who mocked and bullied him, perfectly fit the reigning ideology. The neat tuxedo worn by Chocolat was meant to be ironical. But all the augustes of the time were coming through as half-wit derelicts or unpolished proletarians and peasants, similar in many respects—albeit with marked cultural differences—to the American ill-shaved tramps and hobos.

The whiteface did not take root in American circuses. And it soon disappeared from the Russian cultural landscape also, to be replaced there by a humanized clown figure, typically representative of the working class, which, during the period preceding the October Revolution, had played the role of a political catalyst. Under the new communist regime there was no need to act behind the mask of an outcast, and, as a consequence, a new kind of makeup emerged, which enhanced the natural features of the performer. Modern Russian clowns continued this tradition, and the prototype spread globally as spectators and circus artists were exposed to the celebrated Moscow Circus and high-profile clowns. These clowns included Popov, the jovial jester with his enlarged workingman cap, and Karandash, the little mustached common man who was particularly famous for two acts—"the broken statue" and the "uncooperative mule." In the first act, he was ordered by the ringmaster to dust a replica of the Venus of Milo with a feather duster. In attempting to complete this menial task, he inadvertently knocked down the statue, which broke into several pieces. Confronted with various body parts scattered on the ground, he tried to put the statue back together but kept making hilarious mistakes. The act with the mule staged his struggle to make the animal pull a cart. However, despite his efforts, the mule would not budge. In the end, the mule was seated in the cart and the clown was pulling the cart out of the ring. This latter act was so popular that the Soviet Union printed a postal stamp honoring Karandash, showing the mule sitting in the cart being pulled by the clown.

In today's European circuses and their outreach, we can observe two paradigms: on the one hand, traditional teams formed by a whiteface, now often played by a woman, and one or two augustes; and, on the other hand, clowns who perform solo, occasionally using the ringmaster as interlocutor or bringing into their interludes some willing members of the audience. "Immersive performances," as this second mode has been characterized, involve the participation of adults as well as children in simple games or comedies under the leadership of the clown, who in this context must appear friendly because spectators are invited to play with him or her. These solo performers truly belong to the category of augustes, but their makeup is much more subtle and preserves most of the communicative potential of their natural face, while enhancing some features that contribute to their charisma. Their general appearance situates them outside the norm, but not to the same extent as the extremely refaced whiteface and auguste exemplified by emblematic troupes such as the Fratellini or the Pauwels, in the first and the second part of the twentieth century, respectively (Figure 1.13). In contrast with these colorful styles of makeup, the hues and patterns through which contemporary clowns create their performing identities are greatly toned down.

July 27, 2013. During the afternoon performance of Zirkus Charles Knie, photographer Zbigniew Roguszka has taken many shots of the clown André for the illustrations in this book. As the circus is emptying at the end of the show, André joins us and, as we chat, agrees to be photographed on the spot. Zbigniew, who holds high professional standards, protests that the now-dimmed light is not right for the shots. I insist because it is, for me, a unique opportunity to have a visual document that allows a close analysis of his makeup. I simply ask André to kindly produce the series of emotions he expresses as his bathtub act unfolds. Zbigniew fiddles with the camera and quickly starts shooting. In this face-to-face situation, I can clearly observe how his makeup is crafted with judicious, minimalist additions to his natural features and how this style enhances the visibility of the attitudes and emotions he projects toward the audience.

FIGURE 1.13 *Auguste Pépète (Alfred) Pauwels (1912–1989) with his sons, whiteface Charlie and second auguste Marquis (from the author's collection).*

Now at my desk, as I am writing this chapter, I review the thirty-seven color photographs Zbigniew sent me a few days ago. The one I enlarge on my computer screen shows the details of the makeup as if it were under a microscope. I can easily reconstruct the successive steps that André had followed in front of his mirror. The whole face had first been smeared with a light base. Then, red was uniformly added, except within the ocular orbit, to produce a warm, pinkish color that turns more intense on the upper cheeks and on the chin. The natural eyebrows are hardly visible under this first layer of makeup, but two slightly curved lines of black have been traced just above their upper borders, starting in the middle of the eyebrows and following the orbits toward the temples. The tip of the nose was reddened. White patches were added on the upper and lower eyelids, but a fine line of black also *underlines the eyes under the lower eyelashes. The lower lip is whitened. Finally, two small black dots are painted, on the upper right cheek and slightly off center on the chin (Figure 1.14).*

The black-and-white rendering of the color photograph described above does not make it possible to perceive the chromatic nuances that provide the spectators with meaningful signs. The marked redness of the tip of the nose, for instance, is not visible in this picture and, as a consequence, the absence of the visual anchor point forming a triangle with the two eyes draws the first impression more toward a normal adult face instead of the rather childish gestalt that is foregrounded during the performance. The emphasis on this red portion indeed reduces the length of the nasal appendage, as would the addition of an artificial bulbous red nose, but without totally offsetting the human quality of André's face. It may also hint at the clown's jovial inebriation. However, the high definition of the various shades of gray in this photograph conveys a sense of the richness and radiance of his performing face. The reduction of the eyebrows has the same effect as what we observed earlier in Chicky's makeup. It precludes the possibility of frowning in a hostile manner. But the arcs that have been drawn very lightly just above the eyebrows contribute to the creation of an expression of surprise and innocence congruent with the other neotenic features (infantile face) of this makeup, and their position with respect to the underlying muscles of the face allows them to be visibly moved up and down in the course of dynamic expressions. Finally, the whitening of the eyelids and the lower lip, although it is less marked than

FIGURE 1.14 *Clown André expressing happiness.*
Photo credit Zbigniew Roguszka.

in many traditional augustes, emphasizes the natural signals of friendliness and trustworthiness conveyed by the sclera and the upper teeth. When we analyze the content of some of André's interludes later in this volume, we will see how easily the public reads the signs of the various emotions he flashes on his face as the performed narratives unfold. Quite obviously, this kind of light but smart makeup serves well the artists whose humor selectively taps the communicative resources of the human face by strategically enhancing some of them and toning down others.

André's minimalist but semiotically effective makeup is symptomatic of a new paradigm that emphasizes the humanity of the clown and steers its made-up face away from the unsettling traditional, unnatural patterns and colors. As we will see in the next section, the very process of transforming the natural appearance of an artist into his/her performing identity can even be made a part of the spectacle.

When clowns go postmodern

So far, this chapter has introduced and discussed the makeup of European traditional clowns as they could be observed and documented for approximately three centuries, from Joseph Grimaldi to contemporary performers who perpetuate this tradition. However, as we progressed through the chapter, we witnessed the emergence of more subtle kinds of makeup characterizing modern clowns both in the circus ring and on the stage. All professional entertainers use some amount of makeup to enliven their faces and compensate for the deadening effects of the spotlights, but modern clowns are very specific in deliberately producing these moderate facial transformations, as we saw in André's case. The role of the auguste is thus humanized, while remaining distinct from the appearance of ordinary persons. It is nevertheless still a kind of mask that is complemented by a typical costume and demeanor, squarely situating the clown out of the cultural norm and setting the performing persona as strictly distinct from his/her civil identity.

However, in the wake of postmodernism, some clowns have made the process of their facial transformation a part of their very performance. Through a kind of visual "deconstruction," they expose the tricks of the trade, making the audience witness the metamorphosis of one face into another and, then, at the end of their act, undoing it before leaving the ring. This spectacular disclosure does not seem to have a detrimental impact on the appreciation of the artist whose performing identity quickly captures the attention of the audience and erases the memory of the bare face, which by comparison lacks the salient shapes and colors signaling the powerful circus code. As will be amply documented in this book, playing with codes of any kind is indeed the hallmark of clowning. This can even apply to the clowns' own performing identities.

Vienna, September 2011. As I wait in line to get access to the tent of Circus Roncalli, I notice that this year's program features David Larible, an Italian clown of international fame. He is a modern auguste who usually performs alone, bringing some members of the audience into the ring to have them participate in games or plays he directs, in which they are the butt of his fairly aggressive humor. I am familiar with his look and performance. I have watched him several times when he was touring North America. His makeup is typical of his genre: warm colors and white patches, bulbous red nose, and shaggy hair give him a jovial, childlike expression that nevertheless lets his strong personality emerges through this charismatic mask. His made-up face is nevertheless very natural from a distance and is very effective in the large arenas in which American and Canadian circuses are wont to perform. His forceful presence succeeds in reaching out to the last row of seats. I wonder how he will score in the quite intimate atmosphere of a European circus such as Roncalli—my thought as I proceed to my seat in the rich environment produced by the red velvet and gold décor that evokes a Baroque theater, suffused with the scent of the adjoining stables.

The time for the show is approaching. As I leaf through the printed program, the lights are unexpectedly dimmed and a stern-looking man casually enters the ring and walks toward the small ordinary table and chair that have been placed at its center. He sits down, lights a candle, and takes from his pockets a mirror and some little boxes. A discreet spotlight provides the scene with more visibility. The suggested atmosphere evokes the dreariness of everyday chores in a colorless world. Now, the audience gets the point: this is the clown, who starts applying makeup to his face. The transformation is swift and surprising. The man's long nose suddenly disappears behind a little red ball; his hair gets abundant and undisciplined. The man dons an oversized jacket. Like a Phoenix surging from the ashes, David Larible arises from the common world into the bright realm of the circus, and the show can now start with the fanfare and intense light that form the natural setting of his radiant presence.

He will appear on several occasions during the show, at times shadowed by a ghostly whiteface clown whose presence is an aesthetic, nostalgic homage to the tradition. David Larible's forceful persona fills the ring and the tent. As an auguste, he has emancipated himself from the dependency on a dramatic partner. He engages the audience, whose members are invited to "play" with him and selectively dragged to the center. Willy-nilly, they are made to provide comical content for his acts. This has become a more-or-less accepted part of circus shows under the name of immersive performance—a phenomenon we will discuss further in this book.

The program is now winding down. A chair and a table are brought to the center of the ring. The clown follows, hangs his oversized checkered jacket at the coatrack, sits down, takes the mirror out of his pocket, and starts wiping off his makeup. Soon, the red nose has gone, as well as the shaggy hair and the colorful garments. As the light is dimmed, the music turns sad. The one who ushered in the wonders of the circus vanishes in front of the audience. The world of everyday pains and angst briefly engulfs again the public, which wakes up from the dream. But the circus magic takes over again as the music flares up and all the artists march around the ring and take their bows to the audience under fireworks, which rain tinkling tinsel from the top of the tent.

I now remember clearly having noticed the harsh facial features of this man—who was hanging around in front of the entrance, leaning on the fence that encloses the circus, ogling the crowds with the imperious air of a dominant personality—as I was endlessly waiting to gain access to the tent. When he displayed his transformation in the ring, some people may have been surprised by the stunning difference of the two faces. But as soon as they step outside, the spectators are again confronted by the large posters and banners showing the face of this clown, and there is no doubt that their brief glance at his natural features is quickly obliterated in their memory by the powerful icon they recognize and the glamour of the spectacle they have experienced.

All deconstructive processes can cause a cultural shock of some level of intensity, depending on the force of the norms whose artificiality is thus suddenly revealed. Such a critical multimodal discourse is at the heart of the art of clowning, as we will see later in this book when I describe and discuss the narratives performed by the clowns.

2

The Costumes of the Clowns

The clowns' trunks

Circus is primarily a trade through which individuals, family, and corporations make a living, even quite often a fortune. It requires entrepreneurship, capital, and technical knowledge. It also necessitates the employment of workers who work for a fixed salary or a fee. Clowns, among other artists, are professionals who perform their acts as part of a program, under the constraints specified by their contracts. Whether they can work most of the year in profitable conditions depends on the entertainment market, unless, of course, they are part of a circus owner's family, a situation that usually guarantees their employment. Some high-profile clowns who have successfully managed their career and have attracted the attention of the media command a higher price commensurate with their capacity to attract spectators; others, of lesser status, perform under rather unfavorable circumstances. Most clowns are not highly regarded by other circus artists. But it is hard to find a circus poster that does not feature at least a clown face. Indeed, circus owners know that their audiences expect to see clowns when they purchase a ticket to the show. These expectations bear not only on what clowns do but also on the way they look from head to toes.

In the previous chapter we saw that each clown has a unique makeup, a kind of trademark that together with a stage name establishes his/her performing identity. It is considered the property of the performer who has created it. Attempts have been made to formalize a kind of copyright protection, like the repository of clown faces painted on eggshells that was established in England in the mid-1940s by the International Circus Clown Club, now called Clowns International. This undertaking had limited success because it had far from the international coverage it claimed. It also soon lost its professional specificity when many amateur clowns were included in the collection. The latter tend to invent makeup patterns on a freewheeling basis, irrespective of the various cultural traditions that map the identities and characterizations of circus performers. The market value of a clown depends not only on the effectiveness and charisma of his/her makeup but also on the typical stage costumes he/she wears.

The semiotic creation and daily re-creation of a clown's face is a minimal professional expense. But special costumes are an essential part of the art of clowning. Traditional clowns travel with large trunks. The wear and tear of daily performances—often in dusty, rainy, or muddy environments—takes a toll on the fabric, color, and shape of these garments, which always have to appear in prime condition, even in the case of tramp outfits whose tears and shreds have been carefully crafted. This requires that clowns carry with them several sets of costumes. The whiteface clowns who, as we will see in the next section, notoriously sport valuable glittering attire, need long vertical trunks in which they can hang their robes. Augustes also wear costumes that are colorful and need care, in addition to their wigs and traditionally oversized shoes.

The splendor and sophistication of the whiteface

In the previous chapter, we encountered the typical makeup, in its various versions, of the whiteface clown that became a staple of a 200-year-old circus tradition. The key words that define this kind of clown are elegance, sophistication, dominance, rhetorical excellence, and more generally cultural competence. There is a great variety of models, but all the whiteface costumes are characterized by their fine materials, such as brilliant silk; colorful satin and rich velvet; and cotton studded with pearls, beads, sequins, tinsel, brocade, or tiny reflecting mirrors. All these are often combined with embroidery. They also have a unique shape: a single-piece gown with padded shoulders and upper sleeves, relatively narrow waistline, and laterally expanded sides along the thighs. In many cases, the calves are left visible, fitted with white stockings. The shoes are delicate, similar to those of ballet dancers. This type of dress has sometimes been compared to the glittering garments of Spanish bullfighters, although the global pattern perhaps evokes the refinements of feminine high fashion to a greater degree. Regardless, clown fashion definitely constitutes a unique, iconic type. It is symptomatic that the role of the whiteface is at times performed by a distinguished woman wearing an evening dress.

The decorations embroidered or painted on the whiteface clowns' costumes are most often geometrical. But this is not an absolute rule. There are examples of stars and comets being represented on the fabric, as if the clown were a priest or magician endowed with cosmic power (e.g., Hoche et al. 1982: 48–49). We also encounter costumes on which musical scores have been embroidered. It seems that anything cultural can find its way onto the whiteface clowns' costumes. For instance, some of them display icons of famous narratives such as folktales or songs. But by and large the most frequent decorations are abstract designs of great aesthetic value.

The costume of the whiteface clown is indeed an artistic medium that befits his/her intimate connection with the realm of high culture. Pipo (Gustave Sosman, 1901–1970) was one of the very best clowns of his generation. His demeanor in the ring was elegant; he was charming toward the audience; and he treated his partners with authority but without being excessively aggressive. When I was a student in Paris in the 1950s, I relished the acts he was producing and performing at the Winter Circus. Pipo, Dario, and Mimile formed a successful team in which Pipo, when he was not playing the traditional whiteface part, variously impersonated a military officer, a policeman, a gentleman, or an impresario engaging his two auguste partners in hilarious comedies. One of Pipo's sons, Philip Sosman, started a circus career as a gentle and subtle auguste but, after his father's death, took the family mantle and performed as a whiteface, using the same makeup as his father. Pipo Jr. has now been displaying for several decades, with his own talent, the same style of costumes and impersonations that had made his father famous. During an interview I conducted with him in 1983 at Circus Knie in Switzerland, he mentioned that his father had a costume that had been specially designed before the Second World War by the French painter Robert Delaunay (1885–1941), the founder of Orphism. A few weeks later he kindly sent me a photograph of his father wearing this outfit, which features the geometrical patterns that were the trademark of this avant-garde artist (Figure 2.1).

As it happens, the Sosman family, who ran their own circus in the early 1900s, keeps its archives in good order. An article on this dynasty features a 1944 photograph of Pipo, dressed in the Delaunay costume, as he interacts with the auguste Rhum, who was his partner at the time (Chevillard 2013: 28). See Figure 2.2.

There also exists a website in which the rich iconography of the Sosmans can be found (clownevolution.blogspot.com). We discover there that at age four or five Philip was photographed wearing whiteface makeup. Interestingly, the trademark eyebrow of his father was designed on the child's forehead, but on the opposite side. However, after his father's death, when Pipo Jr. himself became a whiteface clown, the drawn eyebrow occupied the right side, like his father's. In the 1983 conversation, which was recorded in Stephen Riggins's autobiography (2003: 252–253), Pipo lamented what he perceived as a decline in the attention given to the artistic excellence of clowns. He mentioned in passing his interest in the American cinema, specifically the

FIGURE 2.1 *Whiteface Pipo had a costume designed by Robert Delaunay (from the archives of the Sosman family).*

FIGURE 2.2 *Rendering of a photo showing Pipo interacting with the auguste Rhum (from the archives of the Sosman family).*

Artwork by David Blostein.

films with Fred Astaire, whose ways of walking and dancing he yearned to emulate. Whiteface clowns are indeed likely to perform fancy footwork and elegant acrobatics. This is why their costumes must be compatible with the dynamics of their demeanor and not interfere with their virtuoso agility. By contrast, as we will see below, auguste clowns waddle awkwardly and drag their feet, often falling and tumbling.

A few fabric designers have specialized in producing whiteface clown costumes. To be sure, this is not something that can be left to amateurs. In France, Gérard Vicaire (b. 1927) has specialized for decades in such costumes, which are referred to in French circus lingo as *sacs* [bags]. Before probing further the whiteface's typical costume and its sociosemiotic implications, let us turn to the markedly different attire of the auguste.

The auguste's misfits and tatters

There is a range of outfits that characterize the auguste clown. The universal feature, though, is that whatever might be the style of the costume, it is in some ways the opposite of all the features of the whiteface clown. The auguste can appear dressed in a proper black suit, even a tuxedo, but one that does not fit because it is either too small or too large. In most cases, auguste clowns wear oversized two-piece suits cut in fabrics whose hues or patterns are at odds with the standard norms of the contextual culture. These suits may include accessories such as vests, suspenders, large buttons, or huge safety pins. The costumes usually display very bright, lurid, gaudy colors, qualities that magnify the disproportions between the costume and the body. It does not fit the clown's body, nor does it reflect the current male fashion. This kind of costume would immediately be identified as an auguste's attire if it were encountered on a crowded street among numerous other styles of garments, including provocative ones. When current fashion is used as an inspiration for an auguste's outfit, it is implemented in an exaggerated, caricatured manner. It is significant that the costumes worn by Joseph Grimaldi, at the dawn of the modern art of clowning, were parodies of the male fashions during the Regency in England.

A brief review of the illustrations found in Hoche et al.'s book on the great clowns of the past 200 years offers a demonstrative and colorful panorama (Hoche et al. 1982). Note that this volume contains sets of a dozen pages of photographs, which are inserted in the text but numbered independently from the text. Consequently, the references indicate the two pages of text within which specific images can be found. The photographs, though, are numbered from 1 to 115 across the volume. Illustrations 28 to 41 document the celebrated Swiss auguste Grock (Adrian Wettach 1880–1959). Interestingly, they offer examples of ill-fitting costumes on both ends of the spectrum. The parody of a piano recital performed in the early twentieth century shows Grock being cast in a too-short and too-tight tuxedo (35–36); but his auguste trademark figure provides striking examples of oversized coats and trousers (28, 41a and b). The chapter devoted to the celebrated Russian auguste Popov (96–97) includes several color photographs showing the huge French cap that the clown was wearing over his long, straight, yellow hair. It is cut in a black-and-white checkered fabric whose squares are greatly enlarged. Other illustrations present Popov impersonating a cook playing with plates or parodying a nurse treating a patient. In each case, the clown wears appropriate professional outfits over his auguste costume, which remains ostentatiously visible. As appropriate, his iconic cap is traded for the typical hats of the professions he mocks. Pictures of Popov in his trademark outfit can also be found in Lipovski (1967: 39–53).

Among the many other illustrated books on clowns, Bolognesi's (2003: passim) offers photographs of Brazilian augustes that for the most part appear to perform in circuses much less affluent than those of the former Soviet Union. Their garb, however, provides examples of minimal implementation of the same dress code governing the designs of the costumes worn by Grock and Popov. Karandash, the celebrated Russian clown whom Popov considered his teacher and mentor (Lipovski 1967: 61–70), wore a large cap or a pointed peasant hat. His costume was an oversized black suit and a white shirt with a string tie. He waddled through his solo acts, usually encountering unmanageable situations. While Popov evoked the persona of a common workingman, Karandash looked more like a dressed-up countryman. It is in order here to remember that the original meaning of *clown* in English was "peasant." Those toiling in the fields and tending to farm animals have been the butt of jokes on the part of city dwellers who think of themselves as representing the apex of civilization. When farmers dressed up for special circumstances, they appeared awkward and lacking poise. Urbanites relished making fun of them.

At the other end of the spectrum of the auguste's styles of costume we find the torn, patched, shredded apparel that traditionally characterized the derelict bum (the French *clochard*) and the American tramp or hobo. There is a range of variations on this dress code. In the act by Tom and Pepe that we will analyze in Chapter 7, the two augustes performing as a team impersonate homeless people. They enter the ring pushing a cart full of disparate objects that appear to have been picked up in a garbage dump. Tom's costume is a stunning representation of the tatterdemalion. There is no doubt that designing and sewing this garb took more time than producing a whiteface costume. Not a single patch has been left unshredded, to the point that it is an icon of economic dejection, like misery under a microscope.

The sociosemiotics and biosemiotics of clown costumes

In human societies, the relative status of individuals is signaled by the way they dress and the way they move. Postures, manners of walking, hand gestures, and facial expressions form dynamic patterns that we spontaneously read and use to categorize people's class and function. These discriminatory patterns are necessarily perceived in combination with the clothes people wear—their fabric, style, and freshness. The couple formed by the whiteface and the auguste is a stereotypical icon of social differences. This is obvious observing the first minutes of the recording of a classical "broken mirror" clown act interpreted by Pipo and Zavatta in Paris's Winter Circus of 1966 at http://www.circopedia.org/Pipo_and_Zavatta_video_(1966) [permission to view this video must be obtained from the administrator of the Circopedia website]. We will return to this particular comedy later in this volume, but let us focus on its beginning for the time being. The ringmaster appears to oversee the installation of the props for the act to come. Actually, it is the beginning of the narrative. Two movers enter the arena, each carrying an antique armchair wrapped in protective cover. One of the movers is the auguste Zavatta, who has donned a workingman's blue overall like that of the other mover. Zavatta walks like someone used to bearing heavy weight; his manners are uncouth and somewhat disrespectful. Although he wears his auguste makeup, he seems to fit perfectly into the habitus of the working class he represents. The ringmaster scolds him because they have forgotten the mirror that matches the two armchairs. He mentions that it is important because a famous actor (Pipo) from the French national theater, La Comédie Française, will soon arrive in his dressing room to rehearse his part in front of this mirror, which is a stage prop for the play. Zavatta is unimpressed and replies aggressively that they cannot bring everything at the same time and that he will now go and fetch the mirror. Suddenly, there is a loud noise of glass being broken coming from back stage, and Zavatta returns with only the mirror's decorated frame. After a brief moment of panic, the ringmaster suggests that Zavatta should stand behind the frame and mimic the postures and gestures of Pipo so that the latter does not realize that the mirror is absent. In an attempt to make the reflection credible, Zavatta dons a tuxedo and is given a top hat because, as we learn then, Pipo is just back from an official party and wears the formal suit typical of the cultural elite to which celebrity actors belong. When Pipo enters the ring, he displays distinction in the ways he walks and behaves. In spite of being somewhat inebriated, he makes small, elegant steps and decisive gestures. He talks down to the ringmaster. Like people of his class, he can hold his champagne without losing his countenance. By contrast, Zavatta looks awkward in his tuxedo, showing that wearing such classy apparel is not within his habitus. Nevertheless, he will try to perform as Pipo's image in the mirror in order to save the ringmaster and himself from the anger of their employer; Zavatta is a mover and the ringmaster plays here the part of a kind of butler or foreman.

This scene provides a telling example of class differences with respect to the handling of dress, movements, and space. Pipo's performed "distinction" (Bourdieu 1987) is signaled by his poise and self-assurance, as if he were the owner of the space in the ring—in fact, it is supposed to be his own dressing room in the prestigious national theater—and by his haughty attitude toward the deferential ringmaster. He fits well in the cultural frame formed by the Baroque furniture, even if it is part of a fake theatrical setting. We must not forget that all this is acted out in the artificial realm of representation. Zavatta seems at first embarrassed and ill at ease in an attire that he is not used to wearing. He has to rely on cues from the ringmaster when he is not sure how to negotiate some unexpected situations. The underlying power structure is represented through each step of this micro-narrative, in which—as we will see in Chapter 5 when we undertake the semiotic anatomy of this act in its various versions—there is more at stake than a mere practical joke and a conspiratorial deception.

The point of the partial description of this act here is to focus on the specific qualities of the whiteface clown's attire and gestures, and their symbolic affinities with the social elite of their cultural context. But beyond such a sociosemiotic approach, a relevant biosemiotic code can be deciphered. A cue is provided by one of the whiteface costumes designed by Gérard Vicaire, which has two huge peacocks embroidered on its fabric. Like these male birds, the whiteface clown displays a heavily decorated addition to his physical body and social outfit. He exhibits fitness in terms of resources and stamina. In many species, males prove their fitness by demonstrating that they can afford extra weight, conspicuous marks, and ostentatious gestures that would be serious handicaps for individuals of lesser strength and courage, who would thus be in danger of falling prey to predators. The whiteface clown is emblematic of this behavior, which is deeply rooted in evolution. He represents the tendency of some dominant individuals to catch the attention of their congeners by giving stunning evidence that they can overcome such handicaps, with the result of attracting sexual partners and political followers. But as we will see in the course of this book, the whiteface turns out to be a semiotic bubble. Bluffing may bring results in the short term—and this is what counts in biological evolution, because it may make the difference between surviving and reproducing or not. The game becomes much more complex when it is played in the context of a human society with multiple layers of cultural and social history and memory. Although the whiteface clown, as it emerged in the nineteenth century as one of the staples of the circus comic art, displayed great acrobatic abilities—he was often a former acrobat who had reached the age limit—the accretion of richer and richer decorations and embroideries prevented him from engaging in exacting jumps, dangerous somersaults, and other forms of physically demanding behavior. Early whiteface clowns' costumes were indeed much lighter and compatible with physical exertion.

It is difficult to pinpoint the exact time and circumstances that determined the moment at which the whiteface clown's persona emerged and stabilized as a symbolic type, which since then has shown a remarkable resilience. As the twentieth century waned, it seems that this role and its paraphernalia became a cultural fossil carried over by the force of inertia and sustained by the nostalgic expectations of circus audiences. Creativity has moved to the side of individual performers who do not rely as much on the dyadic structure of their acts, but instead spread the dialogic interactions among the spectators. As many examples will show in the course of this volume, it is the auguste who eventually takes center stage and develops new modes and rules of engagement through what has been dubbed "immersive performance."

Clowns in drag: Cross-dressing and transvestism

Parodying the female body and demeanor by hiding two balloons under their blouse and walking as if they had high heels is often a part of the augustes' antics. In so doing, they rely on cultural stereotypes at their worst. But these episodes in drag are usually brief and aimed at creating a shock because of the discrepancy between the grotesque makeup of the clowns and their attempts at imitating seductive feminine behavior. Some traditional clown acts involve the role of a lady represented by an auguste who simply adds a skirt over his regular garb or dresses as a ballerina. A few examples are documented in Bolognesi (2003: 140) and Levy (1991: 19, 55, 251). The first is a drawing of Billy Hayden, a nineteenth-century British clown, wearing a tutu; the second is a series of photos of Achille Zavatta impersonating a female equestrian doing a routine on horseback; the last one shows Italian clown David Larible interpreting the dance of the veils. Pépète Pauwels (1912–1989) appeared sometimes in hilarious versions of Tchaikovsky's ballet *Swan Lake*, in which he performed the role of the principal ballerina, pretending to be the celebrated Claire Motte, who was then a star of the Paris Opera (Renevey 1977: 98). This is a part of the traditional repertory that usually stages at the end a fall by the woman, caused when the male dancer, the whiteface clown, fails to catch "her" when "she" jumps into his arms. The gag includes the explosion of one of the balloons hidden under "her" blouse and ludicrous efforts made by the auguste to conceal this absence by absurdly moving the remaining balloon to the center of his chest. One of the most popular acts by the Spanish clown Charlie Rivel (1896–1983) featured him dressed as an opera diva interpreting Tosca. He sported a commanding breast under his exuberant red velvet dress, which was covered with gold and silver embroideries and extended by a long train on which he kept tripping. His wide red hat was decorated with huge ostrich feathers and flowers. Many gags interrupted his otherwise fine singing, which managed to lend some artistic credibility to his comical performance.

The targets of such parodies were at times high-profile celebrities. In 1890, then-famous Sarah Bernhardt was playing Cleopatra in a play by Victorien Sardou, *The Death of Cleopatra* [La mort de Cléopâtre], which was a great success. Footit, a former British equestrian who had become a very popular clown with his auguste Chocolat in Paris's circus world, used to bring the house down with his impersonation of a ballerina dancing on the back of a horse. There was some trepidation in the circus when he endeavored to produce a parody of the death of Cleopatra as interpreted by Sarah Bernhardt, who had the reputation of being ill tempered. Censorship and prosecution were always possibilities in Paris. Tension rose when it was known that the actress had decided to attend Footit's performance. Footit appeared in drag with a rubber snake and mockingly mimicked the tragic end of the queen of Egypt in the arms of Chocolat. To everybody's relief, Sarah Bernhardt burst into laughter at the sight of this grotesque caricature of her thespian art (Fréjaville 1922: 194–196; Verne 1930: 157–160).

Parodies of courtship provide another ground for representing women by donning female garments. One such example is the micro-narrative usually dubbed "the nightingales," in which the whiteface clown plays the part of a male bird that attempts to seduce the auguste, dressed in drag. This act will be analyzed in great detail later in this volume, but let it suffice to say for the time being that the "girl" portrays someone who is hard to get with cheap, romantic words and gifts. The auguste uses all the stereotyped gestures of feminine coquetry in a dialogic process that ends in a mock wedding only after serious and valuable goods have been produced by the courtier.

All the above examples are episodic moments in the repertory of clown acts. The auguste does not relinquish his persona in these situations, because his makeup and performing identity are always obvious behind his ludicrous disguise. There are, however, a few cases in which cross-dressing is the very basis of a clown's character. Annie Fratellini (1932–1997) was heir to a clown team, the Fratellini, which had reached international fame in the mid-twentieth century. After beginning a career as a movie actress, she returned to her ancestral circus heritage and performed as an auguste under her own name. Although, as we have noted above, women now often play the part of the whiteface clown, the character of the auguste has attracted very few female performers. There does not seem to be a feminine equivalent of the auguste's costume. Annie Fratellini wore various versions of the typical attire for this role: baggy pants, oversized jacket, and bowler hat, and, along with the costume, waddling awkwardly with an air of innocence, if not goofiness.

Another case of successful cross-dressing is Grandma, aka Barry Lubin, a clown who performs solo, impersonating an old woman. He wears a gray wig over typical auguste makeup: large patches of white around the mouth and the eyes, red nose, light reddening of the cheeks, vertical black lines extending the pupils toward the forehead. He wears yellow stockings and long, white underwear, and his trademark is a bright-red overcoat with a necklace of pearls hanging around his neck. He created an archetypal American granny who may walk as if she were struggling with arthritis but speaks her mind and behaves provocatively, apparently convinced that her age makes her immune to retribution. Like many older women in North America, this "little old lady" dresses in vivid colors, wears makeup, and always keeps her gray hair neatly curled up, fresh from the stylist. She is not fashionably dressed, just showing that she is comfortable with herself and does not give a damn whether you like it or not. She carries a handbag that she uses as a weapon whenever she deems it appropriate to chasten an attendant. One of her wicked pleasures is to pour popcorn on unsuspecting spectators. This character came into existence in 1975 in the Ringling Bros. and Barnum & Bailey Circus and was afterward associated with the Big Apple Circus (http://www.pbs.org/circus and www.barrylubin.com). Grandma has since enjoyed international fame, although her first tour in Europe was met with some puzzlement at a time when a long tradition still compelled older women to wear dark colors, even black if they were widows. In addition, a red dress or coat was the sign by which prostitutes signaled their trade. Grandma was at first shocking in the traditional European cultures, whereas she conformed to normal standards in her native country. There her transgressive qualities were expressed more by her insolent social behavior than by the color of her clothes. Eventually, international audiences became fond of her profile and antics. Barry Lubin definitely developed and expanded the character of the auguste by crossing the gender and age gap.

As this latter example shows, circus traditions are not immutable constraints, but are open to innovations. There are, however, deep principles that apply to the creation of new types of characters. In the North American cultural context, Grandma is a fairly realistic rendering of a social type. However, as an older woman, her persona belongs to a category that is both benevolent and liminal. "She" takes advantage of this status to indulge in impudent attitudes and transgressive behavior.

3

The Clown's Workshop

The semiotics of artifacts

An object can be defined by its function, but this function does not exhaust its meaning. Objects certainly can be considered in isolation for the purpose of a quantitative description. In reality, however, objects are always part of a meaningful context. Like words in a sentence or a text, objects are tools of signification. A plate, for instance, may be used practically to eat a meal while being at the same time a sign of hospitability and a display of wealth and distinction if it is, for instance, part of a Royal Albert set or another fancy kind of china. It can be used as a temporary lid or to keep the water under a flowerpot. Some collectors hang painted or antique plates on their walls, thus excluding them from any practical functions. In domestic quarrels, plates, which can be considered a sensitive symbol of harmonious commensality, are often broken as a sign of anger or frustration. Through semiotic recycling, pieces of shattered plates are at times used as parts of decorative mosaics. As we will see later, in the next chapter, clowns make use of plates in several classics in their repertory of scenarios.

Clowns, however, do not only make use of common objects such as plates, musical instruments, and chairs in their gags. They also produce new objects to be used as functional parts of their performances, either by modifying trivial artifacts or creating new ones. Although some comic artists rely mostly on words and gestures, many employ a number of objects in their acts. These objects are crafted in the clown's workshop, which provides the means of cutting, sawing, sewing, gluing, and welding.

This chapter will review and discuss artifacts used to produce gags. But let us first examine the semiotic potential of objects in the hands of performers who transgress or deconstruct their functions. Unmodified objects can be made to behave in an odd or uncooperative manner. As the clown clears his throat before singing or playing a musical instrument in front of a microphone stand, he realizes that the microphone is too high (or too low). Efforts to adjust his own position with respect to the stand rather than the reverse do not solve the problem, and, to make things worse, the clown becomes entangled in the wires as he moves around trying to reconcile distance and proximity for the sake of an impossible geometry. The celebrated Swiss clown Grock (1880–1959) sat in front of a grand piano in preparation for giving a recital but suddenly realized that the piano stool was too far away from the keyboard. He then undertook with his partner to move the piano closer to the seat. Each artifact implies a range of expectations in relation to its normal function. A microphone stand is designed to be adjustable to the desired height. A piano stool is a movable object that can be easily displaced back and forth according to needs. But a piano is also a movable object. Both piano and stool are members of a syntactic whole. They are in mutual dependence, like words in a sentence. They do not make much sense separately from each other. They are often built of the same material and in the same style. By treating both as equal members of the categorical set of mere movable objects, irrespective of pragmatic considerations, Grock disarticulated, so to speak, the syntax that was at the basis of the spectators' expectations. In so doing, he displayed a logic that reflected the odd, anarchical nature of his mind. Despite such a blatant pragmatic abnormality, we have to acknowledge the limits of the rationality of our expectations when we witness this kind of behavior. It would be an error of appreciation to interpret Grock's gag as a proof of stupidity. It was the displaying of naked logic, so to speak—a kind of logic unbounded from pragmatic constraints.

In the course of this volume, we will encounter many instances of such semiotic treatments of usual objects when we analyze the narratives in which they play a part. In the hands of a clown, a rose is a rose and is not a rose. The lady spectator who gracefully accepts a rose from the clown discovers that she holds only the stem, and, when the clown runs away with the flower and acts as if he smells the petals with an air of ravishment, the rose squirts water on his nose.

In the same way as puns activate unsuspected semantic ambiguities concealed in the phonetic structure of words and phrases, artifacts used in gags are emancipated from their normative functions and unfold in new dimensions to produce surprising, even at times shocking, meaning. We will consider later in this book the toilet seat that Charlie Cairoli transformed into a lyre by adding a few strings across the opening. In fact, it is often impossible to describe such transformed objects because the lexicon is constrained by the referential usage, which prohibits free semantic license except for the production of creative metaphors in special domains such as philosophy and poetry. But language use is quite restrictive if it is to remain functional within a linguistic community. The objects in our natural and artificial environment are categorized, for instance, as "a tiger," "a tomato," "a chair," or a "laptop." In any culture, the local language maintains and updates a stock of such labels that provide categorical information but little detail. Each label comes as a bundle, so to speak, of tacit cognitive and pragmatic information. When we provocatively stray away from common use or encounter novel objects, the referential and expressive capacity of language is strained. How to represent in words an umbrella that "rains" inside, on its holder's head, instead of protecting the person from the rain falling from the clouds? The capability of linguistic expression is challenged by such objects, which stand outside the trodden paths of usual descriptive terms loaded with assumptions. These objects both evoke and deny at the same time a functional classificatory identity. Categorically, Popov's umbrella conforms to the shape and mechanisms of the common artifact that protects us from rain or sun, but its function is tweaked to the point of creating a material oxymoron. Exploring the clown's workshop leads to discovering numerous examples of visual and pragmatic tropes of this kind that are generated by a grammar of rhetoric devices akin to the one that produced the typical images of surrealist poetry and art.

A visit to Charlie Cairoli's workshop

Blackpool, July 2012. The son of Charlie Cairoli, the long-time resident clown of the Tower Circus, has kindly agreed to let me examine some of the artifacts built by him and his father, and have them photographed for illustrating this book. As photographer Zbigniew Roguszka and I are sipping some tea in his living room, Charlie goes down to the basement to fetch a few items: a pail, a guitar, and a contraption in metal whose function is not obvious. A close examination shows that the pail has been transformed by welding a smaller container with the same curvature inside it and adding at the bottom a kind of tap or valve to connect the two spaces. There are thus two containers, one within the other, with the appearance of an ordinary pail (Figures 3.1 and 3.2).

Charlie explains that, in preparation for the act in which this prop was going to be used, the outward space was filled with water, the valve secured, and the inner space filled with confetti. But the artifact in itself is as meaningless as a syntactic tool such as a conjunction or a pronoun isolated from the context of the linguistic utterances through which meaning is produced. The act unfolded as follows: Charlie Cairoli walked around carrying the pail and jokingly throwing confetti on the spectators seated in the first row. They were at first scared because Charlie was moving as if there was water in the pail. The ringmaster intervened and scolded him, saying that it was not a nice thing to do to people who were afraid of getting wet.

FIGURE 3.1 *It looks like an ordinary pail…*
Photo credit Zbigniew Roguszka.

FIGURE 3.2 *But it's not!*
Photo credit Zbigniew Roguszka.

Charlie protested that it was only confetti and that he would not mind if someone threw confetti on him. The ringmaster said, "Really? Let me try," and he grabbed the pail from Charlie's hands. Throwing its contents toward Charlie, who was smiling with an air of triumph, it was water that came out of the pail, soaking Charlie. The ringmaster had discreetly release the valve when he seized the pail, water replacing the confetti that had all been previously scattered on the audience.

We are now presented with a vertical metallic tube that is firmly fixed to a circular heavy base and is curved at the top. The end of the tube is capped with something that looks like a showerhead (Figures 3.3 and 3.4).

"Guess what this is," says Charlie with a broad smile. "I invented it with my dad many years ago. We welded it in our workshop. The base is an old butane

FIGURE 3.3 *A portable shower…*
Photo credit Zbigniew Roguszka.

FIGURE 3.4 ... *with a tricky tap.*
Photo credit Zbigniew Roguszka.

container connected to the tube." Bringing the object closer, so we can see better, Charlie points to a kind of tap that protrudes from the middle of the tube: "This is a 'portable shower.' It was very successful." Charlie chuckles as he thinks of the act in which they used that prop. "Yes, a portable shower, man! I was playing trumpet with my dad in the ring when I was his whiteface clown. We had a partner then who was constantly interrupting us with various proposals, like a salesman. It was of course a part of the act. He came in the ring carrying that thing and started to explain how it worked: wherever you are, whenever you want, you can always take a shower with this portable item; you stand under the head and you turn that tap; water comes immediately, and you get your shower. My dad and I, we pretended at first to be annoyed by this interruption, but the guy was supposed to insist. Then, my dad acted as if he was interested and asked him to demonstrate it again. The 'salesman' was standing under the showerhead, making gestures as if he was under a shower, shampooing his hair, singing, making foam with imaginary soap. My dad, then, winked to the audience and with a mischievous expression sneaked closer and released the tap in order to play a trick and soak the unsuspecting guy. But, in fact, it was my dad who received all the water on his face, because the tube was built so that the water would come this way. Before the act, we filled the base with high-pressure water. That gag was a big hit with the public."

The third object was a plain, ordinary guitar. Charlie chuckles again and seizes the instrument, but after striking a few chords, the back of the guitar springs open and reveals a fairly realistic human bottom. Charlie acknowledges that it might not be in the best taste but points out that it creates a big effect of total surprise, albeit a very brief one. "You see, gags can be extremely short, but they must pop up in the act at the right moment and keep a tempo. The public must have no time to loosen its attention. It must be always on the cusp of what is to come, and we had better come up with something they do not expect." (See Figures 3.5 and 3.6.)

All props are not as simple as those described above. I witnessed in the 1970s two acts performed by Charlie Cairoli in which common artifacts had been modified in a more sophisticated way. The first one was a large guitar inside which a fire extinguisher had been cleverly concealed so that at the end of the act the instrument was made to spurt abundant foam on Charlie's opponents. The other modified artifact was a kitchen garbage can with a tape recorder hidden at its bottom. The act developed as a conflict between the ringmaster and Charlie. The ringmaster wanted to prevent Charlie from playing tunes on his concertina. As Charlie did not comply with this order, the ringmaster seized the concertina and left the ring. Charlie then took a mini-concertina from his pocket and resumed his playing. The ringmaster returned and was angry when he heard the music. He went back stage to get a kitchen garbage can, put it on the ground, and violently threw the diminutive instrument in it with a triumphal sneer. The public was outraged and booed the ringmaster. Charlie was left with the garbage can, which he held in his arms, looking desperate and despondent. Then, timidly, he lifted the cover of the can to look inside, and the concertina music seeped out from its depths. His music had survived, and his joy was shared by the audience. In order for the gag to work smoothly, the whole contraption had to be robust and an unobtrusive switch had to be fixed on the side of the can. All the technical moves had to be integrated into the dynamic of natural gestures.

FIGURE 3.5   *Just a plain guitar…*
Photo credit Zbigniew Roguszka.

FIGURE 3.6   *…almost.*
Photo credit Zbigniew Roguszka.

When clowns play magic

Magic acts in the circus require a great deal of special artifacts that create the desired illusions (Bouissac 2012: 48–57). Some clown acts use magic in the parody mode or as a functional part of the narratives performed in the ring. In the first case, objects are constructed so that they will fail to produce the effects expected in a magic act, or they will be manipulated in a way that deconstructs these effects by disclosing the mechanisms involved. In the second case, it is the apparition, disappearance, or transformation of various items that determines the respective characterizations of the whiteface clown and the auguste. As we will see below, these tricks may be used to reverse the respective statuses of the two performers. But let us consider now an extreme case of involuntary parody that ironically provides a clue for this genre of clowning.

July 16, 1965, Timmins, Ontario. The circus I founded with two partners, a lion trainer and a magician, is running its first season. Our small tent is pitched in a fairground. The first three months have been reasonably successful. Our 90-minute show includes pony, bear, lion, monkey, and dog acts; a juggler; two clowns; and a magician. Today, the tension between the trainer and the magician came to a showdown, and the latter decided to leave, despite my efforts to keep the team together. Losing the magic act, and the second clown, is a major setback. A snap decision is demanded, because the next show is due to start in about 6 hours. A local youth has been hanging around since we arrived in this town and has lent a hand when we set up the circus, in exchange for free admission tickets. He is right here. Could he substitute for the missing artist? He is not shy. Why not hire him for the next 2 days until I find a replacement? He accepts enthusiastically. Brian has to learn the magic act quickly. Most of it is simple, the kind of thing anybody can master in no time, like pulling a bunch of artificial flowers from one's sleeve. But the part in which a rabbit is transformed into a dove is more difficult. It is the only spectacular moment of the act. We have a special table that is made to look more flat than it actually is. The white rabbit comes from a top hat; it is immediately put on the table under a scarf, and the magic formula is uttered. When the scarf is removed, the rabbit has vanished and in its place there is a dove, which takes flight from the table and perches on the magician's hand. The rehearsal works well. After two attempts, Brian performs almost like a pro. Now the problem is to dress him up. We still have the tuxedo of the magician, who unfortunately was much shorter than Brian. Well, that will do for the clowning part, and he will keep it for the magic act. We cannot help laughing when we see our new artist emerge from the trailer where he has changed clothes. A lanky young man in his late teens or early twenties wearing that tuxedo is irresistible. We hope the audience will agree. The show starts. Now comes the moment of truth. As ringmaster, I introduce the great magician who has just arrived from Las Vegas. The beginning goes well. Brian's smile is quite charismatic in the ring. But the vanishing act is an absolute disaster: the rabbit falls through the table and start running around the ring, with Brian chasing it and the dove following the two because it is used to having some seeds when it lands on the man's hand. Surprise: the public makes an ovation and keeps clapping. Art is in the eyes of the beholders. Apparently they all think that it was a clown act making fun of magicians.

The positive reaction of the spectators to the failed performance reported in this anecdote can be explained by the fact that the improvised magician was wearing a tuxedo far too short and narrow for his body size, and was thus perceived as a clown. Nobody could have imagined the underlying story and suspected that Brian had simply pulled the wrong string, the one that was supposed to free the rabbit once the table had been returned to back stage. Comic acts of magicians who deliberately bungle their tricks while pretending to be serious belong indeed to the circus code.

The emblematic top hat, the magician's crucible in which transmutations are traditionally purported to occur, is one of the tools used by clowns in their performances. By its formal design and social connotations, a top hat belongs to the whiteface's accessories, as it symbolizes high culture. While keeping its outward appearance intact, such a hat can undergo some ingenious modifications. In the 1970s, Pierre Étaix, in the role of a whiteface clown, and Annie Fratellini, as the auguste, presented the following act, which I recorded and discussed in a previous work (Bouissac 1978: 246–251). The whiteface pretended to be a great magician and extracted multicolored scarves from a shiny black top hat in order to back his claim. Then, seizing a pitcher full of milk, he poured its content in the hat. The milk apparently disappeared, because nothing came out of this container when the hat was turned upside down. As he was announcing another magic trick with a rope, the auguste entered the ring and interrupted him. Annie Fratellini was carrying a kind of suitcase in the shape of a dog. She opened the suitcase, seized the rope, tied it around the neck of her imaginary dog, and led the virtual animal toward the empty hat, which had been put on the ground, resting on its top. Lifting her right leg as a urinating male dog does, she prompted her invisible pet to relieve itself in the hat, waited a moment, then started to exit the ring as the whiteface appeared to be flabbergasted by what had happened. But she quickly returned to center stage as if she had forgotten something, grabbed the hat, and poured out some liquid, which looked more like canine urine than milk. The common artifact that served as the medium of this apparent transmutation had obviously been engineered so that it included two independent chambers, one in which the milk was stored and sealed, the other containing water that could be released by sleight of hand. The hat, though, had to retain an apparent integrity during the whole process.

Clowns as craftsmen and engineers

At the dawn of modern clowning, in the heyday of the British pantomime, Joseph Grimaldi was famous for the props he used. He was noted for his innovative "tricks of construction," which combined papier-mâché outfits and various mechanisms thanks to which an object could be transformed into another. A color print from 1811 shows him in a scene from the pantomime "Harlequin and Asmodeus," in which he fought with a "vegetable man," a kind of Frankenstein figure made of a pumpkin head, a cabbage body, carrot arms and fingers, beet legs, and a celery stalk sprouting from the top of the skull. As this construction came alive, Joe Grimaldi fought it with boxing gloves in the shape of giant turnips (McConnell-Stott 2009: 276–277).

Minimal modifications of common objects are often all the more efficient for producing gags because there is no obvious sign that the objects have been tinkered with. The audience does not expect that they will not serve their usual functions. This was the case of the pail we encountered above. In a 1978 act that I have analyzed in detail (Bouissac 2012: 147–153), Charlie Cairoli used a specially prepared table to generate several gags. It looked at first like a plain table that had just been borrowed from a plasterer's workshop, and it served its usual function at the beginning of the act. The top of the table was simply a bit longer on both sides than the supporting frame, a normal feature designed to provide an expanded working surface. Two unobtrusive modifications had been made: first, one of the ends would bend down under pressure but would return immediately to its original position because a spring kept it horizontal; secondly, a hinge at one end of the frame made it possible to lift the top of the table and thus create a slope. This table was used for two gags only so that the gags offered a maximum of unexpectedness, all the more so because the two mechanical devices seemed mutually exclusive. The first one occurred when one of the clowns—who had scored a victory over his partner—decided to enjoy a quiet moment of triumph by leaning on the end of the table and fell down because the side of the table gave way before returning to its normal position. This endowed the object with the appearance of maliciousness. The second gag consisted of one of the clowns—who had just been victimized by being covered with foam—lifting the other end of the top and thus creating an inclined plane with the whole top, along which a pail of water slid down and soaked his tormentor.

Some clowns keep an abundance of special-effect artifacts. But they can overwhelm an audience, which may quickly anticipate that they will trigger some unexpected results. This is counterproductive, because expecting the unexpected defuses the power of the gags. Redundancy can indeed kill humor. A contrived object, however ingenious it might be, does not elicit laughter by itself. It has to create in the audience the impression that it behaves on its own, and that can be achieved only if the clown acts out appropriately and expresses a convincing sense of utter surprise. For instance, let us consider Charlie Cairoli's portable shower that we examined in the previous section. It is difficult for anybody who knows that turning on a tap will cause water to squirt toward him or her not to anticipate this effect. Consequently, it would be natural to synchronize a spontaneous withdrawal, however small, when the tap is turned on. But this would undermine the gag, because it would cue the audience about what is going to happen. We have to remember that the spectators are intensely attentive and that the score of a gag is played within a millisecond time frame. Charlie Cairoli had to resist this anticipatory reflex and focus on the intended victim of the trick as if he was convinced that the water would go in that direction. His performed surprise was what made the gag work. It was indeed an essential part of this artifact. We can keep this latter example in mind when we consider the nature and dynamics of gags in Chapter 4.

The clown's barnyard

Animals are used in some clown acts, in which they have the same functions as artifacts inasmuch as they are conditioned to look normal but to perform tricks in predictable manners on their master's cues. For the audience, though, they are perceived as normal animals, which are expected to behave according to their species' ethological program. This discrepancy is exploited to generate gags. The chronicle of the circus over the past 2 centuries offers numerous examples of the association of clowns and trained animals. Not all species, of course, can be employed in such acts. In most cases, farm and barnyard animals are the exclusive domain of the clowns. This section will review several cases and reflect upon the semiotic logic that binds clowns, almost exclusively of the auguste kind, to domestic animals.

A typical example of this sort of performance was observed in Switzerland in the 1973 program of Circus Knie. Clown Dimitri entered the ring with Belinda, a black-and-white dairy cow sporting a traditional Swiss cowbell around her neck. When the ringmaster asked him to get some milk, the clown displayed behavior betraying his ignorance of the most elementary bovine husbandry. First, he placed the container under the cow's udder, waiting for her to produce some milk. Confronted with what he obviously interpreted as her lack of cooperation, he started producing the sibilant sound by which parents sometimes encourage an infant to urinate, thus symbolically transforming the udder into a quadruple penis. Then, as this attempt failed, he seized the cow's tail and moved it up and down as if it were a well pump or an old-fashioned gas distributor. For a Swiss audience largely made up of people familiar with the keeping and milking of cows, these gestures were hilarious. Eventually, the cow—which had been given water sufficiently in advance of the act—often relieved her bladder in time to cause an explosion of laughter. Not only was this inept clown unable to obtain pleasurable and nutritious milk from the animal, but he managed to receive only urine (and sometimes more besides)—that is, the opposite of what he was trying to get. The training was minimal, as it just consisted of getting a calm cow to stand still in the center of the ring.

In the same vein, a whiteface clown presents a chicken perched high atop a pole that he balances on his chin. Now, he imitates the song of a hen that has just laid an egg. He extends his hand and catches the egg that drops from the hen. The auguste wants to copy this easy way of getting a free egg. It is his turn to balance the pole, but what drops in his eye is not an egg—at least he mimics through his gestures and facial expression that the chicken has relieved itself instead of laying an egg. Whether this skit involves a real chicken that has been habituated to cope with the context or the work of a taxidermist to make the animal credible is of little importance here. In any case, the pole has to be a prop with a mechanism allowing the whiteface to trigger the fall of an artificial egg that has been hidden from the sight of the audience. The auguste needs only to be a good mime to exploit the comical potential of the situation.

Other clown acts involving animals presuppose some sophisticated training. Molding the behavior of an animal so that various movements can be elicited on demand through discreet cues is not essentially different from building a contraption with springs and triggers, like the pole used with the chicken. Animals cannot figure out the representation of the narrative in which they are made to act according to the script of the clown. They implement segments of actions out of the habits that have been taught to them or, most often, for immediate, small gustatory rewards that their trainer hides in his or her hand. The spectators integrate these bits and pieces of behavior into the global picture of a narrative. At least two generations of "Old Regnas" have presented a dog act in which the animals appear to run the show and make a fool of their master. Andrea Semprini published a thorough description of this act, which he observed at Circus Knie in 1986 (1991: 319–333). The audience always enjoys a well-choreographed chaos that conveys the impression that the dogs are the willful initiators of hilarious gags, which abound in this act.

4

The Semiotics of Gags

What is a gag?

The terms "jokes," "slapsticks," and "gags" belong to a semantic field that implies nonseriousness and merriment. In practice, they designate identifiable units in a performance from the point of view of both the creator and the audience. For a clown, gags are the building blocks of his/her circus act; for the spectators, gags are the events that trigger laughter. It is at first difficult to relate clowns' "gags" to the common meaning of this word in English as something put in someone's mouth to prevent the person from speaking or screaming. Metaphorically, a judicial or political authority can impose temporary silence (gag) on the press or other individuals involved in a trial. In that case, the semantic connection between the concrete and the abstract is quite obvious. However, understanding the sense of "gag" in circus and theater jargon requires a bit of historical lexicology. There is textual evidence that this term was used in the technical language of coal mining to designate a piece of timber pushed into a gap in order to consolidate or stabilize a tunnel's wall. In nineteenth-century theater slang, "gags" came to refer to words or sentences an actor spontaneously inserted into the text of a part he or she was supposed to have memorized exactly. It could also be applied to gestures or actions the actor would add to the staging he/she was expected to follow. When such deliberate or chance innovations met with success—that is, caused the audience to laugh or express their pleasure otherwise—the artist would repeat them in further performances.

"Slapstick" is the name of an artifact associated with the commedia dell'arte. Literally, it is a stick used to hit someone. Actually, "slap" evokes the noise produced by a hand rather than a stick. But the kind of instrument used on stage or in the ring under the name of "slapstick" precisely creates a slapping impression, because it is designed to make more noise than harm. Technically, it can be built by connecting two slats of wood to a handle so that when someone is slapped the two pieces of wood hit each other without hurting the recipient of the blow, who can, of course, simultaneously mimic pain and fear. Another version of the "slapstick" consists of a pig bladder or a pouch fixed to a rod. Then its impact on the audience is more visual than acoustic, as it looks like a massive club. The term "slapsticks" has been generalized to designate all comical effects produced by physical means rather than witty words. As we saw in the previous chapter, clowns make extensive use of such tools for eliciting laughter.

"Joke" is derived from the Latin *ioca* [word plays, games], the opposite of *seria* [serious speech or activities] (Ernout and Meillet 1967: 322). It covers the realm of whatever is playful, in jest, just for a laugh. In Indian circuses the clowns, who are all of the auguste type, are called "jokers." Anthropologists have coined the term "joking relationship" to characterize some form of mock kinship being played out by individuals outside the constraining family structures. Joking seems to be a universal trait of human cultures as a marker of social behavior that should not be taken at face value. In contemporary societies, we distinguish "practical jokes"—usually involving physical aspects—from "jokes" that are simply told. The pragmatics of joking and clowning extends beyond the domain of entertainment to everyday life. By contrast, "gags" and "slapsticks" belong to the vocabulary of artists whose means of living implies that they have mastered the capacity of making people laugh. Gags have to be semiotically crafted and performed as they are delivered in live communication contexts. This chapter will examine how a gag is constructed and what makes it succeed or fail. But to be meaningful, a gag must be framed by a wider cognitive structure. Usually, a clown act is not a mere succession of gags.

Indeed, clown acts are performed narratives unfolding in the dialogic mode. It is possible, as we will see in the following chapters, to abstract their characters and story lines, and to record their verbal and gestural exchanges. These formal features ground the audience's interest by providing a dynamic framework within which each of the clowns' moves (gags) makes sense. The kinds of meanings they produce cause the spectators to experience mirth, which is expressed as smile and laughter. These psychological reactions do not occur continuously but are responses to specific events that punctuate the performance. Gags and narratives form a syntactic whole in which the former are foregrounded and the latter provide the necessary contexts and logical background even if it is reduced to a functional minimum.

A first step toward a comprehensive understanding of clowning as a semiotic and social phenomenon is to elaborate a morphology and typology of gags. Let us keep in mind that gags are functional units endowed with some measure of autonomy despite the fact that, in actual performances, the sense-making potential of gags is context-dependent. Gags are carefully crafted and tested on the audience. The feedback they trigger (that is, whether they elicit laughter or not) determines their permanent selection as parts of the repertory of a clown. The gags can be moved around and inserted at strategic moments in the score of the narrative. They are also portable across the range of the various narratives that the circus tradition has preserved or that creative clowns invent. We will see, in the course of this chapter, that the construction of a clown act pays utmost attention to the timing of gags. Some are prepared by moves staged ahead of time and contribute to creating misleading anticipations in the mind of the audience. Gags must indeed deliver information in the form of surprises. A gag whose development is obvious and predictable falls flat and generates boredom. The felicitous balance between the narrative and the gags is not usually reached immediately but undergoes a period of trial and error during which clowns monitor the feedback from the audience and fine-tune their act. Some gags may be omitted either to shorten the duration of an act or as a response to the behavior of the audience. Charlie Cairoli once added to my description of one of his acts that a gag I had included was sometimes skipped if he felt the audience had been slow to react to the preceding gags (Bouissac 2012: 150–154).

In their diary of 1926, the Vesque sisters recorded a conversation they had on May 17 with François Fratellini, the whiteface of the celebrated trio who were then the stars at the Cirque d'hiver. The clown expressed his reluctance to perform in the Cirque de Paris, another permanent establishment in the French capital city, because of the huge dimensions of the building. François declared that "he would not like to play in that circus even if they were offered the same price as in the Cirque d'hiver. He would feel crushed by the height and immensity of this space. By contrast he can comfortably hold all the public in a glance in the circus where they now work." This led to some personal comments on the way their clown acts were fine-tuned during the first performances of a program: "when they create a new act, they are not sure whether this or that will produce the effect they were anticipating. When they eventually present a new act in the ring, they pay attention to the audience's reactions, and they often modify the act in view of these effects. After the performance, they add notes to their written scenario, indicating at which point the public laughed or kept silent. The next day, they drop some gags, try other ones. This is why it is crucial for them to be able to scan the spectators from the front rows to the cheap seats at the top" (author's translation). Interestingly, the clown also voiced his irritation when he noticed some colleagues and competitors observing them in order to copy the gags that worked and avoid those that did not.

What makes a gag produce the intended effect will be the main issue we will address in this chapter, with particular attention paid to its structure and its timing—that is, its strategic insertion within the visual narrative of an act. The mention of jokes and slapsticks in the introduction of this chapter is meant to point to the complexity of gags, which often include both verbal and visual components in their production. Gags are functional units in the meaningful performance of a clown act. By themselves, they are purely mechanical events that cannot elicit laughter. We will also reexamine in this chapter some props—that is, artifacts—that are custom-built by clowns for the purpose of producing gags. These props can create comical effects, which depend on their context of use within the narrative of the dramatic structure of particular clown acts.

Gags in context

Two acts will now be described, with special attention paid to the gags they include. The first one was observed on February 1, 1986, at the Ryerson Theater in Toronto (Canada). The Colombaioni, two Italian clowns who presented performances on stage, were on a North American tour. When the curtain rises it reveals a lone chair on the empty, poorly lit stage. The first reaction of the public is to laugh and applaud. This beginning is indeed perceived as a gag. They have paid a hefty price to see a performance by famous clowns and realize that they are being treated to no performance at all by an inanimate trivial artifact in a dreary surrounding. After a while, a man in a semiformal suit surges from the wing, rushes to the front of the stage, and starts addressing the public in Italian. He is speaking and gesturing excitedly. He stops and stares at the audience, realizing that they do not understand what he has said because they do not know Italian. He utters, "Niente capite" [You don't get it] and makes a tapping gesture on his forehead with his index finger, signifying that he considers them idiots. Then he switches to English to introduce with a gesture the clown who is expected to arrive on the stage: "His name is Carlo." He acts as if he is going to bring him from the wing, but it is actually he himself who comes back with a top hat on his head. Then he announces his partner Alberto and keeps looking toward the same wing as the one he came from. After a while, Alberto enters but from the other side, wearing a jacket in tatters, with pieces of torn fabric hanging from everywhere, and looking very dirty and dusty. Carlo is shocked at this sight and scolds him for being so sloppy. But Alberto points to a sign in the theater that proclaims in red letters, "No smoking." Only bilingual spectators who have a European experience can appreciate the joke, because "smoking" is a term that refers in Europe to the formal black suit worn by men for special occasions—that is, a tuxedo in North American English. We will consider later this interesting example of humor misfire when we review some of the gags performed in the Colombaioni act.

Now Alberto pulls out one of his repulsively dirty gloves, searching for a proper place to store it. Carlo, looking puzzled and incredulous, watches, standing with one of his arms extended. Alberto focuses in on the arm and dusts it insistently before trusting his glove to this unexpected support. The second glove seems to be hard to remove. Carlo's help is required to pull it off, but the sleeve of his shirt is stuck to the glove and keeps coming out, endlessly, for the length of half the stage.

After this, Alberto endeavors to take off his ragged jacket with great care, folding it ceremoniously as if it were a precious garment. He emphatically utters the words "Christian Dior," alluding to the prestigious fashion label. He folds the jacket in a single fast move and proudly shouts, "Artista!" [Artist!] as if he had accomplished a brilliant acrobatic stunt. Then he looks for a proper place to deposit it and dusts off a small area on the floor of the stage in front of the audience, where he puts the folded jacket. As he walks toward Carlo, he has a second thought and stares suspiciously at a front-row spectator as if the latter is going to steal the garment. Alberto tells Carlo, "Ah! Ah!" and points to someone while adding, "The mustached guy, there!" Then he repositions the jacket further away from the man, with an air of defiance, while addressing him: "Souvenir Colombaioni, hey?" thus implying that the spectator has intended to run away with the jacket.

Carlo promptly disappears in the wing and brings back a high unicycle. He gestures toward Alberto and introduces him as a great acrobat, but Alberto repeats the same gestures toward the wing as previously, as if someone else is going to enter the stage, and says, "Here he is!" Carlo protests and tells him that he, Alberto, is the great acrobat. Instantly Alberto starts introducing himself as the great acrobat, repeating the same thing in several languages, taking a bow when he utters "acrobat": "Mesdames et messieurs, acrobate"; "Ladies and gentlemen, acrobat"; and again in German and in Italian. Carlo shows exasperation and orders him to stop. He also questions the capacity of the public to appreciate real theater by making the iconic gesture of a rectangular screen with his hands, thus claiming that they have been spoiled by television, or, as some spectators understand, that they are "square," unable to appreciate a subtle esthetic performance.

Alberto, who has disappeared in the wing for a brief while, returns and bows again to the audience while repeating "acrobat" but immediately trips and falls to the ground. He apologizes, looks confused, and loses his hat, which moves away every time he tries to pick it up. (This is a classic trick consisting of discreetly kicking the hat as one bends to retrieve it.) Carlo joins

Alberto, and both pretend they are trying to capture this elusive object that always manages to escape, thus seeming alive and mischievous. They try to approach it in silence, with no success. Alberto catches his own foot and trips when he tries to nab the hat. Eventually, they devise a strategy according to which they act as if they have lost interest in the quest, walking leisurely away while holding each other's hands and looking elsewhere. But suddenly they both jump on the hat and seize it with an air of triumph.

Carlo announces the next trick with a gesture toward Alberto: "Salto della morte!" [The leap of death!]. Alberto walks across the stage, showing the public a card with a large inscription reading "death-defying act." Now, using the support of the sidewall of the front stage, he attempts to climb to the top of the unicycle, but the saddle falls to the ground when he tries to put his right foot on the pedal. He shouts in Italian that the machine is broken. In the meantime, Carlo continues his emphatic introduction to the forthcoming "Salto della morte." At long last, Alberto has fixed the saddle and reaches the top of the unicycle. He makes a short, wobbly circle on the side of the stage area, showing fear and uncertainty. He quickly grabs again the support from which he launched himself. But Carlo resumes his banter and announces that Alberto will now ride the unicycle with his eyes covered, a scarf tied around his head.

As Carlo walks toward Alberto with a black scarf, the latter carefully straightens up the pleats of his trousers as if he is concerned with this perfectionist detail before performing a dangerous trick. The scarf is tied across his eyes, but he quickly lifts it to let one of his eyes see. Then he shifts his position so the public can perceive only the side on which he is blinded. Back on the unicycle, he zigzags across the stage in an apparently erratic manner. He rushes toward the audience as if he has lost control of the cycle but stops right on the front edge of the stage. He then pedals toward the corner of the stage for support so he can climb down, but he fails to reach it, flips his arms up and down to maintain his balance, and in so doing "accidentally" slaps Carlo with his hand. He eventually returns to his point of departure and dismounts the unicycle.

Without transition, they both start mimicking cowboys through their way of walking and playing with their guns. No actual guns, real or fake, are involved, but the brothers mime the range of typical behavior with which the audience is familiar because of their exposure to American Western films. This sequence is probably more effective when they perform in Europe, more particularly in Italy, where these movies are popular to the point of having spurred the production of a genre of movies commonly referred to as "Spaghetti Westerns." This term is loudly uttered by Carlo, who adds after a pause, "No lasagna!" as if he is giving information about the daily menu at an Italian restaurant. Alberto almost strangles himself as he ties his cowboy scarf around his neck. They now engage in a parody of Western movies. They portray cowboys as vulgar and stupid machos by making brutal facial grimaces, imitating horsemen's way of walking, and shooting their guns indiscriminately. In the absence of actual revolvers, they shape their hands appropriately by pointing two fingers and folding the others. Following stereotyped gestures, they pretend to quickly remove the guns from their invisible holsters, throw them in the air, and catch them as they fall back down, making the guns revolve around their index fingers before replacing them in the holsters. While Carlo behaves competently, albeit purely as a mime, Alberto lets his gun crash to the ground. To conclude this display, they both throw the guns high in the air and pretend to catch them directly in the holsters when they fall, like jugglers often do when catching balls in little baskets hung on their belts.

The two now turn mutually aggressive. They challenge and confront each other as if ready to start a real fight. But as they closely face each other, they play a children's hand game at the end of which Carlo slaps Alberto, saying "Justicia!" Alberto collapses and dies, taking all sorts of strange, unnatural positions before reaching the state of a corpse. Carlo proclaims: "He is dying!" and adds, "Dead in 24 positions!" He then asks Alberto, "Morto?" [Are you dead?]. The latter replies, "Si" [Yes].

As Alberto lays motionless on the floor of the stage, Carlo goes and fetches a large piece of cloth and some burial props, which he places on the "corpse." Then he climbs on the chair, makes some magical gestures, and suddenly the body levitates horizontally under the hanging black fabric, with the shoes of Alberto showing at the end of what is supposed to be his legs. However, the trick is soon disclosed as Alberto turns around toward the exit and reveals that he is holding two sticks with his extended arms, at the ends of which shoes have been fixed. He had raised himself on his feet, thus creating the illusion of the levitating corpse because the hanging cloth was hiding his body.

Carlo comes back and presents a juggling act with three circles. He introduces himself as the greatest juggler in the world. During the juggling, he periodically catches a metal ring around his neck. He invites the audience to clap their hands in rhythm so that the clapping coincides with the catching of the ring. But the public does not follow and claps out of time. He looks at them as if they are idiots unable to understand the simplest things. Again he makes a gestural allusion to the television screen, implying by this that they watch too much TV and this is what makes them stupid, or, as was noted earlier, that they are "square." Then, he stops to say, "Actually, I am not a juggler. I am just doing this to kill time while Alberto dresses up." He resumes his juggling, and it seems now that the public follows the rhythm properly. However, he confuses them by misdirecting their attention. When they fail, he gets angry, alludes again to the TV screen, bangs two rings against each other in frustration, and screams in pain because he has caught his fingers between the two metallic objects. He says he needs to concentrate in order to succeed with the next trick and repeats the stupid cowboy's posture that he had mimicked earlier in the spectacle.

As they take their leave at the end of the first part of the program, Carlo wants all the applause for himself and orders Alberto to go away. The unfair behavior of the authoritarian clown prompts the audience to support his victim. Some bickering ensues, but the public's insistence leads to the reconciliation of the partners, and they leave the stage hand in hand.

For the second part of the program, Alberto arrives from the wing, dressed in a beige formal suit and sporting an elegant tie. He gets ready to make a declaration but behaves as if he is bothered by something. He keeps adjusting his jacket and shrugs his shoulders from time to time. The audience is puzzled. Eventually, he removes the coat hanger, which was still inside the jacket. Thus relieved, he declares that until now they have performed "commedia comica" [comic comedy] but that the time has now come for "commedia classica" [classic comedy]. He announces "una tragedia svizzera" [a Swiss tragedy]. At this moment, Carlo appears from back stage wearing a little Swiss hat. Alberto introduces him as "Wilhelm Tell!" but Carlo comments, "Niente capite" [They don't understand]. He makes the square sign and says, "Billie Tell." Then he walks across front stage and grabs the corner of the red curtain, wrapping it around his waist as a kind of gladiator outfit while dramatically proclaiming, "Spartacus." He quickly transforms this improvised garment into a toga with the word "Julius Cesar." Alberto is exasperated: "No! Guillaume Tell!"

They now interpret a classic of clown comedies, which is a parody of an episode of Schiller's play in which a famous marksman, Wilhelm Tell, is forced by a tyrant to prove his skill by shooting an arrow into an apple placed on the head of his young son. Carlo is given an apple, and Alberto picks up the crossbow and starts aiming at Carlo, who suddenly transforms his Swiss hat into a traditional military bicorn hat while taking the iconic posture of Napoleon, one of his hands stuck in his vest. The hat is quickly removed, and he places the apple on his head. But it cannot stay there and rolls down. He then turns to the public, looking for someone with a "testa quadrata" [square head]. The alternative is to eat a bit of the apple so that there can be a flat surface. He succeeds in keeping the apple in balance on the top of his head. Alberto aims, but toward an area lower than the apple. Carlo protests, but Alberto explains that it is a special arrow that goes to its target along a zigzagging trajectory. Carlo takes a tragic posture and says "Adieu Roma" [Farewell, Rome]. Alberto retorts, "melodrammatico!" [melodramatic!], and, while he aims again, Carlo eats the whole apple. Alberto pretends to think that the audience has eaten the apple and threatens them. Carlo spits the pieces of apple toward Alberto, who becomes angry and chases him. Carlo begs for mercy by using a series of tender variants of the name of his partner: "Alberto, Albertino, Albertuccio!" and he takes refuge among the public by sitting next to a young woman. Alberto calls upon the theater director to ask him to remove the intruder, but immediately Carlo pretends to be a legitimate member of the organization by uttering the words "Coffee! Ice-cream!" as if he is peddling refreshments to the audience. Then he switches to the role of a spectator who orders Coca-Cola, treating Alberto as a refreshment seller. Alberto angrily responds, "No waiter! Artist!" Then Carlo says, "Cocacolina?" thus echoing his earlier use of sweet names for his partner, to which Alberto replies, "No," with the intonation of a waiter who is sorry that he does not have what the customer wants. Carlo insists, "Cocacoluccia? The response, "No!" Carlo again: "Pepsi Cola?" Alberto is exasperated by the fact that Carlo has driven him into the role of a servant by pretending that his negations are not a refusal to play his game but a statement meaning the drinks he is ordering are not available. Alberto tries to silence Carlo, but the latter starts telling stories to the woman next to him and speaks loud enough to offset Alberto's voice.

Now Alberto gets back to center stage, picks up a top hat from the chair, and declares that he is going to perform some magic, ceremoniously bowing to the public. Carlo comments, "Catastrophe!" and tells the woman next to him, "While he does these stupid things, let us go have a drink outside." But Alberto persists, explaining the meaning of the Italian words as he shows the objects to which they refer: "la mano" [the hand], "il cappello" [the hat], etc. Then he declares, "Mano: niente, cappello: niente," a simple way of saying in Italian "Nothing in my hands, nothing in the hat," thus implying that he is going to make things appear out of thin air. But Carlo shouts, "Testa: niente" [Nothing in the head]. Alberto announces that indeed he is going to make something appear, and Carlo replies, "Coca-Cola!" triggering the same "No" as before. Carlo reacts by saying that he is going to go to another restaurant with his girlfriend. Alberto puts a scarf on his hand, and something seems to be rising under it, but he soon reveals that it is his own finger, which he has lifted under the scarf. Carlo climbs back to the stage and tries to do the same thing, but nothing happens under the scarf while two fingers are raised on his other hand.

Alberto now declares again that after "la commedia comica" they will perform "la commedia classica." It will be by Shakespeare William. Once again he dismisses the audience as uneducated: "Niente capite!" [You understand nothing], "Que publico!" [What an audience!]. And he expresses this idea with the gestural leitmotiv of the rectangle. He announces Romeo and Juliet, and undertakes to explain the topic of the play by way of mime. First Juliet's father and mother are sleeping; then Juliet escapes from the house and meets Romeo; finally they make love. Alberto himself plays all the characters.

The love scene is performed by making explicit pelvic thrusting accompanied by the sound of a galloping horse. Now it is Julius Cesar whose death he mimes, with stabbing and guts pouring out of Cesar's belly. He mentions Henry and enumerates the dynasty: "Henry one, two, three, four, five, six, etc., etc." But they are going to represent *Hamlet*. Carlo, who is still returning from time to time to the restaurant frame, shouts, "Yes, omelet with Coca-Cola! No! Champagne, please!" And Alberto falls back to the previous context: "No." "Well, cheese omelet then."

The assignment of roles is announced by Alberto. Carlo will be the king of Denmark, and he will be Hamlet. But he asks, "Where is Ophelia?" Carlo replies, "She has left because we did not pay her," then adds, turning toward the audience, "Would there by any chance be an Ophelia for sale among you?" He points to a woman: "Not this one because she has dark hair. We need a blonde Ophelia." Carlo identifies a young blonde girl among the spectators and makes the curvature gesture, signifying an attractive woman. He immediately falls in love with her and says with ravishment, "Wow, the eyes!" Alberto intervenes, "She has two of them!" Carlo moves back toward center stage but whispers to the woman, "Let us meet after the show when they have all left."

While Carlo undertakes to tell the story of Romeo and Juliet as a flashback to the previous description of the play by Alberto, the latter brings from the wing Ophelia, who is represented by a contraption in metal, a tripod whose vertical rod is about the height of a small human being, a blonde wig placed at the top and a long scarf wrapped around a short horizontal support fixed at the spot where the shoulders would be. As Carlo continues telling the audience about his version of the adventures of Romeo and Juliet, he mimics the scene when the father arrives and discovers the lovers, saying in a dramatic tone, "Il padre!" [The father!]. Then he turns around and sees Ophelia: "Oh! She is skinny." But Alberto corrects him: "No! She is slim." Carlo resumes his story about Romeo and Juliet, and confuses Juliet and Ophelia. Looking at the latter, he suddenly grimaces in disgust and notes that she has three legs. Then he compares this Ophelia to the woman in the audience with whom he interacted earlier and expresses his enthusiasm for her.

Alberto hands over to Carlo a red wig and a blanket, which are supposed to be his costume for playing the king in Hamlet. The king sits down on the back of an ordinary chair, but he claims that the blanket stinks, and he shouts, "Gorgonzola," referring to the smelly Italian blue cheese. Alberto replies, "Drammatico!" Now Alberto puts a crown on Carlo's head, but it is actually a pasta strainer. As the public laughs, Carlo gets angry and scolds Alberto: "*Hamlet*, drammatico! Why they: hehehe?" Alberto again evokes the bad influence of television on North Americans. Then Carlo moves the side handle of the strainer in front of his eyes. He claims it is a television and pretends to change channels. Alberto gives him a broom to serve as his royal scepter. Carlo admires the broom: "Che bello!" [How beautiful!]. Alberto now explains how the play goes and tells him that when Hamlet arrives on his horse and draws his sword out of the sheath, he must ask him, "Che tempo fa?" [How is the weather?].

Alberto performs the role of Hamlet, imitates the sound of a galloping horse, and stops in front of the king, but he cannot manage to pull his sword, which is stuck in its sheath. At last it comes out, but he immediately tries to put it back on the wrong side. Then he thrusts it in his pants with a cry of pain. He behaves as if he has hurt his genitals but says, "Wow, it is cold!" While Alberto wiggles with the sword, Carlo says, "Travolta!" When Carlo keeps eyeing the woman in the front row as he pretends to look at Ophelia, Alberto says, "Casanova!" Alberto quickly resumes his impersonation of Hamlet on his horse but discreetly fills his mouth with water from a bottle that has been placed on the ground. When his father, the king of Denmark, asks him how the weather is, he spits the water in his face: "It rains!"

The transcription of this performance can be interrupted here, as these first 60 minutes of acting provide a rich trove of gags. Actually, there is nothing but gags, which succeed each other at a quick rate. The background narrative is minimal, albeit definitely present, formed by the mildly antagonistic relationship between the two brothers. However, a number of subnarratives are inserted in rapid succession to create secondary contexts for the gags. Another interesting feature of this performance is that the props are trivial and very simple. Verbal communication is also kept at a minimum, because the artists are Italian and far from being proficient in English. This is not a liability, though, because they manage to turn this deficiency into a comical asset. Let us now consider another clown act, which is also essentially composed of gags performed in rapid succession without relying on an explicit narrative.

Rob Torres: A solo clown act in New York

New York, December 11, 2010. This is the time of the year when the Big Apple Circus, an institution that has carved its place among the countless cultural entertainments of New York City, sets up its tent next to Lincoln Center. My Swedish friend, Philip Clevberger, happens to be in town for an IT assignment. He gladly accepts my invitation to the circus. In his early thirties, he has never seen a circus. A naïve adult spectator's reaction to a show is always a bonanza for the ethnographer. I will observe his facial expressions and body movements and postures as the program unfolds. But the program, which I have previewed the day before, will also require my full attention, as I will be making notes during the clown performance.

After the first two fast-paced acrobatic acts, a clown comes from the audience at the opposite side of the artists' entrance. He carries a red suitcase. He walks across the ring in a unassuming manner, seeming somewhat despondent. He has a worried look and peers around. Sheepishly, he lowers his head when he reaches the center of the ring, and begins walking faster as if he intends to leave the ring through the artists' entrance, without attracting attention. The public expresses vocal disappointment and starts clapping their hands to encourage him to stay. He hesitates, turns his head back, and sees a rope with a tassel dropping from the ceiling. He pulls it, and the ring is immediately flooded with light. He smiles and acknowledges the applause. But he soon notices that one side of the audience claps their hands more softly than the other. He shames them and prompts each side to try to outdo the other. When the level of noise has reached a sufficient intensity, Rob Torres makes a hand sign to tell them to wait. He extracts a small box from his suitcase, opening the lid toward the public and prompting them to clap louder. They understand that he is "storing" the applause. They stop when he closes the lid and start again more loudly when he lifts it. He asks them again to wait a moment, and gets a much bigger wooden box from the suitcase. People play along and shout when the lid is open and stop as soon as it is closed. Then the clown "controls" the public by successively opening and closing the lid of the big box, creating the impression through a spontaneous collaboration with the audience that the noise comes from the box.

Philip is a brilliant photographer and has brought to the circus his most advanced camera. We are on the front row because he wanted to have an opportunity to get some good shots. The black and shiny protruding lens is very conspicuous. Rob Torres now squats in front of his suitcase and fetches from its recess a very small, undistinguished flat camera. He indicates that he wants to take a picture of the audience and tries several positions but eventually gestures to them that they have to move toward the center so he can get a group photo. Everybody laughs at this suggestion. Then the "photographer" undertakes to make some cosmetic changes to the appearance of his subjects: he prompts a little girl to smile, gives some dental floss to a man, runs across the ring to arrange the hairdo of a young lady. Finally, he extracts a big comb from his pocket to comb a bald, older man. Suddenly, he seems to notice Philip's expensive camera, rushes toward him, grabs the camera, and gives him in exchange his own tiny machine. Now the clown shows off in the ring with that beautiful camera and gets ready to resume his photographing. Philip is not sure how to react, but I reassure him that he should not worry. Indeed, in no time, Rob Torres walks toward him and hands back the camera. However, on his way, he has secured his grip on two spots on the long strap and, as Philip looks relieved and extends his hands to receive his precious instrument, the clown releases one of his hands, causing the camera to quickly drop down—without crashing on the ground because he securely holds the strap in his hand. The audience burst into laughter when they see Philip's angry expression.

Now Rob wants to be photographed by a spectator. He hands his camera to a man, who stands up and takes photos as the clown does several poses at a fast pace: macho, camp, sexy, etc. His next whim is to be photographed with this man in all sorts of situations, eventually ending up by being carried in his arms like a baby.

The clown walks back toward his suitcase. He mimics someone who is not sure of what to do next, looking puzzled or searching for an object, then suddenly seemingly getting an idea that he will implement. His facial expression is similar to the one of the popular Mister Bean when he improvises a silly solution to a new problem. Rob takes three red conical hats from the suitcase and tentatively juggles them. Then he invites some members of the public to play with him by throwing the hats, which he catches on his head. He makes sure, though, that one particular man he has singled out never succeeds. In order to "facilitate" this man's task, he wraps sticky tape around his hair, and the hat lands accurately on the top of his head. But when he tries to get rid of the tape, he grimaces with pain as it pulls his hair. He implores a lady from the first row to help him. She complies and cautiously undertakes to unstick the tape while he cries in pain. Suddenly, the clown withdraws his head and the confused lady holds only a wig in her hands. Rob Torres reveals his completely shaved skull, grabs the wig, and puts it on the head of a bald spectator. The audience laughs and claps their hands. Rob rushes to the suitcase to pick up the little wooden box and hurriedly stores their applause in it. The clown takes a bow and makes a triumphal exit.

Rob Torres returns to the ring in the second part of the program. His performance starts in the same manner as in the first part. Coming from the audience space, he brings his suitcase to the center of the ring and extracts from it two cone-shaped metal goblets. He attempts to juggle with these objects but fails. He scolds a cone, which lies on the ground. He then fetches two more cones and juggles successfully with the four cones. Eventually, he catches three cones in the first one, which he is holding upside down. The audience applauds. At the end of a new attempt, his thumb is caught between two cones as they fall into the one he is holding. He shows that he is in pain, looks around, and walks toward a first-row lady, asking for help while imitating the expression and vocalizations of a child seeking help from his mother. He signals to her that she should kiss his thumb in order to cure it. The woman plays the game and brings his hand toward her mouth for a healing kiss. He *shows delight, but on his way back to the center of the ring, he trips and falls facedown. Now it is his nose that hurts. He returns to the same lady for a second healing kiss, this time on his nose.*

Rob resumes his juggling. Throwing the four cones up, he takes shelter under his raised arms to protect himself from the falling objects. He readies himself for more juggling, when, suddenly, an alarm clock starts ringing in the suitcase. He stops juggling, goes to the suitcase, extracts a big alarm clock, and checks the time, acting as if it has signaled the end of his work in the ring. He packs all the items and prepares to leave, but the public's loud applause prompts him to delay his exit, and he resumes his juggling. Unfortunately, he trips once again on a cone and rises from the ground in pain, holding his genitals as if he has hurt himself. He looks at the same lady and walks toward her with his legs pressed together. This triggers a big laugh in the audience, but he stops walking midway, gesturing "no" with his hand as if he is shocked that the woman is getting ready to kiss his sore spot.

The clown then performs a brief display of juggling talent with the four cones before leaving the ring, but not without taking the wooden box from the suitcase in order to store more applause in it.

The semiotic anatomy of gags

The selection of the performances by the Colombaioni brothers and Rob Torres was determined by the fact that all the gags produced by these professional clowns met with success. While not entirely original, all these gags showed some interesting level of creativity in the framing and interpretations displayed by the artists, somewhat like a pianist can demonstrate his/her excellence by playing a familiar score in a unique, brilliant manner that makes it sound new. In spite of the difference in style of the two acts and the 25-year gap separating their performances, the similarities between the two suggest that all gags are generated by the same algorithm or, to use a linguistic metaphor, the same grammar. Moreover, although all the gags bear witness to a long tradition of slapstick comedy, the ways in which they were performed are telling examples of the emergence of a new clown culture that breaks away from the traditional patterns of clowning and is characterized by a high degree of self-irony. They also rely heavily on immersive performance. The Colombaioni stay clear of the polarization between the whiteface and the auguste by ignoring the makeup and costume codes, and constantly switching from one role to another. Rob Torres exemplifies the modern tendency to perform solo and to extensively involve the audience to provide the dialogic structure essential to humor. Another important reason for choosing these two acts is that they are formed by a large number of gags of various kinds, independent of any explicit narrative. This, of course, does not mean that the acts are randomly composed, but rather that they are markedly different from the more traditional acts we will probe in upcoming chapters.

As complex, multimodal acts of communication, the performances by the Colombaioni and Rob Torres are not a mere accumulation of gags, but are endowed with a rhetorical structure. They are indeed obviously perceived by the audience as consistent wholes that unfold in time until they reach a closure. They can be analyzed as texts or discourses that articulate in their own codes (gags) implicit semantic or ideological contents.

Anaphor is one of the main tools of textual consistency. In linguistics, it designates the use of pronouns or any other indexical units to refer back to another word or phrase in the text. It links together parts of sentences and bridges the grammatical gaps between clauses, which is a consequence of the linearity of language. In rhetoric, anaphors are repetitions of words or structures that build up the cohesion of discourse and create momentum toward a climax. In multimodal communication, words, gestures, objects, or musical tunes can play the same role by reminding the receiver—that is, the spectator in the case of a performance—of signs and events produced earlier in the act. In the Colombaioni performance, for instance, Carlo jokingly puts down the North American public by implying that watching too much television blunts the mind. He does this by noting that they do not understand what he means when he speaks Italian, and he conveys the idea by tracing in the air a rectangle with his hand, thus producing a schematic representation of a television screen. At the same time, his facial expression signifies contempt. This sign recurs several times during the performance, thus referencing his claim to belong to a more sophisticated culture in spite of the many blunders, bad manners, and contradictions the two clowns display in their act. As the performance progresses, this iconic gesture becomes more and more schematic when it occurs, because now everybody in the audience understands that it refers to earlier, more redundant instances of this multimodal statement. It ends up functioning like a pronoun, an empty form that can produce meaning only in the present context by virtue of the moment in which it appears. It certainly lends a valuable consistency to this clown act characterized by the fast succession of unconnected clusters of gags.

We can identify at least three kinds of anaphors that give strong cohesion to Rob Torres's acts and play an important role in the construction of his gags. These anaphors convey a sense of textual integration within each one of his two acts discussed here and help bridge the time gap between the act in the first part of the program and the one in the second. The first anaphor concerns the storing of applause in a box. At the beginning of his first act, the audience quickly catches the implied metaphor: applause is the treasure of a performer; therefore it should be saved and used when needed, like money trusted to a piggy bank. Rob periodically repeats this trick, which, at the end of the second act, brings his performance to a closure while securing a good measure of resounding approval from the public. The second anaphor, which also bridges the first and second acts, is purely formal; it is the geometry of the objects he manipulates—conical red hats in the first act, conical metallic goblets in the second. The third anaphor that grounds one of the main gags in the first part repeats a stereotypical behavior: when a child gets hurt, he/she tends to rush to the mother for soothing help. Kissing the affected part of the body is purely symbolic but effective, as it provides the reassurance of direct contact. The kissing of the thumb is a moving evocation of the clown's childish nature and his/her loving relationship with an audience. This brief episode causes people to smile. Then, the kissing of the nose brings the contact closer and suggests that the clown is exploiting his chance of benefiting from the kindness of the lady he has chosen for this purpose. However, as it involves the face, which is a more intimate area of the body because the nose is dangerously close to the mouth, the trick becomes ambiguous and evokes a transgressive behavior. The childish mimic of the clown, though, prevents any obvious sexual innuendo. It nevertheless brings out some laughter in the audience as audience members begin to see through his gimmick. After all, Rob is a fully grown adult male even if he behaves somewhat like an innocent child. The third instance focuses on the genitals, and it suddenly becomes clear that Rob's ultimate goal might have been to reach that situation. The stereotypical behavior to which the successive episodes refer is used in this act as a rhetorical anaphor leading to a climax. By his sudden gesture of declining the help of the woman, Rob implies that she has expressed her willingness to comply, although there is no indication in the attitude of the woman that this was the case. But, of course, the public's attention is focused on the clown pretending to be in pain, and Rob simply creates through his gesture of shocked refusal the illusion that the kissing was going to occur again on the spot that was hurting.

We can see in this latter example how anaphoric devices contribute to the construction of gags. The first two instances of kissing are semantically self-contained, so to speak, and do not make the third situation predictable. This rather complex gag, which develops over time while the clown displays some juggling skill, is construed like a logical proposition in which the first two instances of kissing form the premise and the third instance the conclusion. But the assumptions created by the childish situation that the premise evokes do not naturally lead to the conclusion unexpectedly thrown in the face of the audience—at least as a potential breach of sexual taboo. The situational anaphor yields maximal information when the argument reaches its conclusion. This analysis shows that gags are cognitive events endowed with strong logical structures, a logic that runs wild as it emancipates itself from the pragmatic constraints dictated by the rules prevailing in the cultural context.

Let us now consider the sequence of gags introduced as "commedia classica" in the performance by the Colombaioni. Following the circus tradition of the past 200 years, clowns often perform parodies of classical plays, operas, and ballets, which they render in condensed and simplified forms without much regard for the original scripts. These revered symbols of highbrow culture are mocked; famous characters and scenes from particular works are interpreted in the grotesque mode. The Colombaioni refer to this comic tradition by cramming into a brief period of time three different icons of the European artistic heritage: Wilhelm Tell, Romeo and Juliet, and Hamlet. In each of the gags the clowns produced the basic premises are provided by the cultural knowledge of the audience. The term "premise" is not taken here in the sense of formal logic, but refers to cultural logic, the set of tacit knowledge and norms governing expectations. When the Colombaioni evoke *Hamlet* and assign to one of them the role of the king (who immediately perches on the back of a chair representing his throne), the set of assumptions constituting the premise of the gag includes the stereotypical paraphernalia of kingship: a crown, a royal coat, and a scepter. These objects are theatrical props commonly used on stage in historical plays. Clowns also occasionally use such props in their parodies. But in the case of the Colombaioni gag, the conclusion of the argument comes in the form of totally unexpected artifacts: a pasta strainer instead of a crown; a torn-up blanket as a coat; and a broom for a scepter. These items introduce a maximum of information because they are associated with the opposite of the royal function, the class of servants: the utensil of a cook (the strainer); the cover of a homeless beggar (the dirty and torn blanket); and the tool of a cleaner (the broom). The staging ensures that these objects are kept out of the view of the audience until they are propped up in quick succession to provide the emblems of the "king." Then, the Colombaioni invent a scene in which a military Hamlet arrives by his horse before his royal father, who is supposed to ask him, "How is the weather?" The question is incongruous and the answer unexpected, because "Hamlet" has discreetly filled his mouth with water, which he spits on the king, implying the answer "it rains."

Material culture is not an undifferentiated collection of artifacts. Objects are mapped on a cognitive map. They are categorized according to functions, morphology, symbolic value, and gender and social class indices, to name only a few broad criteria. A celebrated gag of Joseph Grimaldi that was recorded in a color print shows him dressed as a hussar, one of the heroic cavalrymen in the time of the Napoleonic Wars (McConnell Stott 2009: 276–277). Following the same principle that we observed in the case of the latter Colombaioni gag, Grimaldi's outfit is constructed of items associated with the material culture of the home, and more particularly women, thus yielding the less expectable conclusion with high information value (Bouissac 1977). Grimaldi's boots are made of two coal scuttles; various female garments are used for his furry hat and other parts of a typical hussar's military uniform. He is represented throwing a puppet dressed as Boney (Napoleon Bonaparte) in the mouth of a bear. Obviously, the premise is maximally denied by the conclusion of the argument.

The use of coal scuttles as boots is a good example of another productive source of gags: visual metaphors enacted in the form of gestures or novel artifacts. Objects belonging to diametrically opposed cultural categories may have similar formal features to which we are blind in everyday life. The more cognitively distant these categories are from each other, the stronger are the gags that bring them together by creating hybrid artifacts. Among Charlie Cairoli's props, we found a guitar whose back is a three-dimensional naked bottom painted in fleshy pink (see Figures 3.5 and 3.6). As long as the clown plays or pretends to play the guitar, it seems to be a perfectly normal instrument because the back of the guitar is hidden from the audience. However, as soon as the clown turns it, the backside flashes its wicked icon. The ground for this effect, of course, is the shape of this kind of musical instrument, which exhibits symmetrical curvatures typical of the morphology of a young woman. Men often vulgarly refer to attractive ladies by producing a gesture that traces in the air, with both hands, two circular shapes related by a narrow waist. This mimicking can be considered demeaning, as it reduces a person to an object, in fact, a mere geometrical figure endowed with sexual significance; but such a gesture never evokes a guitar or other string instruments. This gag reveals a culturally repressed homology that is all the more shockingly funny—that is, informative—because the guitar is symbolic of romantic courting. Breaking cultural taboos through visual metaphors generates efficient gags that, at times, reach the limit of psychological or moral acceptability. For instance, another example of Charlie Cairoli's creativity in inventing gags was the use of a toilet seat as a frame for a lyre, which he pretended to play while wearing a mock angel outfit. In that case again, two culturally incompatible artifacts— one belonging to the material culture of defecation, the other connoting highbrow music, poetic inspiration, and heavenly life—are collapsed into a single one by virtue of a geometrical homology.

In the Colombaioni act, one of the gags that triggered loud laughter at the performance I attended was the introduction of Ophelia in their instant interpretation of *Hamlet*. As they assign roles, they discover that they needed an Ophelia. Carlo rushes to the wing and brings back a freestanding metallic coat stand crowned by a wig, to which he adds a scarf. Alberto jokes that "she" is very skinny and compares "her" to the nice lady in the audience with whom he interacted earlier. This gag elicits laughter because it creates an extreme metaphor that brings an inanimate artifact into a relationship of equivalence with one of the most famously tragic young heroines in the literary dramatic tradition. It foregrounds the fact that here are some undeniable abstract similarities between the two: both a woman and a tripod coat stand are erect, freestanding, endowed with appendages, and carry clothes. A realistic manikin would not have achieved the same effect. This gag implemented an unexpectedly big cognitive split, so to speak, by equating a metallic structure adorned with a piece of fabric and a feminine icon of the Western cultural heritage.

But is the radical discrepancy we noted between the premise and the conclusion of a gag a sufficient explanation? Not all non sequiturs necessarily produce laughter. Random associations are not sufficient to create meaning. Like the surrealists' images (Breton 1974 [1924]: 19–22), the relation between the distant realities must be relevant, albeit occulted in the realm of common sense. It is not merely because of their categorical difference that the two syntactic components of a gag trigger laughter. The two referents must be culturally disjointed with the force of a taboo. There are obviously degrees of cultural prohibition. In general, the stronger the objective similarities or continuities, the greater resistance there is to think of them together or to associate them with a single behavior or artifact. The argument of a gag must reveal a repressed truth.

The examples of Charlie Cairoli's props described above offer a striking example of this process. Both objects, the guitar and the lyre, belong to the realm of music; that is, they are instruments designed to create sounds. These sounds pertain to highbrow culture. However, the props are intimately connected through synecdoche to the sounds produced by the human digestive system. From this point of view, a bottom is a wind instrument and a toilet seat is closely associated to it. Flatulence, however, is a social taboo in the contextual culture, and it would be scandalous to consider this natural phenomenon as musical in spite of the fact that it can yield a range of acoustic variations. Relating these two categories is culturally "unthinkable," but the gags connect them visually by bridging the difference between chords and wind. Let us note that we are here in the presence of two extreme cases in a paradigm that is very productive in clowning. It is common to see a clown trying to play an occluded trumpet, making efforts until a noise is produced that sounds like a fart, thus putting nature and culture on a continuum that is fiercely denied by social institutions—for instance, schools, academies, and etiquette. Some clowns resort to such gimmicks to secure easily obtained laughter from their audience. There are countless variations on this theme that can be observed in popular circuses in many countries of the world.

The gag produced by the transgressive visual metaphor of the toilet seat transformed into a lyre depends on the specific categories involved. Not any

U-shaped or oval object would obtain the same result. Although only an actual substitution of a component in a live performance could prove this claim, a simple thought experiment is to imagine that the clown uses a draft-horse collar, a mirror frame, or an oversized magnet fitted with strings. It is doubtful that this prop, how surprising it may be, would trigger laughter. Regarding the example of the guitar, let us fancy that the back side reveals a face, a pan, or a cabbage instead of a human bottom. The categorical distances between the two objects are not sufficient to construct a gag. The premise and the argument of a gag must be culturally relevant, although their relation must be socially inhibited. Unfortunately, it would be impossible to convince a clown to accept to cooperate in such experiments at the cost of failing to make an audience laugh.

The Commedia Classica of the Colombaioni offers a cluster of gags of a similar kind. The three literary works that form the premises of the gags are representative of the highest esthetic and moral values celebrated by the traditional European cultures: loyalty to the father or the king, paternal bond, and romantic love. The arguments of each gag present conclusions that deny the cultural idealism through bluntly displaying the natural behaviors underlying these cultural norms and the arbitrariness of their symbolic representations. These conclusions include the degradation of the props of royalty, the reduction of romantic love to some pelvic motions, and the transformation of filial submission into mockery when the son of Wilhelm Tell eats the apple and Hamlet spits at the face of the king. These gags address the fundamental basis of the traditional patriarchal society by denouncing the delusional sacredness of its values and the artificiality of its symbols.

This chapter has attempted to selectively document the semiotic mechanisms of gags by showing that all gags are generated by a single matrix or an algorithm consisting of connecting two strongly disconnected cultural objects (artifacts, behaviors, concepts, or ontological categories) that nevertheless are part of a formal or material continuum. It has proposed to consider that all gags can be analyzed on the model of arguments comprising a premise and a conclusion. However, this semiotic logic that may have descriptive or heuristic value does not explain why we laugh and why we feel euphoric when we do. After all, even the most accurate account of a gag usually does not cause laughter. It might just prompt an appreciative smile or trigger a kind of cognitive pleasure. The daunting question of the nature and function of laughter will be raised in the concluding chapter of this volume once we have further explored a large body of clown acts both from the past, as they were recorded by observant spectators, and the present, as they can be experienced nowadays in contemporary circuses and theaters.

The physics of gags

Cesar Dias was the clown star of the Zirkus Charles Knie in 2013. We met him earlier in the introduction to this volume. He was the young, unassuming man whom I interviewed before his act was to be photographed. Every single time I watched him perform, the circus tent was filled with resounding laughter, but not the kind of canned laughter that is synchronized as if all the members of the audience were simultaneously producing these vocal sounds as a well-disciplined choir. This laughter had the hallmark of spontaneity, which is characterized by an irregular acoustic texture. Irrepressible bursts of laughter exploded among the audience like multiple-rocket fireworks and triggered waves forming successive crescendos. Reflecting upon his act will help us understand a crucial aspect of gags: their temporal structure. The gags themselves were not very original, although they had a personal twist that reflected the unique personality of Cesar Dias. By his own admission during our interview, he credited his model, the great George Carl, for his inspiration (Bouissac 2010: 128–136). But gags cannot be imitated. They have to be re-created at a new tempo. There cannot be even the smallest lagging time between the premises and the conclusions. It is a matter of milliseconds. The proof of a gag is in the surprise it causes, its maximal information value.

When a clown enters the ring, he/she takes possession of the space for the purpose of making the space produce meaning. It may be a gesture of ownership, determining where the center is and taking possession of all its dimensions. This is what André and Cesar Dias do when they appear in the ring to mark the beginning of the show (Figures 4.1 and 4.2).

FIGURE 4.1 *André and Cesar Dias open the show together. They bring the performing space to life and capture the attention of the audience.*
Photo credit Zbigniew Roguszka.

FIGURE 4.2 *The clowns inaugurate their contact with the public and set the pace for the actions to come. They will perform alternately during the program and will bring it to a close by returning together to take their final bow.*
Photo credit Zbigniew Roguszka.

This is what the clown André does when he steps into the ring and starts chasing a troublesome mosquito with his hat before grabbing a broom. After a few rhythmic swipes of the broom, he keeps being bothered by the mosquito, whose presence is indicated by the high-pitch sound produced by the orchestra. He tries to monitor the path of its flight, moving his head up and down, right and left, but the pest keeps evading his attempts to hit it. Whenever the sound stops, André marks a brief pause as if thinking that the mosquito has been killed. Instantly, though, the sound resumes its infuriating vibrations. Now it appears that the mosquito has landed on the head of a bald man seated in the front row. The clown cautiously approaches, holding the broom as if he intends to violently hit the insect on its resting spot with the hard wooden stick. The man is spared the blow because the insect resumes its flight. Through these successive actions, the clown has constructed a three-dimensional space that encompasses the whole performance frame. At the same time, he has initiated a gestural rhythm that determines the pace of his whole act and controls the attention of the spectators, who vicariously follow the meandering trajectory of the fictive mosquito and share the clown's frustration. From one move to the next there is no place in the spectators' mind for reflecting on the plausibility of this situation. The time frame of their attention is saturated and coincides with André's performing agenda (Figures 4.3, 4.4, 4.5, 4.6, 4.7, and 4.8).

Alternatively, the space of the performance may be construed as a hostile milieu by a clown who first steps into it cautiously as Rob Torres does when he crosses the ring hesitantly, slightly stooped, and carrying his red bag as a traveler who is just passing by and dashes toward the exit until the audience

FIGURE 4.3 *This mosquito is annoying. Let me try to kill it!*
Photo credit Zbigniew Roguszka.

FIGURE 4.4 *Good! I think I got it.*
Photo credit Zbigniew Roguszka.

FIGURE 4.5 *Now, let us bury it.*
Photo credit Zbigniew Roguszka.

FIGURE 4.6 *May it rest in peace!*
Photo credit Zbigniew Roguszka.

calls him back, and thus give him self-confidence. He will then progressively take possession of the space by standing at the center and moving at regular intervals toward the periphery as the act requires before reasserting his central position. It is from there that he manipulates the audience into laughing on command through the trick of the treasure chest in which he

FIGURE 4.7 *To make sure it stays there, let us put this big stone on top of the tomb.*

FIGURE 4.8 *What is that? The stone is moving!*
Photo credit Zbigniew Roguszka.

stores their applause. Once a clown has taken hold of the time-space that engulfs the spectators' attention, gags can blossom as long as there is no slackening of the tempo.

Let us now return to Cesar Dias. Solo clowning is particularly challenging. It is indeed somewhat easier for a duo to set a rhythmic dynamic that can spread to the audience. Cesar Dias, like André and Rob Torres, is alone in front of the crowd. He must quickly engage audience members, capture their attention, and impose the tempo that will rule his act until it reaches its climax. I asked Cesar if he was timing his act by actually counting like a metronome as he proceeded with the successive gestures and gags. He said he was not but that he felt unconsciously possessed by the right tempo as soon as he stepped into the ring. All performers need to be in a kind of state of trance that gives them a high for the duration of their act and is enhanced by the positive feedback they receive from the audience. The spectators must be kept on the brink of time so that they have no possibility of pondering what will come next. They must entirely rely on their cognitive automatic pilot, so to speak. They must have no other choice than to anticipate the most expectable conclusion of the premise the clown throws at them, which he will disprove in a split second, thus assaulting their cognitive balance with pure information (Figures 4.9, 4.10, 4.11, 4.12, 4.13, 4.14, 4.15, 4.16, and 4.17).

FIGURE 4.9 *Cesar Dias cultivates a proper look. He wears just a touch of makeup, with a thin, braided lock of hair hanging on his forehead as his signature. The glasses are also a part of his clown outfit.*

Photo credit Zbigniew Roguszka.

FIGURE 4.10 *Now let me sing a nice song!*

Photo credit Zbigniew Roguszka.

FIGURE 4.11 *Damn! Something is wrong with this mike stand.*
Photo credit Zbigniew Roguszka.

FIGURE 4.12 *As Cesar attempts to fix the problem, he becomes entangled in the wires and the mike falls into his trousers. Trying to extract it causes him to lose face.*
Photo credit Zbigniew Roguszka.

Cesar Dias is a good singer, but he has problems with the mike and the mike stand, which do not cooperate. This leads to a cascade of accidents during which Cesar gets inexorably entangled in a mesh of wires and tubes. Each move he makes to extract himself seems to drag him further down in chaos. He will eventually triumph, but not until two dozen quick gags have been produced at a fast rhythm. The premises are the solutions that seem to be obvious to the audience; the conclusions are

FIGURE 4.13 *Ouch ... he forgot to put something back in his zipper and he confuses the rose from his lapel with the mike!*
Photo credit Zbigniew Roguszka.

FIGURE 4.14 *Where is it? I had a comb in my hands just a second ago!*
Photo credit Zbigniew Roguszka.

his unexpected movements that worsen the entanglement. His perfect timing is what makes his act bring the house down.

In another memorable act, which has been recorded and is available online (http://www.youtube.com/watch?v=CUzZUZXHaJs), Cesar Dias enters the ring walking at a fast pace, which sets the time structure of the whole performance. He rhythmically balances his arms back and forth as he reaches the center of the ring in front of the mike stand. He starts to play music on a harmonica, which he has quickly extracted from his pocket. But he cannot

FIGURE 4.15 *Toying with a flexible hand saw can be dangerous.*
Photo credit Zbigniew Roguszka.

FIGURE 4.16 *It can knock your glasses off.*
Photo credit Zbigniew Roguszka.

succeed because the microphone is too high. Through a series of jerky movements, he first attempts to lower it by pushing it down, then jumps up, and eventually manages to slide it down by endlessly mimicking the unscrewing of the stand with a suggestive, repetitive gesture closer to his crotch than to the stand. But, alas, the mike tube now stands between the harmonica and his mouth. He makes several complicated moves to try to disentangle himself from this situation, including transferring the musical instrument through a detour from the front of his body to the back by pushing it between his legs

FIGURE 4.17 *It is safer to wear a helmet when one plays music on a saw using a coat hanger as a bow.*
Photo credit Zbigniew Roguszka.

and thus moving the harmonica back and forth in the genital area. He emerges from this uncomfortable position with an unlikely posture that has his arms tightly meshed around the mike stand. However, he now produces music because the harmonica turns out to be close to his mouth, and, to everybody's surprise, he moves sideways free from the apparent entanglement that bound him to the mike stand. He punctuates each episode with stereotypical laughter of the kind used in social media: "hehehehe" or "hahahaha" with triumphal or sarcastic intonations depending on the assumed attitude of the audience in reaction to the gags. He then introduces a brief juggling display with his hat, which he eventually throws toward the mike stand, on the top of which it lands. He is now going to resume his music, but the braided lock of hair on his forehead interferes with his playing. He tries various jerking head movements in order to send it back to the top of his skull, but without success until he fetches a large white comb from his pocket and tries to use it to tame the rebellious lock. In a moment of distraction, the comb remains fixed in his hair and Cesar desperately looks for it on the ground.

Cesar can now continue playing the harmonica. But a strange ringing similar to the sound produced by ancient cell phones prompts him to extract from his pocket a new harmonica, which he brings to his ear and mouth to say "Allo?" upon pulling out an antiquated antenna. This is a quotation from old George Carl's act that has been carried over by Cesar Dias, despite the fact that this bulky communication artifact has become obsolete—but not completely forgotten by the more mature members of the public. Cesar suddenly starts playing the French Cancan tune, but the circus band takes over and blasts the music while the clown stays idle. After a brief while, the music stops and the clown bows to the audience as if he has produced all the music alone. As he lowers his head, the comb falls to the ground to his great puzzlement.

Before the act started, a small table and a chair had been placed at a short distance from the center of the ring. This is where Cesar threw the hat after his juggling interlude. He picks up a large handsaw that was lying on the table, which nobody in the audience could have noticed because the fast pace of the succession of gags saturated its attention capacity. He now toys with this unexpected object. He tests its flexibility by bending it away from his face, but he "accidentally" releases his grip on the extremity of the tool and is hit on the face. His glasses are knocked off. He quickly gets ahold of the saw again, sits down, and plays music using a coat hanger as a bow. For a few seconds he extracts beautiful sounds from this unlikely instrument. As he smiles in recognition of the public's applause, the audience does not notice that he is bending the saw to release it again and be hit violently a second time. He marks a brief pause as if reflecting upon a solution, and, quickly turning his head toward back stage, he whistles to prompt a circus hand to bring him a yellow hard hat of the kind workers wear on construction sites.

The spectators' minds are saturated by a bundle of visual and acoustic novelties: yellow hat, metal tool, coat hanger, melody. The first hit by the saw elicited some laughter, but the second one triggers much louder laughter because the audience has spontaneously inferred that Cesar learned a lesson and is unlikely to make the same mindless mistake another time. This is calculated, of course. But when we laugh, our motor and cognitive competencies are impaired, and we are more prone to be surprised by the sudden impact caused by an unexpected conclusion. The almost-undecipherable scribbling of my field notes during my first experience of this gag bears witness to this phenomenon. The reader might watch again with profit the recording of this fast-paced act, which lasts 7 minutes on average. In some performances, the laughter and applause of a particularly appreciative audience may extend the length of Cesar Dias's act by 1 to 2 extra minutes.

It is noteworthy that, at the end, the clown acknowledges the positive feedback he has enjoyed, gestures toward the whole public, and exits by marching on the top of the ring's enclosure while generating with his triumphal steps and arm movements the same tempo that he has sustained for the duration of his act. He now enjoins the members of the audience to clap their hands at this rhythm and experience a climax of collective enthusiasm and emotional fusion.

5

The Game of the Rules

The language of clowning

In the first four chapters we have reviewed and documented what can be considered the lexicon of the multimodal language of clowning: makeup, costumes, props, and gags. As we saw, each class of elements forms a subsystem of its own, which is founded on differences and oppositions for the makeup and costumes, and on relatively more elaborate algorithms for the props and gags. Their local meaning can be defined through these relations. But a lexicon is not sufficient for creating meaningful texts. This requires a grammar. With these functional elements, clowns produce complex narratives embodied in multimodal discourses. A clown performance is indeed an act of both signification and communication. As words or phrases by themselves without any context represent only semantic potential, so do makeup, garb, artifacts, and gags. These building blocks need to be integrated into a narrative structure in order to produce a fully articulated signification. The framework may be kept to a functional minimum, as we saw in the case of the isolated gags that were discussed in Chapter 4, but in general clown acts are organized along a story line. This chapter will endeavor to explore further the language of clowning and to show how signification is created by selecting and combining the elements of this language.

Let us consider first a brief example by a clown who performs solo: the auguste André, who was introduced in the first chapter of this volume. André ceremoniously walks toward a standing microphone, he clears his voice, and then he starts singing an Italian opera with all the appropriate dramatic gestures and facial emotions. He is credible for a few minutes because many clowns also happen to be good vocal artists and musicians. This one could indeed be a good tenor. The public is not sure, though, where this performance is going to lead because they know that he is a clown that appeared a couple of times during the first part of the program. Suddenly, they hear the soprano voice of a female singer. It is now obvious that it is the recording of a duo and that the clown was just silently mimicking in synchrony with the singing of the man. The auguste is taken aback and shows a moment of panic until he notices a mop that has been left on the side of the ring. He rushes toward it, rips off the whitish mop head from the handle, and puts it on his head as a long-hair wig. His face is totally transformed by this prop, and he resumes his fake singing, miming the facial expressions of a woman as he had done for the male voice. But the voice of the man returns and again André has to switch to the appropriate appearance by dropping the improvised wig. When the two singers alternate their passionate duet at a faster pace, it becomes difficult for the clown to cope with the timely changing of hairdo and mimic. Each time, there is an overlap between the voice and the gender of the singer. It ends in confusion when the music reaches its climax and the two singers sing together. Defeated by the situation, the clown runs away from the ring. He will briefly reappear, though, to take his bow while the audience applauds.

By its very nature, humor is dialogic and interactive. A solo performance does not mean that the clown is absolutely isolated in the ring. The clown constantly relates to the surrounding public, in contrast with a team, which performs an act in front of an audience without interacting directly with any of them—as is the case of the Fornasari, whose act will be introduced in the next section of this chapter. The solo type of clowning emerged a few decades ago from the activities of street performers and the subsequent development of immersive performance. André addresses himself to the audience, which is one of the two poles of the communication arc. There is always an implicit contract between an artist and the public that has paid to see the show. Therefore, André is bound by the circus code to deliver some valuable experience. The behavior he displays when he enters the ring makes a strong claim of vocal artistry. He looks serious and seems to be concentrating on his singing in earnest. The first few seconds appear to demonstrate his competence. But this is the story of a deceiver. The audience laughs when the female voice is heard. The lie is revealed and the illusion collapses. The first rule of felicitous performance, the principle of *accountability*, has been flouted (Bouissac 2010: 151–155). This character is an impostor. Although he has been unmasked, he will persist in making desperate efforts to remain credible by impersonating both the male and the female singers engaged in their love duo. He is not apologetic and ignores the etiquette regulating the rapport between performer and spectator, thus transgressing the social *congruence* of the performance. The principle of *semanticity*—that is, the cultural consistency of the act—is tainted by the prop he uses as a wig. Nothing could be of a lower status than a mop. The visual metaphor is effective because it connects two domains that are maximally distant in the contextual culture: the hairdo of a prima donna and a rag meant to absorb and collect dirt. The *rhetoric* principle is inverted as the clown becomes less and less convincing and sinks further and further down in his abysmal failure. His mastery of timing goes awry. His gender versatility is put to the test when the situation would logically force him to impersonate both a male and a female at the same time when the duo sings in harmony. It is at this very point in time that the act is literally zapped.

The narrative line presents what could be characterized as the negative of a performance, in the sense that the rules of performance are systematically inverted. These rules are usually taken for granted and therefore can be considered invisible. André's brief act literally puts the implied normative system inside out.

The straight, the tight, and the loose

In the preceding chapters the profile of the auguste in all its avatars has emerged as an agency that is defined by its position outside the cultural norm. This position at the margins of society makes the clown immune to the usual retributions that sanctions the transgressions of the rules according to which the body politic sustains its consistency and permanence, because the auguste is already excluded. Clowns are ostracized in the sense that they have by definition the status of outcasts. In the American context, the clown is the "tramp" or the "hobo"; in Europe, the "clown" nobody takes seriously. Like a young child, the clown can get away with breaking the rules. Such behavior does not call for legal repression through the tools of the law but elicits laughter that ridicules transgressors and acts as a form of mobbing. Why mirth is associated with this essentially aggressive reaction on the part of the audience is a daunting problem that this volume will endeavor to address in its conclusion.

Most of the rules that define the cultural norm of a society are tacit in the sense that they are not explicitly and formally stated in the law of the land. They constitute, however, a set of injunctions forming the basis of social education and class membership. As "common sense" or "good manners," they imply respect for the existing social hierarchy and regulate the interactions between individuals. Although most of these rules can be considered relatively trivial— for example, abstaining from producing physiological sounds in the presence of others or refraining from interrupting a superior who is speaking—some are truly the very basis of both the harmony and dissymmetry that are the basis for civil society in any of its cultural versions. Even the most arbitrary conventions are integral parts of a whole, and there are no truly innocuous violations.

The rules of the games people play, either as full-fledged members of an institution or as participants in various activities such as chess or card games and competitive sports, are the only guarantee against chaos and violence. They are the absolute conditions for the maintenance of the social order. During their cultural learning, children—and immigrants as well—are allowed to make mistakes that can be formally corrected through instruction or repressed in a more spontaneous manner by being ridiculed. Occasional lapses can be repaired through apologies. But deliberately and systematically flouting these rules, even minor ones, is always a serious matter, because the norm must be unquestioned as a whole if it is to remain the norm. It must impose itself as absolute lest its progressive loss of status unleash chaos. Its arbitrariness, though, makes it a fragile construct that is permanently threatened by disrespect and irony.

With all this in mind, let us turn to a traditional clown act and follow its development step by step. Comments will be inserted in the course of the description. This act was observed several times during the 1980s. It belongs to a rich paradigm offering variations through which the same basic narrative is implemented. Its interpretation by the three-member team of the Fornasari, an Italian family then performing in North America, will be the focus of this analysis. This description is based on observations made in February 1984 and 1985 at the Garden Brothers Circus, which was playing in a sports arena in Toronto. The act was part of a program that toured Canada and the United States. Although the two programs were different from one year to the next, the act by the Fornasari remained unchanged. This indicates that it consistently met with success and provides evidence of its cultural relevance.

This act involved three characters that I will label with reference to the type of costume they were wearing—Straight, Tight, and Loose—thus metaphorically hinting at the same time at their attitude toward the norm. This terminological move indicates at the outset that the rendering of the act as a descriptive text is elaborated in a theoretical perspective. Such labeling is not arbitrary, however, because it is grounded on objective features of the actors through the properties of their garments and demeanors. It is also made necessary by the fact that the three clowns are introduced collectively without specifying the personal stage names of each one. Consequently, the spectators have to distinguish them on the basis of visual cues and behavior.

"Straight man" is a common expression in the technical jargon of the circus. It designates someone who is not dressed like a clown or an acrobat but instead resembles a professional in civil society. He wears more-or-less formal attire, at times a tuxedo, but it may also be a colorful suit for the sake of striking a circus note by avoiding the usual drabness of business outfits. In the Fornasari act, the Straight plays the role of the whiteface clown. North American audiences are generally not familiar with the appearance and function of the whiteface, which usually puzzles them. It belongs to the traditional circus code of Continental Europe. That is why this functional character in duos—as we saw in the case of the Colombaioni—or in trios dons a formal garment to symbolize the norm in its highest embodiment.

The other two characters formed a striking contrast: Tight was an exaggerated version of Straight in the sense that he did not wear the heavy makeup of an auguste. Let us say that he had a "straight face." However, his suit was very tight, with sleeves and pant legs that were much too short. Loose was a typical auguste, with his face made up in red, white, and black patterns of the kind we discussed earlier in this volume. His garb and shoes were ill fitting, much too big for his size. His reddish, unkempt wig was crowned by a miniscule hat. His movements and gestures were awkward. We will see in the course of the act that these two characters are defined by their respective attitudes to the rules governing the contextual culture, with the Straight in the role of the umpire.

As the clowns enter the ring, Tight declares to Straight that he and his partner are going to perform some acrobatics. As he strikes a preparatory pose, Loose argues about what exactly they are going to do. Eventually it appears that they have agreed that Loose will stand motionless in the center of the arena and Tight will perform three somersaults above his head. As Tight walks away in order to take up a position at a distance, Loose follows him instead of staying at the center. Tight brings him back to the spot where he should stay, with the help of Straight, and the two force him to bend and stand on all fours. Once again, Loose does not comply, stands up, and follows Tight. The same sequence is repeated and, at last, everything seems to be in order. When Tight is ready, Straight gives him the signal by shouting, "Go!" Loose runs away as if he is in a marathon, because he thinks the order is addressed to him. Loose is put in place again, and Tight makes two somersaults above him. Tight resumes his initial position and announces before starting to run, "and three!" But Loose, who thinks the sequence is finished, rushes at the same time toward the exit and bumps into Tight. Maddened by the collision, Tight shouts, "Ah! You want a fight! You will get it!" Straight stops them and declares that the fight should be in the form of a boxing match.

A few observations are in order at this point before moving to the second part of this act. The sequence of actions has established, on the one hand, Tight as a dominant master closely associated with Straight, and, on the other, Loose as the underdog, a kind of insubordinate servant who lacks intelligence, courage, and discipline. In the traditional function of the whiteface clown, Tight displays outstanding skill, in this case acrobatic competence. Loose is forcefully reduced to the role of material accessory, a mere obstacle designed to help demonstrate the excellence of Tight. Furthermore, he is transformed in the process into a quadruped—that is, an animal—because he is compelled to get down on all fours. But his persistent reluctance to comply with the orders he is given after the appearance of having reached an agreement with the master construes him as a stubborn rebel who, literally, steps out of the social contract. His behavior progressively hints at feigned stupidity, and, at the end of the first sequence, his revolt shifts to violence. The masters, though, insist that the conflict should take the form of a boxing fight regulated by the rules of the game, and Loose is drawn, willy-nilly, into this cultural frame imposed upon him through the cooperation of the two dominant characters. At this point, the audience can legitimately wonder how he is to fare under the constraints of the system of confrontational sport.

Straight fetches boxing gloves and hands them to Loose and Tight. Loose puts them on his feet and mocks Tight, who is fixing them on his hands. Straight tells him that he should indeed use them as gloves. Then Tight gets ready for the fight and starts skipping from one foot to the other like boxers do in order to warm up before the action starts. Loose looks puzzled and interprets this as a dance. He starts dancing too, but in a funny, nonfunctional way, and declares that Tight has become crazy. But Straight says, "Go!" and Tight punches Loose, who pulls a white flag from his pocket and bitterly complains to Straight that he has been hit. Straight tells him that it is all right and that he can punch back. Loose rushes to Tight and kicks him, but Straight stops him and reminds him that he must use only his hands in a boxing match. The two engage in a series of fast fighting motions involving acrobatics jumps and falls. At one point when Tight is lying on the ground, Loose keeps pounding and stomping him on the backside. Again, Straight intervenes to remind Loose that it is against the rules to hit an opponent who is lying on the ground. Loose asks him to repeat this and seems happy to hear that. As Straight and Tight are talking during the pause, Loose punches Tight and immediately lies down. Then, he quickly stands up, hits again, and lies down again so that he can avoid being punched back. Straight objects to this behavior, declares that it is not fair play, and out of frustration gives up his role as umpire: "Now, anything goes!"

Philosophers have distinguished two kinds of cultural rules: "regulative rules" specifying how natural activities should be performed, and "constitutive rules," which create by their very existence particular social activities. The former include, for instance, table manners, etiquette, and fashion; the latter fully account for card games, chess, and, to a large extent, poetry. The rationale for this distinction is, for example, that humans need to eat to survive, but each culture produces its own norms regarding how this activity must be accomplished—from the way food is prepared to the manner in which it is ingested (chopsticks, hands, or fork and knife). By contrast, constitutive rules do not regulate activities that exist prior to their elaboration, but instead determine the form and meaning of the activities they create. This distinction should not be taken as an absolute dichotomy, however. There are gray areas that the clown act we have discussed so far will now lead us to explore.

Boxing is at the interface of nature and culture. Violent confrontation has been codified in the form of a sport institution. Fights are conducted in the bipedal position, exclusively with the fists, which are protected by leather gloves, and under the supervision of an umpire. When the argument between Tight and Loose turns physical, Straight stops them and imposes the codified version of aggressive behavior. There is an obvious social dissymmetry among the three actors of the narrative that unfolds in the circus ring, soon to be transformed into a boxing ring: on the one hand, Straight and Tight are socially dominant and embody the cultural norm; on the other hand, Loose is on the side of the oppressed members of society because he is ordered to serve as a tool in the acrobatic demonstration of Tight. In the second episode of the act, the dominant characters know the rules because they belong to the class that has created them. Loose flouts these rules and, in doing so, foregrounds their arbitrary nature. The rules are revealed to be naked, so to speak. Their force depends of who has the power to enforce them. Then Loose denounces the irrationality of these rules by generalizing them and exploiting to his advantage an extreme parody of the "work to rule" strategy in order to win the confrontation. He brings to light the whole ideological discourse of which the explicit rules are only the expressible tip.

We see now how this clown act toys with the constitutive rules of a familiar sport in a way that metaphorically unmasks the deeper institutional violence inherent in the contextual society inasmuch as it is founded on social inequality. As we will see when we move to the third episode of this act, the denunciation of the arbitrariness of the rules leads to the collapse of the social order.

After the decision by Straight to give up his role as the umpire who makes sure that the rules are followed, a new dynamic is created. *Tight and Loose continue fighting in a disorderly manner, eventually mixing boxing gestures with other combative behavior, and progressively acting as robots who at times do not even face each other, as if they were mad machines. Loose makes Tight face him and claims that he is going to punch his head off. Tight, at first, looks stunned and stays motionless. But, as Loose steps away from Tight so that he can aim his blow better, Tight makes a handstand. When Loose turns back toward him, he is confronted with his behind and immediately makes a gesture of disgust and pinches his own nose to signify that it stinks. A short scuffle ensues, and Loose throws Tight over his shoulder as a dead load and carries him out. They will then all come back to the center of the ring to briefly play some music and take their bow.*

Loose has demonstrated how fragile the rules are. First, he mocked them. Then, he showed how easily they can be ignored, even simply canceled. As a result, the hierarchy loses its relevance. Straight and Tight are deprived of their identities. The former resigns; the latter becomes a mere robot. No need to behead him; he already stinks like a corpse. If we compare the state of play at the beginning with the novel situation that concludes the action, there is an obvious inversion of values. This transformation has been obtained through denying the rules their absolute power by toying with them and even discarding them. By the same token, this game reveals its metaphorical pertinence, as it implies that all social rules can be subverted in the same way. The game of the rules is not mere entertainment. The auguste is uniquely qualified for such a ritualistic flouting of the social order.

Identity: One in two, two in one

In the chapter dealing with the makeup of clowns (Chapter 1), we addressed the sensitive issue of the relationship between identity and appearance, and we pointed out the tacit rule that is the bedrock of social life: the stability and consistency of the link between the two. Such a fundamental principle was bound to be the target of clowns' semiotic manipulations.

Let us consider now an ancient Sanskrit drama of the farcical type (*prahasana*). This popular comedy was formally written by Bodhāyana in the second or third century of the present era but likely rests upon a more ancient oral tradition. It is still often performed in India, notably in Kerala as a part of the Kuttiyatam theater repertory. Its title, *Bhagavadajjukam*, has been variously rendered in English as *The Yogi and the Courtesan* and *The Hermit and the Harlot*. It starts with a dialogue between an ascetic wanderer and his reluctant disciple. The latter has abandoned his strict Brahmin family because he was dissatisfied with their diet; he had first joined Buddhism in the hope that he would be better fed by the monks, but he was disappointed by their bland food and eventually followed the yogi. Their exchange is evocative of some dialogues between the whiteface clown and the auguste. One expresses only pieces of lofty thought, while the other has only food on his mind. They visit a garden where the yogi plans to experience the peaceful emptiness of contemplation, but the disciple looks for things to eat or otherwise enjoy. They meet a courtesan and her servants, who are seated on a bench. The play emphasizes the contrast between the lady of pleasure and the ascetic old man. A messenger sent by Death (King Yama) kills the courtesan. The yogi demonstrates his power by introducing his own soul into the dead female body, which apparently comes back to life. But it happens that the messenger has made an error and taken the life of the wrong person. King Yama sends him back to restore the courtesan's life. It annoys him to discover that the yogi has interfered with higher powers and decides to play a trick: he put the girl's soul in the body of the yogi. There are then hilarious dialogues in which the female speaks and behaves like the wise old man and the yogi expresses frivolous and amorous attitudes toward the girl's lover, who has rushed there after hearing that the woman had died. The boyfriend is surprised that she is still alive, but taken aback by her strange talk, while at the same time recoiling in horror from the advances of the yogi. All this goes on for the amusement of the audience until normality is reinstated by the messenger, who reconnects proper identities and appearances.

It is now well established that the nomadic entertainers who peddled their skills in Europe since the Middle Ages originated in India, where such nomads can still be observed nowadays plying their trade as street and market square performers. Their immemorial art is the ultimate source of all the disciplines that formed the core of the modern institution of the European circus, including the representation of comical interludes. It is, of course, impossible to retrace with any certainty the genealogy of a particular clown act, let alone the archaeology of performance in general. But there are homologies and recurrences indicative of probable continuity. The cultural evolution of oral traditions generates innovations and adaptations, while preserving some models whose resilience depends on the deep significance of the issues they implicitly address. The theme of identity is bound to be one of these recurring themes, especially when we consider that ancient cultures were rife with stories of supernatural agents taking up the appearance of animals and humans, or magicians able to transform themselves and others into different guises. Contemporary technological societies are far from being immune to this kind of anxiety, as witnessed by the heavy bureaucratic apparatus devoted to the securing and policing of identity kits and their reliability. The stealing of identities and the impersonating of others are considered serious crimes that are difficult to control.

Let us now return to the circus and observe a few other acts that echo this fundamental preoccupation. An auguste is crying loudly as he is seated on a bench, looking despondent. "What is wrong with you?" asks the ringmaster. The answer is a tragic story of lost identity: "I used to be a beautiful little girl loved by everybody, but one day a mean fairy came up, took me away, and put in my cradle the ugly boy I am now. And nobody loves me anymore." Note the role of a supernatural agent in this micro-narrative.

A successful clown act that has been performed by so many augustes that it would be unfair to attribute its origin to any consists of playing a four-person melodrama singlehandedly. For instance, the auguste Quito auditions in front of the whiteface Rex to be in the cast of a play. He claims that he can play all the characters. Indeed, Quito carries four items in his bag (a bowler hat, a woman's wig, a helmet, and a police cap). Deftly putting the bowler hat on his head, he says good-bye to his wife while replacing the hat with the wig and hugging himself perfunctorily. Suddenly, the helmet introduces the lover, who rushes to the woman, now under the wig, miming a wild embrace: "Alone, at long last!" But the husband reappears under his bowler hat, draws a gun, and shoots the lovers. Here comes the policeman, blowing his whistle. He pulls handcuffs from his pocket and captures the murderer. I witnessed this very brief episode several times by the duo Rex and Quito at the Cirque d'hiver in Paris in the 1950s. It was so brilliantly executed in less than a minute that it left an indelible trace in my memory. The action was punctuated by the hurried voice of Quito: "C'est lui! C'est elle! C'est l'autre!" [It's him! It's her! It's the other!]. Then the strident whistle brought the drama to a close.

Playing with the rule of univocal identity provides a matrix that includes two possible transgressions: one identity with two or more appearances; one appearance with two or more identities. The above examples offer a variation of each. But the most elaborate game on this theme is a traditional clown act called "the broken mirror." It has been, and still is, interpreted by many duos including a whiteface and an auguste. We will focus on this act as it was performed in 1966 by Pipo and Zavatta at the Cirque d'hiver in Paris. This act was recorded by French television and remains accessible at www.circopedia.org, a well-run website that is more likely than others to endure the passing of time and technology. Like many clown scenarios, it is pointless to assign authorship and to trace its source back to an original creator. Clown historians have found evidence that the broken mirror gag was part of a seventeenth-century Spanish play that was likely inspired by still-earlier popular performances (e.g., Towsen 1976: 244–248). We have already examined some aspects of this act in Chapter 2.

Let us return now to the moment when the ringmaster welcomes the two movers who are delivering some antique-looking furniture to the ring. In this case the ring is supposed to be the dressing room of a famous actor of the Comédie-Française who will shortly arrive in order to rehearse his part before the performance. One of the movers is the auguste Zavatta, who after depositing an armchair returns back stage to fetch the mirror in front of which the thespian will practice his acting. The noise of shattering glass is heard, and Zavatta explains that he missed a step and broke the mirror. All that is left is the freestanding frame. The ringmaster panics and suggests that the auguste should pretend to be the reflection of the actor and mimic whatever the latter may do on the other side of the absent mirror. Zavatta is quickly fitted with a tuxedo and a top hat because this is how the actor is dressed. When the latter, played by the whiteface Pipo, enters the ring, it is obvious that he is tipsy as he comes from a formal dinner party with his colleagues. He still holds an empty bottle of champagne, which he hands over to the ringmaster before looking at himself in the mirror. He notices "his" red nose, but the ringmaster tells him that it is because of the wine he drank. Zavatta is a good mime who manages to perform well at the beginning, but a series of gags follows based on the fact that Pipo's behavior is more and more challenging to imitate—such as the lighting and the actor smoking a cigarette, the cleaning of the mirror, and the swallowing of an egg for clearing the actor's throat. Discrepancies between the model and his reflection reach a critical level beyond which the credibility of the situation is bound to collapse. We will reconsider these gags in more detail in the paragraphs that follow, but let us leap to the end when Pipo turns to the final scene of the play he is rehearsing and draws a gun with which he is supposed to shoot his wife's lover while uttering vengeful words. Forgetting his passive role, Zavatta protests that he is innocent and, having thus disclosed his deception, he is chased by everybody as an impostor. He suddenly pretends to have a heart attack, sits down on the floor of the ring, and, while they all stop the chase and show concern, he dashes out of the ring at great speed. Pipo and Zavatta return to the center of the ring to take their bow and acknowledge the applause of the audience.

The first noticeable feature of this narrative is that an auguste—that is, a character of lower social rank—is led by circumstances to deceptively act as the reflection of a whiteface, thus virtually erasing the differences of identity, with all their social and cultural connotations. Let us note that the auguste has caused the accident that triggered the whole process. Once the paradoxical repair strategy is adopted, the situation provides many opportunities for gags. Each clown team that has performed this traditional act developed their own set of visual jokes and met with various degrees of success. The reference act by Pipo and Zavatta, described above, shows variations in comparison with the same narrative as interpreted some 15 years earlier by Pipo and his then-partner Rhum. This act was recorded in writing in 1950 by Tristan Rémy (1962: 187–191). Clowns sometimes present reduced versions of the story as a mere pretext to stage a few worn-out gags, as did the traditional but unimaginative Chickys in their lackluster performances in the 1980s, thus unwittingly providing fodder for a postmodern anthropologist (Little 1993: 118–119). In fact, the kinds of gags as well as the type of story line that frames them are worthy of a closer examination. How the act ends may puzzle viewers if the ethnographic details are glossed over and if one looks for a logical conclusion without truly understanding what is at stake in the narrative.

But there is more. Whatever fictitious narrative is invented in order to motivate the action and establish its superficial credibility, such as the assumed awkwardness of the mover or the drunkenness of the whiteface, the whole story starts with the breaking of a mirror. This is an object loaded with significance. From as far back in time as we can know about, since this artifact was created, it is associated with magic. Breaking a mirror is still believed nowadays to bring 7 years of bad luck or to foretell a death in the family. In

Christianity, it has been variously attributed to the devil, who can use this tool to capture souls, or to a divine gift that offers a faithful representation of the true self of a person. Mirrors play a role in the folklore of vampires, in which they are credited for not reflecting vampires' images because they have no souls. In modern times, even from a strictly secular perspective, mirrors are no less significant as tools of identity that not only contribute to developing our visual notion of the self but also constantly allow us to check and manage the permanence of our appearance. Breaking a mirror can thus always be considered an ominous sign. It challenges the imperative of keeping up the appearance and deprives the self from the eye control that then becomes literally alienated from others' gaze. In this clown act, the mirror significantly belongs to the sphere of prestige and power. The shattering of the mirror by an agent of low social status creates a crisis incommensurate with the accidental breaking of a common object. Attempting to repair the lack of true reflection by garbing an auguste to match the status and image of the whiteface subverts the social cohesion based on unbridgeable hierarchical differences. The transgression is compounded by the fact that the auguste himself is the perpetrator of the crime—the killing of a virtual image. Miming is an artistic technique that can reach perfection. Two professional mimes could easily create a perfect illusion of reflection if they were required to do so. However, if we focus on the details of the gags, it becomes obvious that the systematic failure of the auguste is built into the script and that the process necessarily leads to his drastic demise.

The 1966 recording of the broken mirror act is a valuable research document. It was filmed at close range in black and white for a TV broadcast, and all gestures, movements, and facial expressions are clearly visible. The sparse but meaningful dialogue is also audible. Pipo obviously follows the pattern of his earlier routine with Rhum in the 1950s, but there are some changes that we will note as we proceed to examine the successive gags. When Pipo first stands in front of the mirror, he projects his hands forward as a kind of welcoming gesture to himself, and Zavatta imitates him in almost perfect synchrony. He expresses some surprise at noticing the red nose of his image and cracks a joke with the ringmaster concerning the champagne he had been drinking that evening. Then, he sits down and so does Zavatta. Facing the mirror, Pipo crosses his legs, lifting the right and then the left leg in rapid succession, while Zavatta hurries to follow his lead. But when Pipo lifts his two feet at the same time in a gesture of exhilaration, the auguste loses his balance and tips over the chair. Pipo does not notice, because from time to time he addresses the ringmaster, turning his face away from the mirror. Pipo now gets rid of his white gloves and throws them on the ground. This action is exactly duplicated by Zavatta. Both now stand face to face, and Pipo executes some movements with his elbows, which are accurately imitated by his partner. So far everything goes smoothly except for Zavatta's fall from the chair, but because Pipo was distracted at that moment, this episode was only a close call.

The audience, however, tends to identify with the auguste and starts experiencing some anxiety based on empathy. How long will Zavatta be able to meet the challenge of impersonating the dynamic image of the authoritarian whiteface? Tension starts building up when Pipo removes his top hat, then puts it back on his head, while Zavatta does the same thing but mistakenly presses down the collapsible top hat, which appears flat. Pipo calls the ringmaster to voice his surprise, pointing to the discrepancy he has perceived in the mirror. But when the ringmaster redirects Pipo's attention to the mirror, Zavatta has again propped up the hat and both now look alike. Pipo is puzzled, but once again alcohol is blamed for this brief hallucination. Pipo strikes his chest with his fists in a gesture of self-stimulation and defiance, and reaches to the inside pocket of his jacket to get his silver cigarette box. Smoking will help him sober up. Zavatta picks up a cigarette from the box at the same time as Pipo but does not release his grip on the box and puts it in his own pocket, in a gesture that appears to be the reflection of Pipo's action. Pipo looks at his empty hand and once again is puzzled by the disappearance of the item, turning inquisitively toward the ringmaster. But when the latter brings him back to the mirror, Zavatta shows the box and Pipo is satisfied in spite of the fact that the auguste again pockets this valuable object while Pipo seems to think that he is the one who has done this. They now both hold a cigarette, and Zavatta gets close enough to the virtual mirror to light up his cigarette from the same lighter. They blow the smoke in each other's face, and the word "echo" is uttered by the ringmaster as an explanation that will be called upon again in the course of the act. However, a new problem develops, because they both hold their cigarette in their right hand. Zavatta has not taken into consideration the optics of mirrors, and Pipo is troubled by this inconsistency. He changes hands, and Zavatta mindlessly does the same. Once again the ringmaster is summoned, but when Pipo wants to show him what is happening, Zavatta is now holding the cigarette in his left hand. All is well, although Pipo starts showing some skepticism and the drunkenness hypothesis progressively loses its validity.

The ringmaster now claims that the mirror must be dirty and that this accounts for the blurred vision generating the problems. Pipo grabs a white piece of cloth. So does Zavatta. They wipe the glass of the mirror in perfect synchrony, to the point of creating the brief illusion for the audience that there is indeed a mirror, thus demonstrating that the two artists are accomplished mimes. Upon taking a close look at the result of their cleaning work, they hit each other's nose. This is explainable: the mirror is a hard surface. Suddenly Pipo realizes that he now holds two pieces of cloth instead of one. He has inadvertently grabbed Zavatta's during the action. But when he looks again, Zavatta has recovered his cloth. As Pipo takes a dramatic posture to rehearse his part before the performance at the Comédie-Française, the ringmaster suggests that he should swallow a raw egg to clear his voice. "Yes, bring me an egg!" he says; the egg is delivered, and Pipo places it on a plate resting on the chair. Zavatta panics because there is only one egg. He quickly seizes the egg, but Pipo notices that it has disappeared from the plate. He is flabbergasted. He again summons the ringmaster, while Zavatta puts the egg in his pants pocket in order to avoid detection. "Look! That is extraordinary: there was an egg, and the egg has vanished!" Pipo emphasizes his declaration using a common gesture of great surprise, which consists of hitting his thighs laterally with his hands. Zavatta has no choice but to imitate him and eventually crushes the egg hidden in his pocket.

At this point in the dramatic development, the act has clearly taken the form of a game in which each move of Pipo's is a challenge that becomes increasingly difficult to meet and mistakes made by Zavatta are less and less easy to repair. The climax is represented by the broken egg, which Zavatta undertakes to extract from his pocket and whose remains drip on the floor while Pipo requires a revolver to practice the last scene of his play. Pipo rises menacingly from his chair, and Zavatta follows suit. As they face each other, Pipo utters a guttural sound of threat, to which Zavatta, forgetting that mirrors do not speak, replies with a higher-pitch noise. Surprise! "It is the echo!" says the ringmaster. "Ah, yes, of course, the echo!" repeats Pipo. But the confrontation between Pipo and his "mirror image" heats up, and as the action accelerates, they meet face to face outside the frame of the mirror. In the confusion that follows, they change sides, and now Pipo (pursuing his acting practice) reproaches his virtual rival of having slept with his wife, while aiming the gun at his heart. Suddenly, the fictitious game collapses. Zavatta panics and protests his innocence, but Pipo continues his diatribe. They literally move out of the frame of the mirror and, by the same token, out of the narrative. Zavatta is now the culprit, who tries to escape. He is chased around the ring, not only by Pipo but also by the ringmaster and all the circus hands that were standing nearby. They all freeze on the spot when Zavatta raises his hand to his heart, sits down on the side of the ring, and gives signs of being sick. "Heart attack!" says Pipo, and everybody stands to attention, showing concern. Zavatta seizes this opportunity to jump to his feet and sprints toward the exit, where he disappears, followed by all the others. Pipo and Zavatta are quickly brought back to the center of the ring to bow to the audience and acknowledge their thunderous applause.

The readers who check the URL where this act is found will discover that the above written rendering has not done justice to each and every detail of the dynamic interactions of the three characters. This will be more and more obvious if the video is run repeatedly, thus providing supplementary observation time. As in a live performance, the semiotic saturation constrains the spectator to somewhat schematize the whole experience as it unfolds. In that case, the dynamic of the plot leads to a tipping point when Pipo understands what is happening and cleverly merges fiction (the play he is rehearsing) and reality (the deceptive game of which he is the victim) within the fiction of the clown act itself and the relative statuses of its actors. This latter aspect is quite important and has generally been overlooked by those who have found the clown act thought provoking. This is, to my knowledge, the only traditional narrative of the circus repertory in which the whiteface is represented as being drunk. Behaving in a disorderly manner is part of the auguste persona that always walks awkwardly and displays a red nose. But the whiteface is an epitome of self-control and decency. His identity is stable, or at least consistent, across the various avatars that he may be required to impersonate by the nature of the various plots: conductor, officer, magician, or—in the case in point—famous theater actor. One of the effects of alcohol is to interfere with the cultural norm of identity. People commonly disown their action under the pretext that they were under the influence of a personality-modifying substance. The broken mirror act is unthinkable if the whiteface had not first renounced his identity in one way or another, drunkenness being the most socially acceptable cause in the contextual culture, mainly if it is caused by an elite drink such as champagne or whisky, congruent with the high status of the whiteface. But under whatever name, alcohol is alcohol: the self is alienated and afflicted by a drastic impairment of judgment and change of personality to the point of acting "out of character" or being unrecognizable. In the circus code, a drunken whiteface is as scandalous as a drunken pope or a drunken president would be in the religious and political realms.

This initial transgression makes possible the flouting of the identity rule by the auguste. If, as I will try to suggest in the following chapters, clown acts are modern remnants of long-lost master narratives of a mythical nature that have survived in the fragmented forms in which they can nowadays be observed, we can attempt to elucidate the basic structure and its transformations accounting for the "broken mirror." As in folktales, the short narratives that organize the semantic contents of clown acts can be expressed in an abstract manner. In this act, the temporal order in which the events appear in the ring does not necessarily reflect the logical relations that account for its deep meaning. As the embodiment of the rules that found and sustain culture, the whiteface commits a transgressive act by drinking a substance altering the integrity of his identity. He requires a mirror—that is, the most sensitive and fragile artifact, whose function is to guarantee the continuity and permanence of identities. Trusted to the hands of an auguste, who is the lowest-ranking member at the opposite end of the spectrum of society, the mirror is broken.

This constitutes the second transgressive move, because it can be considered an occupational mistake or a rebellious gesture. This triggers a major violation of the foundational rules of the stability of identities and the basis of social hierarchy: the auguste becomes the symmetric image of the whiteface. Trapped in the frame, in which he endeavors to reduce two identities to a single appearance, the transgressor eventually pays for this crime. First he is increasingly at the receiving end of the gags, and finally he is mobbed out of the circus, a metaphor of the circle of civilization. It is symptomatic that some commentators have noted what they consider "a weak ending" (e.g., Little 1993: 122). Given the magnitude of the transgression, the only logical conclusion would be the killing of the transgressor of lower status, who becomes the scapegoat. In the Pipo and Zavatta interpretation, the death of the auguste is briefly evoked as a last deceptive trick, but the chase soon resumes to exclude the perpetrator from the community. This is indeed a strong ending commensurate with the virtual semiotic crime he has committed.

6

Clown and Trickster

Master of tricks

Despite all his refined demeanor and rhetoric, the whiteface clown is not a benevolent character. He very often indulges in playing cruel tricks, the usual victim of which is the auguste. Self-assured and at times arrogant, the whiteface entices his apparently less gifted partner into playing rigged games or participating in self-defeating schemes. But the contemporary version of the whiteface is a somewhat polished, restrained version of its early nineteenth-century prototypes. The violence and nastiness of the British clown Footit, for instance, were legendary. It is around this time that the auguste appeared as a full-fledged character and became the butt of much humiliating vexation. However, it can happen that the roles are reversed and that the auguste eventually outsmarts his tormentor, as will be seen below. But this is not the rule, and the shifting of roles, when it occurs, counts as a transgression of the circus code, thus creating a powerful gag.

This chapter endeavors to review and discuss the rich paradigm of narratives that could be subsumed under the category of the "trickster cycle." These acts are part of the traditional repertoire. They are the origin of the romantic notion of the clown—that is, the auguste, as "the one who gets slapped." But the clowns who are represented and pitied in the literature are different from the clowns whose performances can be observed in the circus ring. Poetic elaborations have picked up a mere aspect of this phenomenon and have extrapolated an existential misery that has contributed to reinforce the outcast status of the auguste in the public imagination. But, as we will see in this chapter, ethnographic evidence is more complex. The auguste transcends his scapegoat destiny by playing tricks of his own.

A typical version of such an act was documented in writing by Tristan Rémy, who observed it in 1920 (Rémy 1962: 236–237). The Fratellini was a renowned team formed by three brothers, including François (the whiteface),

Paul (the first auguste), and Albert (the second auguste). The latter embodied the lowest status through his heavy makeup, outrageous costume, and childish demeanor. The working title for the narrative we will look at is "the coin in the funnel." The performance goes as follows: François asks Paul if he wants to easily earn a valuable coin. It suffices to keep the coin resting on his forehead with his head being tilted backward. A funnel is slipped under his belt and if Paul manages to make the coin drop in the funnel at the signal of the whiteface, the coin will be his. This is an easy way of making money. François will count "One! Two! Three!" and Paul must drop the coin when he hears "three!" As his head is tilted backward, he cannot see the whiteface who, in the meantime, receives from a circus hand a decanter full of water, which he pours in the funnel just before uttering, "three!" Paul's pants are soaked, and he expresses his anger at the whiteface who has tricked him into agreeing to play this stupid game. "It was only a joke!" says François as Paul leaves the ring walking awkwardly because of his wet pants. At this very moment, Albert emerges from the curtains. François makes him the same offer, to win money without effort. And so it goes. However, the water from the first decanter does not soak Albert's trousers. He keeps his head tilted backward waiting for the signal. Several decanters are thus poured without effect until the assistant says that there is no more water. Suddenly, Albert raises his head and the coin slides but is stopped by his huge red nose before falling into the funnel when he hears "three!" He then pockets the coin while extracting from his pants a large bottle that has collected the water, because he has smartly inserted the end of the funnel into it.

Another version of this scenario was presented in December 2012 at the Cirque d'hiver in Paris by the Spanish José Michel clowns. Note that almost a full century separates this from the previously discussed performance, thus bearing witness to the resiliency of the narrative. In fact, the José Michel troupe has been performing this act over the past decade in many major European circuses, including Circus Benneweis (Denmark), Circus Finlandia (Finland), and Circus Krone (Germany). At times, the whiteface was a woman. In the 2012 version, the whiteface was Alberto Caroli. In all the interpretations of this narrative by the José Michels, the funnel is simply held by the victim high above his head, and the game consists of catching in it the coin thrown by either the ringmaster or the whiteface. Earning a coin among the contemporary European currencies is hardly worth the effort. When the Fratellini performed this act, much higher monetary values were available in the form of coins. Therefore, another motivation had to be built into the story. In 2012, the whiteface tells the first auguste that the prize is a drink. After the latter refuses and walks away, the whiteface mentions a meal. To both offers the auguste replies "no!" But the whiteface shouts, "It will be free!"

The auguste stops walking and says "yes!" Then the game can start. Another variation in their interpretation consists of developing the water theme into a series of slapstick events during which the augustes are soaked.

The general pattern of the act that remains constant despite the variations that can be observed is that a deal is offered that sounds like a good way of earning an advantage without really working for it. Once the offer is accepted, it turns out that it was a bad deal. The victim has been tricked into playing the game out of greediness or gluttony and is eventually soaked with water. With this in mind, let us follow the two versions performed in 2010 and 2012 by the José Michels, both of which are generated by the same matrix.

First version: The ringmaster asks the whiteface to play the game, and the two augustes are the ones who bring the water in various containers. But instead of pouring the liquid in the funnel, they either spill the water before reaching their target or inadvertently soak themselves. They try to sneak up close to the funnel, which is held high by the whiteface, but do so awkwardly and attract the curiosity of the whiteface. As soon as they realize that they have been discovered, they attempt to "repair" their behavior by transforming it into another kind of gesture or action. This provides the opportunity for many water gags of the slapstick kind. The attention of the audience progressively turns toward the two augustes, because it is clear that they will never succeed in dousing the whiteface with water. The rhetorical organization of these gags leads to a climax as the augustes use larger and larger containers, which spill more water each time. At the beginning, they bring water in goblets, and when the whiteface looks at them suspiciously, they hide the goblets in their pockets, thus wetting their pants. At the end, they pretend to be rowing in a huge bucket, which they treat as a boat. An alternative to this finale consists of one of the augustes pretending that he is swimming in the spilled water, and he slides across the ring while miming front crawl strokes. For acts involving the spilling of water, the sawdust or carpet of the ring is covered by a plastic sheet, which quickly becomes slippery.

Second version: The whiteface entices one auguste into playing the game with the promise of an easily obtained profit. The second auguste is the one who provides the water but fails to achieve his task and undergoes the same ordeal as in the previous version. What these two versions have in common is that the whiteface is directly or indirectly the trickster who avoids getting wet and causes the augustes to get soaked.

Let us now turn to another popular narrative that is often performed nowadays as it was over a century ago—one whose roots likely reach far into the past of human cultures.

Too good to be true

As we have seen above, the offer of a free ride by the whiteface is a classic opening of an abundant set of narratives found in the traditional repertory of clowns. We will now examine one of the most popular clown acts from this paradigm. It is variously called "the bees" or "the honey." It was documented at the beginning of the twentieth century and can still be observed nowadays. I witnessed five interpretations of this act by various clown teams between 2010 and 2014. The reference for this section is a 1920 written version of "the honey" by Dario (the whiteface), Bario (the auguste), and Loyal (the ringmaster) (Rémy 1962: 183–187).

After a musical opening, the whiteface declares that now it is time to work. The auguste Bario replies, "What? Work? I am fed up with that. It does not pay. I don't want to work anymore." The whiteface appears to be upset and tells him that this decision raises very serious issues unless, of course, he suddenly becomes rich. But this is not the case. Bario declares that he will simply wait for people to provide him with what he needs to live. The whiteface protests, "But this is not a legitimate system!" to which the auguste replies, "So what?"

Confronted with such a problem, the whiteface comes up with a solution: "Listen. I will teach you how to drink and eat without having to work. Do you like honey?" Bario loves honey. The whiteface is going to transform Bario into a queen bee seated on her throne in the hive and waiting for the worker bees that bring her nectar and feed her with honey. When the little bees come back to the hive and bow in front of their queen, she just needs to order, "Give me some honey!" Bario finds such a system exceedingly appealing and keeps repeating, "Eating and drinking without having to work for it … what a great idea!"

The whiteface Dario thus undertakes to metamorphose the auguste Bario into a queen bee by performing some magic gestures and having him sit on a chair. Then he claims that he is a worker bee and dances around the happy-looking auguste, pretending to gather nectar but secretly filling his mouth with water from a bottle that has been placed at a distance. When he returns in front of Bario and bows, the latter is ecstatic and shouts, "Little bee, give me some honey!" The whiteface then spits all the water in his face.

Bario is furious to have been tricked into this hoax and threatens Dario with one of his shoes. But the whiteface suggests that he too could have fun by playing the same trick on the ringmaster, Mr. Loyal. Fair enough. The auguste summons the ringmaster and starts explaining that he has discovered a method of eating and drinking without having to work. Once he has caught his interest, Bario declares that he is going first to transform him into an animal, a camel. Bario obviously mixes things up, and the whiteface intervenes to correct him: "Not a camel, Bario!" "Sorry," says Bario. "I will transform you into a cow…No! I will transform you into a mother-in-law!" The auguste is confused, and the whiteface has to whisper the correct words, which Bario misunderstands. He utters instead other inappropriate words that are phonetically close to "queen bee," such as "cookie" or "Frisbee" (my English rendering of the original French homophony *abeille* [bee] and *corbeille* [basket]). He eventually gets it right, but soon gets off track again by listing the plants he will visit to gather the honey: "carrots, turnips, cabbages…" Dario protests, "No, idiot! You will gather the nectar from flowers!" "This is right," says Bario. "Cauliflowers!" And he proceeds with the explanation of what will follow. However, the auguste does not manage to keep the water in his mouth, either because he stumbles on the way or cannot help laughing at the thought of the trick he is going to pull on the ringmaster, who in the meantime fills his own mouth with water. As he remains silent when Bario succeeds in standing in front of him with his mouth full, nothing happens except that Bario swallows the liquid and reminds the ringmaster that he should say, "Little bee, give me your honey!" at which point the ringmaster spits in his face the water he was holding in his mouth. The whiteface had indeed conspired with the ringmaster to play a double trick on the auguste.

I observed in 1974 a similar interpretation of this narrative by the auguste Dédé Gruss and his son, the whiteface Alexis. This act was described and discussed in an article on "the meaning of nonsense" (Bouissac 1982: 203–209). Pierre Robert Levy (1982: 112–113) has summarized another version of this act as it was performed by the same clowns and has documented the version of the funnel in which the auguste, who has been soaked by the whiteface, undertakes to trick the ringmaster but fails to victimize him because a cork has been secretly introduced to prevent the water from running out of the funnel. The auguste keeps pouring water and is greatly puzzled by the lack of effect until the ringmaster tips the funnel toward the auguste, who thus gets doused for the second time. Photographs showing snapshots of this act, albeit performed by other clowns, are found in Levy's abundantly illustrated book (1991: 152–153).

Transgression and consequences

All the narratives we have reviewed so far in this chapter exhibit a distinctive pattern: the whiteface tricks the auguste into renouncing one of the basic rules of social life—rules that are in their multiple forms the bedrock of civilization or, more generally, culture. Symbolically, the auguste chooses to get a free ride at the expense of others, or he simply accepts to willingly regress to a state of nature. "The honey" is doubly symptomatic, because the deal offered by the whiteface includes not only the advantage of surviving through the work of others without contributing anything to society, but also of being transformed into an animal, thus embracing nature wholeheartedly. But the deal proves to be too good to be true. The auguste is abundantly doused with water, a traditional way of punishing transgressors with various degrees of severity, from the simple humiliation of wetting his pants to the drastic custom of drowning the culprit.

This performed behavior has social and political implications. The use of bees as a sociopolitical metaphor is particularly significant as it refers back to hunter-gatherer cultures and possibly to the first domestication of the insects responsible for honey production. It is difficult to uncover for how long in human history such a narrative and its conclusion may have provided the collective meaning we can observe in today's circus performances. The interesting point is that being doused with water is the retribution befalling the transgressor. In the standard version of this act, the victim is placated by the suggestion that he can play the same trick on another clown or on the ringmaster. But taking the role of the trickster backfires, and the clown ends up being doubly soaked in water as the whiteface strikes an alliance with the second clown or the ringmaster and conspires to douse him with more water. But as we saw above, the unexpected shifting of roles is always a possibility, and the trickster can be tricked in turn.

Splashing water on someone is a classical prank. It is also a ritual behavior that can be observed nowadays in most South Asian cultures. It is, for instance, practiced in the Holi festival in India, which is marked by a loosening of social restrictions associated with caste, gender, age, and economic class. Colored water, or simply water, is abundantly splashed and poured on unsuspecting people, with total disrespect for social norms. It accompanies jokes and mocking laughter. Playing with water is a recurrent theme in clown acts. In the greatest number of cases, it is the pants of the clown that are the target of the splashing. In the funnel game, the clowns behave as if they have wetted themselves, thus reversing to a state of pre-enculturation like babies or de-enculturation like senile people. The control of sphincters is indeed the hallmark of civilized social life. This soiling of the pants is performed with more or less subtlety, as is the symbolic production of flatulence through wind instruments and accompanying gestures that signal the embarrassment of the perpetrator or the protest of the whiteface partner. This belongs to the range of transgressions that characterize the trickster's persona, manipulating the realm of cultural innovations both as a provider, a spoiler, and a rule-breaker, ignoring the fine line separating proper from improper social behavior.

Master of fire

The first clown act described by Tristan Rémy in his collection of documented scenarios is titled "the match or the waxed taper" (1962: 35–37). The fact that the date indicated is 1900 and that the actors are designated only by their function (the clown, that is, the whiteface; the auguste; and Mr. Loyal, the ringmaster) suggests that Rémy did not witness this act but used indirect sources. For such a dialogue to be recorded anonymously in such detail, it must have been both commonly performed and found memorable— therefore, particularly relevant to deep cultural concerns.

As the whiteface proudly steps into the ring, he addresses the ringmaster, boasting that he has become an outstanding sharpshooter. He further informs him that, in view of this new talent, he is going to ask the circus director to raise his salary. The ringmaster replies that he will be pleased to make such a recommendation as long as the clown gives him evidence of his new skill. The whiteface is indeed prepared to demonstrate the accuracy of his shooting at targets, but he needs a courageous man to hold a burning match so that he can extinguish the fire with a single shot. The ringmaster agrees to do so after having been reassured that the clown never fails.

They strike a match, and the ringmaster holds it at a distance with his right hand. The whiteface takes a revolver out of his pocket and slowly walks across the ring; then he turns toward the ringmaster and tells him that he must take the time to collect himself, making sure that he is in the correct position. Suddenly, the ringmaster utters a cry of pain, because the flame has reached his fingers. He realizes that he has been tricked into playing a stupid game.

This is indeed a joke, and the whiteface has a big laugh, but he suggests that the ringmaster could also have fun by playing the trick on the auguste, who enters the ring at this moment. The whiteface exits discreetly. The auguste becomes the mark of the ringmaster. The dialogue reveals the stupidity of the auguste, who eventually agrees to hold the match when the ringmaster tells him that if he misses the target and kills him inadvertently, he will pay him a pension. The same outcome occurs, and the auguste gets burnt. But the ringmaster convinces him to play the same trick on someone else, and, because the whiteface emerges from the curtain just then, the auguste announces to him that he has become a remarkable sharpshooter. A comical dialogue ensues in which the auguste mixes up the explanations and is corrected by the ringmaster.

Now it is the whiteface who holds the burning match, and the auguste takes his time to aim: he changes position, flexes his arm, squints, looks around, walks to the right, then the left. The match is still burning in the whiteface's hand, without hurting his fingers. The auguste is puzzled and wonders why the whiteface does not cry in pain. The latter laughs and says it is because he is smarter, and he shows that he had replaced the match with a coiled wax taper.

If the making of fire is generally considered to have been the first step toward human cultures, controlling slow combustion and instant explosion is the hallmark of civilization. In the above narrative, the whiteface demonstrates his mastery of the latter two skills, with an emphasis on the technology of risk-free, continuous burning as a source of light, heat, and energy. Skills based on the controlling and manipulating of fire are found in abundance in the circus, which variously exhibits fire-eaters, fire jugglers, humans or animals leaping through flaming hoops, and magic acts featuring combustion and explosion. The following opening act of a circus program deserves especially to be mentioned here because this act interestingly straddled the usually distinct genres of clowning and daredevil. Hubertus's Master of Hellfire act is liminal in many respects, to the point that some in the audience find it absolutely scandalous in spite of its enthusiastic reception. But let us first put this in the context of the circus tradition.

Although the categories of spectacular skills in the modern circus code are well defined, some blending occasionally occurs in the staging of acrobatic acts. For instance, one of the members in a flying trapeze troupe may join the others under the guise of an auguste and comically perform some failed stunts before shedding his camouflage and completing outstanding exercises in a regular leotard. In the 1950s, equilibrist Kervich presented a daring balancing act on a single trapeze, but he first pretended to be a drunken sailor among the audience and kept interrupting the ringmaster while the latter was deceptively introducing a female acrobat who was supposed to be the trapeze artist. Kervich managed to force his way into the ring, climb the rope with lots of near misses, and reach the trapeze bar, on which he suddenly stood upright, keeping his balance without holding the ropes with his hands. Then, his extraordinary act could unfold, which included standing on a chair resting on two of its legs on the bar of the trapeze or reaching forward while balancing on his knees to catch a burning cigarette in his mouth. But let us return to a more dramatic version of the pyrotechnic theme in the circus ring.

Bordeaux, January 17, 2013. The premiere of Cirque Arlette Gruss is about to start. This is one of the very best European circuses. The public is visibly expecting a spectacle of the highest standards. The printed program is not yet available. Therefore, the acts that will commence in a moment will yield a maximum of information because they cannot be visually anticipated by leafing through the usual illustrated booklet. The background music stops. The spotlights are turned on and focus on the elegant and serious ringmaster, who proceeds toward the center of the ring to welcome the audience and delivers some warnings about various regulations such as turning off cell phones, not using a flash if they take pictures, not recording copyrighted material, and, most importantly, absolutely not smoking. The spectacle can now start. Well, not quite yet. As he finishes the last sentence, he notices smoke coming from the first row of the audience. Someone is obviously smoking a cigarette. The ringmaster politely reminds this person that he has to go outside if he wants to smoke. The public can see a young man with long hair who calmly keeps puffing on his cigarette, seemingly unconcerned by the words of the ringmaster, who walks toward him and repeats his warning. "Sir, do you understand French?" The reply comes with a heavy accent: "Non! je suis allemand." [No! I am German.] The ringmaster makes some effort and explains that it is dangerous to smoke in a circus. The dialogue heats up. The young man raises his voice: "Dangerous? You have seen nothing yet! I am the Master of Hellfire!" As he emphatically makes this pronouncement, the young man stands up, the sleeves of his coat catch fire, and flames are rising high as he joins the ringmaster. The show has started as the sudden irruption of something totally unexpected: the breaking of a law and a taboo. Once in the ring, the rebel displays stunning feats of fire eating, ending with a huge jet of flame from his mouth, while two fiery fountains at his sides spit out geysers of fire. The seamless fabric of everyday life in a province town where most events are predictable, including the usual rituals of the opening of a circus show, have been torn apart. Hubertus—the name of the artist—will return twice to the ring during the performance to again shock and delight the audience with pyrotechnic skills and truly never-seen-before stunts. These include the setting on fire of his nipples, the apparent aspiration through his nose of the white contents of a huge glass jar, and, in the second part of the program, a wild ride on a pink motorized excavator sporting rabbit ears, which bucks and rears on its back wheels while, of course, spitting fire.

Hubertus Wawra, alias Master of Hellfire, is a German-born comedian, licensed pyrotechnician, and holder of the Guinness World Record for High Speed Fire Eating. As his Facebook page declares, "He integrates his fire tricks with his comedy show—a show in which his explosive verbal bombs destroy the stereotype of the fire-breathing 'daredevil' and offer us instead a glimpse of a bright and burning future ... he will charm you and will educate you. ... "

The mixture of mischievousness and transgressive behavior situates Hubertus in the same liminal region as the clowns. The fringe culture he represents in an expressionistic style suddenly takes over the heart of the circus. The audience is at the same time scared and liberated. Hubertus exemplifies to some extreme extent the traditional role of the trickster who violates the norms without ceasing to be a cultural hero. He synthesizes the symbolic pair formed by the whiteface and the auguste because he uses his mastery of fire to upset and transcend the arbitrary rules of safety and decency.

The trickster and his avatars

To suggest that there is a direct filiation between the clowns of the circus and the tricksters of the myths and folktales of a particular cultural area would be doubly ill advised. On the one hand, there seems to be only some superficial similarities between the behavior of mischievous gods and heroes, and that of circus whiteface and auguste clowns. Such resemblances have been allusively pointed out by anthropologists and philosophers (e.g., Diamond 1972: xiii; Radin 1972: xxiii; Hynes and Doty 1993: 23–24, 206, 220; Williams 2012: 225–240). But in most cases references are made to ritual performers who have been metaphorically categorized as "clowns" in the metalanguage of ethnography rather than to actual circus clowns. In these writings, the latter are conceived and imagined intuitively as a part of taken-for-granted common cultural knowledge without having been researched and documented with the precision and method this volume attempts to achieve. Western anthropologists have paid attention to exotic "clowns" as belonging to the religious sphere of native populations and thus relevant to prestigious academic topics but were reluctant to delve into the actual circus, which was considered the lowest level of popular culture, thriving in their own backyard.

On the other hand, dealing with oral traditions and live performances considerably limits the possibility of gathering valid evidence beyond a narrow temporal scope. In addition, as Michael Carroll (1984: 105–107) noted, modern scholars use a very broad, not entirely consistent definition of "trickster." However, some very suggestive clusters of functional features can be noted when tales and performances are formalized as narrative patterns and characters are reduced to their distinctive qualities. If we compare the properties and functions generally attributed to the mythical figure of the trickster with those that define the clown, some striking resemblances can indeed be identified.

But before reviewing these similarities, an important note is in order. Like some other cultural phenomena, the complementary pair of the whiteface and the auguste may show a remarkable stability in Continental Europe over a relatively long period of time, but these two markedly distinct characters emerged from a more compact set of features that can be inferred from what has been preserved from the performances of the likes of Joseph Grimaldi in the eighteenth and early nineteenth centuries. The early modern clown, which later evolved into the whiteface, embodied then some of the properties that later became the exclusive domain of the auguste. Viewed from the more expansive temporal perspective of cultural evolution, the dynamic of clowning shows a great fluidity with the constant shifting of roles and the emergence of new characters. The modern auguste embodies qualities that once belonged to the *stupidus* of the ancient Latin comedy and, later, of the Harlequin of the Commedia dell'Arte, which was victimized by the domineering Brighella. Harlequin, however, evolved into the master of cunning and deceit, to the extent that his traditional costume and behavior have prompted some to define him not only as a direct ancestor of the modern whiteface but also as a typical trickster often associated with the devil in Christian cultures (Oreglia 1968: 56–70). In the contemporary circus, the solo clown achieves again a merging of the two roles: he appears under the guise of an auguste, but he most often leads the games and ridicules the spectators, whom he tricks into playing games with him. The general acceptance of immersive performance turns some willing members of the audience into functional augustes in the sense that they are being ridiculed for the enjoyment of other people.

Vienna, September 19, 2011. Circus Roncalli features on its posters and banners the Italian auguste David Larible of international fame. I look forward to watching this popular solo clown perform again; my last encounter with his immersive style of acting goes back more than a decade. He was then picking up four men from the audience and, using a chair as a resting point, was persuading them to sit on each other's laps in such a way that when he suddenly withdrew the chair with a mischievous smile, they did not collapse but unexpectedly remained in the same position above the ground, without any other support than their combined, locked-in sitting position. After a while the clown had to lend them a helping hand so they could disentangle themselves and rise to their feet.

In the 2011 Roncalli program, his routine is different. He invites a younger man, an older man, and a young woman to join him in the ring. Whether they are stooges or genuine spectators is irrelevant as long as they appear to the audience to be ordinary people who are willing to play with the clown. This has become such a regular item in circuses that some children and adults seem to be eager to take part in these games even though they usually become the butt of jokes or are tricked into mildly embarrassing situations. Larible lines up his three playmates and undertakes to make them rehearse an Italian opera. The two younger improvised singers become the lovers, and the older man is supposed to be either the husband or the father of the woman. The clown equips them with light period accessories such as a wig, a hat, a scarf, a sword, etc., and they are instructed to mime the action as brief excerpts from the recording of an opera are broadcast. He mocks the actors because of their awkwardness and lack of poise, and demonstrates to them how they should express deep love, jealousy, and anger in synchrony with the music. The audience laughs at them when these proper Austrians attempt to mimic Larible's Italian exuberance. They are eventually applauded heartily when the clown thanks them, makes them bow, and leads them back to their seats.

Bad Durkheim, April 15, 2013. The purpose of my 2-day visit to Zirkus Charles Knie is to see the new program, with special attention to the clowns and to prepare the photographic session I plan to organize in the summer. Some acts from the previous year have been kept in this program. As I am led to my seat by a uniformed usher, I recognize the smart young man in a suit who scans the crowd as people enter the tent. He is Kenneth Huesca, the musician and ventriloquist whose act I had recorded in writing the year before. Like Hubertus, he is a clown, but not in the sense that he wears any typical makeup besides the color enhancement of his face and a subtle black line that underlines his lower eyelids. All artists need such face grooming lest they appear pale and disheveled under the spotlights. His stage costume is elegant, with discreet dashes of spangles on the lapels of his jacket. His act is divided into three parts: First he displays his outstanding ventriloquist skill by manipulating a set of animal dummies engaged in hilarious verbal jousts. The concluding part will be a musical performance featuring a romantic tune on the saxophone, and, as a finale, he will present an exhilarating piece on the xylophone. But let us focus on the second part of his act, which is a unique variation of the routine of David Larible.

Before the show started, Huesca was observing the spectators as they walked toward their seats, in order to identify those who would be good choices for taking part in his act. He needs a young woman, a young man, and an older gentleman. As I have witnessed this act many times, I know that his criteria include a proper-looking young and pretty woman, a somewhat nerdy young man, and a respectable middle-aged man, preferably with a belly and some facial hair. Experience tells him which ones are more likely to accept the invitation to join him in the ring when the time comes. When he quickly walks toward his marks and entices them to follow him, he must be polite and seductive, but also persistent and persuasive. Some spectators are reluctant to play that game, and Huesca must have identified alternative potential playmates in the crowd so that he does not antagonize anybody if one of his choices stubbornly refuses to enter the ring. Every time I saw this act, it was a smooth process, although it was obvious that sometimes people agreed to follow him willy-nilly because they were finding it more embarrassing to resist in front of an audience than to step into the spotlights of the ring. Of course, they did not know what to expect because usually nobody, except circus ethnographers, attends a show several times in a row.

After lining up the three persons side by side, Huesca teaches them the rules of the game: First, they must open and close their mouths repeatedly without producing any sound. Secondly, they must do so only whenever he grasps their hands. Then he puts ridiculous hats on their heads: pink rabbit ears on the woman, insect antennas on the man, and a Viking helmet adorned with bull horns on the older man. What follows usually brings the house down. Huesca asks questions with his natural voice, amplified by the microphone, and produces the answers himself thanks to his ventriloquist skill while he has his three improvised partners selectively move their lips as if the sounds and words were coming from their mouths. Treating them as dummies, he creates the illusion that they are speaking with strange voices and uttering unexpected replies totally out of character. Sexual innuendos abound in the dialogue, notably when Huesca asks the men if they like the woman and the questions trigger howls and moans. At one point, the woman emits a sonorous belch. The act ends with the three spectators being coiffed with shaggy wigs and pictured as singing wildly like a rebellious rock band.

Like Hubertus, Kenneth Huesca is not made up or dressed either as an auguste or a whiteface, but his act is more akin to clowning than to any other circus specialty. Clowns both upset the cultural norms and the expectations they generate. Huesca makes the audience laugh at the expense of the few spectators he tricks into being manipulated like dummies under the pretext of playing with him, while, in fact, the jokes are on them, and he emerges as a triumphant hero in the manner of a whiteface clown.

It is clear that the clown under all its guises is a trickster in the literal sense of the term. Clowns play tricks on each other and on members of the audience. In the former case, the auguste is the victim; in the latter case, the auguste or the straight man targets ordinary people, either stooges who play this role or actual members of the audience when immersive performance becomes an accepted form of entertainment. It is with reference to the examples reviewed in this chapter that comparing circus clowns with tricksters found in myths and folktales makes sense. This is all the more true because, as in texts recorded by ethnographers and mythologists, the circus trickster is himself occasionally tricked. Roles are reversed and lessons are taught.

As in biological evolution, there is a fundamental continuum among cultural forms that emerges over time. Their differences are caused by variations on earlier forms that were selected because they provided their consumers with cognitive and affective gratifications as well as being the source of economic advantages for those who could deliver these cultural forms to appreciative audiences, be they storytellers, priests, or mountebanks. The narratives performed by modern clowns did not appear suddenly from nothing. We noted earlier that the broken mirror story that was described in Chapters 2 and 5 is documented in a Spanish comedy of the sixteenth century. If less is known about the history of slapsticks and clowning than about political regimes and military events, it is because popular cultures have always thrived below the radar of scholarly interests and historiographers. In their written forms, myths and folktales have received a great deal of attention, but oral traditions and ephemeral performances suffer from historical invisibility.

Tricksters and clowns indeed share in common some defining properties: they are entertaining and make people laugh; they use deceit to trick their victims; although there may be verbal components in their interaction with others, their tricks involve concrete actions in the form of practical jokes; their characteristics and actions are excessive with respect to the social norms of their cultural context; they punish those who fall into their traps because of greediness or stupidity; they are themselves occasionally the objects of reverse victimization; they transgress the cultural rules; at the same time, they transcend these rules; whatever they do has deep cultural relevance; in any case they are always cultural heroes, either as defenders of culture or as fallen angels; eventually, they always escape in time and even get away with murder; they are endowed with a kind of immortality—i.e., the trickster reappears under other names from culture to culture and from story to story like the clown in its many guises reenters the ring in the next performance and starts its antics anew.

There seems to be robust ground for considering circus clowns and tricksters as avatars of the same symbolic social entity and embodiments of similar values in the parallel media of storytelling and live performances of narratives. These cultural properties can be distributed among several characters and personae such as the whiteface and auguste in the modern circus, or bundled into a single type as is the case of the contemporary solo clown. We will further explore the transgressive behavior of the clowns in Chapter 9, which will focus on the ritualistic profanation of the sacred.

Admittedly, the narrative cycles of Hermes (Greece), Loki (Scandinavia), Agu Tomba (Tibet), the Monkey King (China), Fox (Europe), Maui (Hawaii), Coyote (Winnebago), or Raven (Tlingit) (Radin 1972; Hynes and Doty 1993; Williams 2012) cannot be put on par with any single clown act that is constrained by the practical conditions of live performances. But these relatively short narratives that numerous audiences enjoy under circus tents or on stages may represent mere episodes of a much larger story in which the clown tricks humans into coming face to face with the arbitrariness of their culture and the fragility of their identity. This grand narrative is delivered in the fractal mode through countless multimodal episodes performed by masked characters that all wear the generic name of Clown either as whiteface or auguste.

Understanding tricksters and clowns

Two main theoretical approaches have endeavored to explain the quasi universality of tricksters and clowns. Both go beyond the semiotic description and analysis of these cultural types in terms of signs, signification, and narratives. They use the data provided by ethnographic and semiotic research as the basis for their speculative generalizations. The first approach is psychological; the second is anthropological. Both interpretations assume that unconscious factors determine the forms of observable phenomena and their appreciation by an audience.

The former relies on the notion that deep psychological forces explain the behavior of clowns and tricksters, and the interest children and adults take in watching them perform their ritualistic antics or hearing about their deceitful feats in tales and visual stories. They are either considered as stirring up repressed desires of chaos and regressive gratifications or construed as universal archetypes profoundly rooted in the human mind. Freud and Jung and their respective followers have probed the links of clowns and tricksters with unconscious psychological motivations and affects. Primal impulses are released through identification with clowns and tricksters. In the wake of Freud and Jung, David Williams (2012) has called upon cognitive neurosciences and evolutionary psychology to propose updated psychological explanations for trickster narratives (125–135) and clown performances (225–240). However, the latter pages refer exclusively to the ritual clowning found in numerous world cultures from the Americas, Asia, the Middle East, and medieval Europe. Similarly, West African ritual clowning has been discussed by Pelton (1980). It is noticeable, however, that these authors stay clear of the topic of modern circus clowns, despite the fact that a 1931 dissertation by Julian H. Steward, which the authors occasionally mention and quote, lists characterizations of the "sacred clowns" that point to undeniable resemblances with their circus counterparts: "the mocking of important ceremonies and persons; the breaking of societal taboos; comedy based upon sex and other bodily functions: such as scatology and gluttony. In addition there is a type of humor based upon sickness, sorrow, misfortune, and need" (Williams 2012: 227). Typically, these works do not offer precise ethnographic evidence but only generalities derived from secondhand anthropological observations. The same applies, of course, to the circus clowns that have not been seriously documented to date. This lack of ethnographic writings, which this volume attempts to start remedying, undoubtedly accounts for the relative invisibility of the circus in the literature.

Cultural anthropologists can provide another kind of explanation based on the notions of "tacit knowledge" or "cultural unconscious." In this approach, problems of interpretation are framed in a cognitive rather than affective perspective. In the heyday of stucturalist anthropology, it was tempting to consider that clown narratives might be variants of myths. For instance, a clown act such as "the honey," described earlier in this chapter, can be construed as a symbolic resolution of the tension generated by the contradictory attractions of culture and nature (Bouissac 1982: 199–209). From this point of view, the assumption is that the human mind fosters unconscious or subconscious cognitive conundrums that can be reactivated, if not fully articulated, through experiencing a performance that represents the terms of the problem and its tentative solution. In his landmark volume *From Honey to Ashes*, Lévi-Strauss notes that "matrimonial alliances are perpetually threatened on their borders: on the side of nature by the physical seduction of strangers; and on the side of culture by the risk of infighting among members of the same household. Similarly, the institution of cooking is exposed to the danger of tipping over entirely on the side of nature through the encounter with honey or on the side of culture through the conquest of tobacco, although, theoretically cooking should represent the harmonious union of nature and culture (1983)." Honey is indeed a naturally processed food that does not require the transformative work of cooking in order to be consumed. Tobacco, on the other hand, is a form of overcooking because it is consumed through total combustion.

This approach is symptomatic of a conception of cultural codes that map unto each other. Homologous relations allow the transfer from one order to the other in the intellectual processing of social experience. Thus, cooking according to the rules of a given culture and copulation within the matrimonial institution of this culture can be thought of as forms of optimal balance between nature and culture. Privileging one side over the other creates the dangerous risk of returning to the state of nature, like animals, or, in the opposite direction, becoming overcultured or oversocialized like bees are believed to be. In this particular clown narrative, the transgressor who embraces the seduction of honey that dispenses him from working is punished by water in the form of spitting rather than splashing with the contents of pails or decanters. The farfetched stucturalist interpretation calls upon the longstanding European habit of frequently spitting in public, which has been controlled only recently and became associated a few centuries ago with chewing tobacco, thus making this clown narrative match the mythical patterns observed in the myths of other cultures that are exposed to both honey and tobacco.

Let us recall that the transgressor is the auguste, who is already close to the side of nature, and that the whiteface is an exaggerated cultural embodiment. The trickster teaches a painful lesson to the culprit who has unwisely rushed toward honey by administering to him a high dose of the cultural antidote represented by tobacco. For such an explanation to be found credible, we would have to ignore the recent introduction of tobacco in Europe and to accept the unlikely possibility that the system of semantic values it presupposes has been preserved in a layer of unconscious cultural memory and still resonates in some ways in the experience of modern audiences. But how to account otherwise for both the antiquity and the apparent relevance of this clown narrative, which remains one of the most popular in contemporary circuses? The hypothesis of an ancient ritual carried over a long period of time through the force of cultural inertia can be considered. Forms can always be reinvested with new meanings. It is symptomatic, for instance, that in the versions of the act that I witnessed between 2010 and 2014, the initial dialogue about the refusal to work and the counteroffer of honey is most often skipped. The action starts with the proposal by the whiteface to procure honey as if it were a game, and then the emphasis is on the spitting and splashing of water. The narrative is truncated, and the gags and slapsticks are foregrounded. Clown acts are fluid dialogic structures that are more or less loosely anchored in narrative kernels whose origins are lost in the remote, undocumented past of cultural traditions. It is probable that modern clowns are the continuators of secularized ancient rituals, without being aware of their origin, because their cultural memory rarely goes back more than two or three generations. The victims of the trickster are clowns who represent ordinary people, often emblematic of the lowest rungs of their society. But the augustes themselves can shift their role and perform as tricksters toward members of the audience or even, through a dramatic reversal, toward the whiteface.

Peering into the cultural past:
A reasoned speculation

Attempting to identify the origins of the European modern clowns beyond historical figures such as Joseph Grimaldi is a daunting challenge. It is, however, possible to engage in reasoned speculations in order to outline a range of plausible hypotheses. The general interpretative frameworks discussed in the preceding section—namely the psychological theories of clowning as an innate drive of the human mind and the stucturalist speculations that construe clowning as a metacultural discourse of universal relevance—are much too abstract to account for actual instances of clown performances in their historical sociocultural contexts. There is too wide a gap between those timeless theoretical elaborations and the data provided by ethnographic research on today's circus clowns. As noted earlier, cultural phenomena do not burst into existence out of nothing. They are the results of evolutionary processes constrained by the dynamics of continuity and change. Joseph

Grimaldi gained historical visibility through the celebrity status that London society granted him at a time when the urban entertainment trades prospered and the printed media developed. But this was not an absolute beginning. Grimaldi came, like many others, from a long lineage of acrobats and comic performers. How far can we peer into the distant past in search of common cultural ancestors? It does not make much sense to look for such antecedents in distant cultural phenomena such as African jesters or the Pueblo so-called "sacred clowns." This is why any reasonable speculations regarding some forms of cultural continuity should be limited to the part of Europe in which trade, conquests, and migrations have woven a complex and compact fabric of cultural traditions during the last millennia. We must be mindful, however, that we are dealing with a cultural palimpsest, because after the Roman colonization of most of Western Europe, Christianization endeavored to erase the beliefs and rituals that had survived, or at least to modify them in order to make them compliant with Christianity. But some traditions were more resilient than others and still persist nowadays in the form of folktales, underground cults, and superstitions that have preserved to a large extent their cultural relevance among large segments of the European populations. The Niebelungen have remained a fascinating window on the religious past of northern Europe, and parts of these pre-Christian myths have reemerged in Western consciousness through Wagner's operas.

The last frontier of Christianization was Scandinavia and northern Germany, whose religious oral traditions and rituals were recorded from the tenth century on by monks who provided written versions of the heathens' sacred sagas. The reliability of these texts is doubtful, as the scribes were not wholeheartedly accomplishing the task of perpetuating such unholy traditions. But they cannot simply be discarded, because they are the only sources at our disposal. These works have been scrutinized by philologists, historians of religions, and anthropologists. All students of these traditions (e.g., Dumézil 1948; Rooth 1961; Toynton 2011) have noticed the particular status of a character named Loki whose ambiguous function in the context of the Northern pantheon stands out as an anomaly with respect to the norms prevailing in the realm of the gods. Loki is indeed generally considered as a trickster inasmuch as he transcends the divine order and freely breaks the rules, both bringing chaos and solving problems through cunning and mischievous behavior (Cawley 1939; Rooth 1961: 1890–1930). Although information about Loki is sparse because it is distributed among many fragmentary texts, this character is ever present as a troublemaker or a problem solver. His stories create "traditional humorous cycles" blending cunning and wisdom (Rooth 1961: 190), and he is a central figure in the comical tales found in the Old Norse myths (Rooth 1961: 195). In one of the most famous episodes, Loki succeeds in making a maiden who had never laughed in her life laugh for the first time, and thus acquires the precious gold jewels she was holding (Dumézil 1948: 114–115). In his characterization of Loki, Dumézil uses the terms "buffoon" and "clown" as appropriate approximations to define his function (116). He describes his persona as "lovably awkward, mischievous rather than noxious, but also capable of serious misdemeanors" [my translation] (149). There is a reference in his facetious deeds to a sticking stick whose mere name evokes some kind of gag.

Loki appears at times as being deformed, or as a dwarf, thus embodying the anomaly he represents in the mythical landscape. He can also transform himself into a female or an animal, or even a female animal when, for instance, a divine stallion impregnates him as a mare, which gives birth to a magic eight-legged horse. In her attempt to come to grips with the complexity and puzzling actions of Loki, Gwendolyn Toynton notes that the trickster "shows us the hidden dimension of the naked orifices under the clothing of civilized and rule-governed life" (2011: 23). In light of the scholarship that has elucidated the northern traditions in recent decades, she points out that "Loki's social interactions display criticism, rebellion, and protest against existing structures, against boundaries, against the seriousness of order, and constructs which are socially and ritually acknowledged. [...] Loki [performs] tasks that the other gods cannot or will not do [and] serves as both a scapegoat and a bearer of impurity" (23). Moreover, as all students of the Scandinavian and northern German myths and legends have noticed with some puzzlement, Loki is closely associated with Odin, the god of law and order, as his inseparable brotherly shadow (23).

It is worth noting that the scholars who have thus attempted to define the character and function of Loki through scrutinizing ancient narratives do not appear to have any precise knowledge of traditional European clowns and their performances. The above remarks by Toynton are obviously made independently from any reference to contemporary popular culture except in the form of surviving underground cults and a concern for the revival of these ancient religious beliefs and rituals. However, the readers of this book cannot fail to sense the way in which what is known about Loki, as fragmentary as this may be, resonates, so to speak, in the persona of the modern clown.

Naturally, the lack of historical data precludes the possibility of establishing the continuity of Loki's legacy within the confines of Europe. Could some rituals have survived under the radar of the official culture that reigned supreme in the wake of Roman colonization and the ensuing "cultural revolution" that was violently brought about by Christianization? After all, we should not forget that theatrical and circus performers were long persecuted by the church authorities as demonic manifestations. The documented ordeal of the mountebank William Banks and his trained horse Marocco in the sixteenth century bears witness to the relentless hostility of Christianity toward surviving ancestral traditions (Bouissac 2012: 59–62). As we noted above, cultural evolution presupposes continuity and change. Modern clowns did not appear overnight. Mikhail Bakhtin (1968) and Peter Burke (1978) have amply documented through literary and historical evidence the resilience of ritualistic transgressive behavior in centuries of popular culture in Europe. However, until further research yields new information on the hypothetical link between the Loki legacy and modern clowns, this cultural continuity can only remain in the realm of pure speculation. Speculation, however, might provide a heuristic perspective that could inspire that needed sound research in that direction.

7

Clowns and Gender Play: The Politics and Economics of Sex

Beyond sex and gender

Most acrobats and some animal trainers, whether male or female, wear tight outfits that enhance their gender morphologies, thus playing out the erotic qualities of circus performances (Bouissac 2012: 170–180). Clowns of all types, by contrast, mask, deform, or blur the natural features of their faces and bodies. Their makeup and attire are not designed to enhance their physical attractiveness, but instead to construct psychological and social characters that are beyond the scope of sex and gender. Both the whiteface and the auguste are situated outside the range of the stereotypes of desirable appearance prevailing in their culture. The whiteface embodies a cultural refinement in his garments and behavior that in some aspects verges on androgyny in spite of his traditionally authoritarian demeanor. The elaborate fabric and glittering quality of his costume, his usually narrow waist, and his white stockings evokes feminine fashion. However, the exaggeration of the width of his shoulders and the commanding tone of his voice bring forth traditional qualities associated with male stereotypes. Significantly, this character is nowadays sometimes interpreted by women who successfully blend assertiveness, elegance, and charm. But the whiteface persona does not engage in ambiguous, seductive behavior. He/she is meant to represent high standards of propriety that entitle him/her to dominate others, whether they be ringmasters or augustes.

The auguste, on the contrary, exhibits ill-fitted suits, unkempt hair, and oversized shoes. His makeup, voice, and behavior are too gross or too childish to create natural or conventional sexually attractive patterns. He can be endearing like an infant, a good-natured tramp, or an eccentric old man, but most spectators would undoubtedly consider him as an asexual entity.

Women who occasionally perform as augustes are nearly indistinguishable from men, mainly if their roles involve gestures and music rather than speech.

Paradoxically, however, sex and gender are prominent themes in clown acts. The object of this chapter is to document and discuss these recurring representations of the attributes of gender and their role in the narratives performed in circus rings.

Images of desire

The big top of French circus Arlette Gruss is an impressive monument nicknamed "the cathedral." All white except for a few curving marks of red, its peaks and spires reach heights never seen before in a traveling tent show. The big top takes 2 days to build, but this circus is so popular with the inhabitants of large French cities that it often performs several weeks in some locations. It visits mostly the same towns annually but never presents the same program 2 years in a row. The audience is treated to high-quality spectacles, comfortable seating, and respect. Like every year, the premiere of the 2013 season was scheduled in mid-January in Bordeaux, an affluent city on the Atlantic coast of southwestern France.

For an inquiry that aims to include in its purview circus clown performances in the twenty-first century, the Arlette Gruss Circus is a good place to start. Its website announces that Tom and Pepe are part of the new program. Because their contract was renewed from the previous season, we can assume that they were successful with the 2012 audiences and that, according to the principles of this circus, they have produced different acts for the new program. These two considerations are strategically important for our purpose because, on the one hand, their success with the public authenticates their cultural relevance and, on the other, these new acts will offer examples of variations and creativity within their genre of performance. But, in this particular case, there is another research advantage in monitoring the first performances of a year's program. Although the circus had been set up one week ahead of the premiere in order to provide plenty of time for dress rehearsals in the ring, it continues to fine-tune the spectacle during the first month of performance, in view of the feedback of the public. The staging and lighting are assessed by the management and often are modified to achieve better results. Actually, in that circus, the production of a printed program is delayed several weeks until the spectacle has reached its perfect balance so that, for the rest of the year, spectators will be offered an accurate guide to the performances they attend. At the end of the first show, which was a bit too long, a member of the direction was overheard saying, "We have to cut at least 15 minutes." Dress rehearsals, indeed, cannot take into account the actual duration of the applause and ovation that some acts trigger in the public. These moments blend into the texture of the show and cumulatively add to each act a warm climax that may significantly extend them timewise. These remarks are all the more relevant here because measurable changes were made over the first three performances of the program, some of them involving its comic components.

We will focus in this chapter on the contributions of Tom and Pepe to the second part of the program, but we must take into consideration the performance of another artist who played a crucial role in the first part. Indeed, each act is not a completely isolated entity but may use the semiotic resources provided by other acts in the program to which it makes implicit reference.

We have to keep in mind that the audience is fostering at least a sketchy memory of Hubertus (introduced in Chapter 6), who is associated with transgressive behavior and sexual license, when they witness the performance of the clowns Tom and Pepe just after the cage act that opens the second part of the program. While the steel arena is being dismantled, the two augustes appear at the top of one of the side aisles and proceed to walk down toward the ring but stop midway. They shout, "Hello! Hello!" and the spotlights make them conspicuous to the whole audience. They wear Turkish turbans, and Tom carries an oversized teapot. It quickly becomes clear that they will summon the genie of the Arabian tale found in the *Thousand and One Nights*, which is imprisoned in a jar or a lamp and grants three wishes to whoever frees it. There are many versions of this narrative, depending on the cultural context in which it is represented. Variants involve the form and function of the container and the kind of wishes expressed. The moral lesson all these versions convey is that human greediness usually brings unhappiness. For wanting too much too quickly, the transgressor who has freed the genie experiences at the end a frustrating loss.

According to some traditions, the process can start by rubbing the container with one's hand. This is what Tom does, obviously making a wish at the same time. Suddenly, an attractive woman in a white wedding gown appears under a spotlight in the opposite aisle. Pepe takes his turn and, after having donned Tom's bigger turban, rubs the teapot with an air of keen anticipation. Instantly, the wedding gown vanishes and the woman appears half naked, wearing only scant apparel. The third attempt causes the sudden appearance of Hubertus, dressed in a fancy pink suit and acting exuberantly gay. The two clowns rush up the aisle in terror and get out of the tent. Obviously, their wishes were of a sexual nature. Whether the final gag was designed simply to shock and to surprise, or whether it was meant to carry a deeper message of inclusive sexuality is difficult to decide in the absence of insiders' information. As our concern in this book is to study the interface between the audience and the performance rather than the process of production of the acts, let us note that the public reacted with laughter when the bride was transformed into a scantily dressed woman and with still louder laughs when the gay man in pink unexpectedly appeared. The assessment of the degree of hilarity is naturally a matter of broad appreciation. It is a statistical effect that may vary from performance to performance, even from city to city, and be relative to sociopolitical contexts. But the effect was consistent over three performances in a row, thus giving some weight to the impressionistic evaluation. This act was observed in France in January 2013, at a time when a legislative project to make same-sex marriages legal was triggering intense public debates. Cultural stereotypes were undoubtedly at play in this brief act, and the folk narrative provided the syntax that allowed the clowns to articulate a strong sexual content with respect to current institutions. The first wish produced a bride, the second transformed her into a sex object, and the third brought up a gay groom. One may wonder what will come next. There is no conclusion. The two clowns flee in disarray. They have indeed opened the Pandora's box of sexual desires. A brief blackout precedes the next act.

A further remark is in order. The man in pink is not unknown to the audience, although some features of his new persona are. He is identifiable as the rebel who insisted on breaking the law by smoking in the tent just before the show started. In fact, he is the real initiator of the spectacle "Master of Hellfire" (Chapter 6), who by his act of insubordination started it all by literally lighting up. He appeared again in the first part of the program, immediately after the horse display, to present a fire-eating act loaded with visually provocative sexual allusions and punctuated by the word "Erotik," both inscribed on a panel and uttered as a leitmotiv with a German accent. His behavior was camp, and his partial striptease was accompanied by the iconic music of this genre of entertainment. Sadomasochistic elements were also introduced in the form of nipple clips, which he set on fire after the cord that linked them exploded on his chest. This act went well beyond the classic fire-eater to overlap with the gay leather subculture. Later on, in the second part of the program, still dressed in the pink suit, he will be the crazy driver of a motorized excavator disguised as a monstrous pink rabbit with long ears and sharp teeth that will jump and madly turn and, of course, spit fire as it leaves the ring.

An odd couple

This provides further evidence that the meaning produced by individual clown acts depends to a large extent on the multimodal discourse of the whole program. Anaphors and cross-references knit together the performance and amplify its density of signification. When three acts later the spectators witness the entrance of two tramps pushing a cart full of battered boxes and suitcases, they immediately identify Tom and Pepe, who have donned for their final contribution to the program the guise of slovenly tatterdemalions who hesitantly walk across the ring showing all the stigmas of derelict and homeless old men. Their ragged outfits and sheepish looks convey a poignant sense of hopelessness. Suddenly, they notice a public bench inside the ring. They contemplate it for a few seconds and express relief and joy as if they have found a promised land. Then a moving process of homebuilding starts. Within a short while they extract from their packages of recycled garbage typical living room items to transform this bare object and its bleak surrounding space into a cozy place: two cushions change the bench into a couch; a teddy bear adds a touch of intimacy; an improvised lampstand and its shade suggest the comfort of a home; then comes a small portable TV plugged into one of the suitcases; knick knacks in the form of a plastic flower and a windmill set in motion by a tiny fan is placed on top of the TV. Pepe is now comfortably seated, and Tom tries to turn on the TV, which is a vintage model with a movable antenna. Pepe signals that the image is blurred, and Tom orients the antenna with loving attention until it works. Tom sits down next to Pepe, and a friendly dog rushes toward them and takes a place on the couch between the two men. For a very brief time the audience is presented with a happy family tableau, when suddenly a thunderstorm with lightning and the sound of heavy rain bring an abrupt end to it all as the two tramps raise their hands with an expression of disbelief and resignation. Thus ends the act on a note of tragic irony that cannot fail to call to mind the dramaturgy of Samuel Beckett. But there is more to it.

Tom and Pepe form an odd couple that nevertheless conforms to a range of stereotypes. Laurel and Hardy, film stars of a symbolic type, have generated over the years a comic formula that was probably grounded in more ancient traditions. The contrast between a tall, corpulent, and assertive character and his short, skinny, and subdued sidekick can produce situations rich in comic potential. Moreover, the popular representation of homosexual couples projects on the partners of either sex the complementary images of masculinity and femininity. As we noted at the outset of this chapter, clowns are asexual but not ungendered. As we will see below, they toy with the cultural attributes and social roles of genders in their creative narratives. In all their contributions to the 2013 program of the Cirque Arlette Gruss, Tom and Pepe appear as two men in various disguises. But Tom is always the leader and Pepe acts submissively as his assistant, or his helpless and hapless partner. In a brief piece of performance toward the end of the first part of the program, while the net of the flying trapeze act is being dismantled, Tom enters the tent from the top of an aisle. He sports a gaudy fairground parade uniform, a proud belly, and a large curled-up mustache. With a defiant martial air, he balances poles of increasing length on his chin. Pepe looks at him in admiration while he hands over and collects the poles his partner uses. In their last act, they impersonate the two male tramps who are wandering in a world in which they have no place. Their appropriation of the public bench and their meticulous crafting of a dreamlike, albeit elusive, home implement the complementary gender roles of a mainstream heterosexual couple: Tom takes charge of the technology as he installs the TV and regulates the antenna, while Pepe is comfortably seated on the couch. Does the conservative ideology of the sociopolitical context in which they perform determine the tragic outcome of the act, which spells out the impossibility of economic and sexual outcasts finding a place in the public space? In fact, the Bordeaux audience seemed to be more sensitive to the amusing irony of the narrative than compassionate toward these two tramps yearning for a cozy home.

There are indeed multiple layers of possible understanding and appreciation in regard to such an act. This is the last installment of these clowns in the program. The public cannot fail to recognize them and, at the same time, evaluate their skill at representing the particular socioeconomic category they have endeavored to portray. Their personalities shine through their new avatars. Anybody can don a tramp outfit, but it takes a consummate actor to create by his gait and gaze the open space in which a tramp lives and moves in search of an opportunity to settle down, even briefly, before his wandering must resume. Tom and Pepe do not surge forth from the back stage, but enter slowly, setting nevertheless through their pace the sustained rhythm that will structure the attention of the audience for the duration of their act. A kind of reflexive mood is induced. No word is uttered. All the meaning is produced by postures, gestures, artifacts, and facial expressions. There is no lagging of interest in the audience because each of their moves carries information— that is, something unexpected. One example is the way in which a living room lamp is constructed out of recycled items that are suddenly endowed with new functions. The resourcefulness of homeless people who often transport huge loads of bags and boxes is foregrounded. From this cornucopia emerge all the basic components of a modern, happy home: a couch, cushions, a television, a teddy bear, decorative knick-knacks, and even the family dog. These, of course, are mere symbols that are assembled with a great economy of means. They magically demonstrate how a public space can be transformed into a private place.

Watching this act again reveals several layers of signification that might have been kept latent while the immediate information flow and the subtle gags it created had to be processed. A second viewing may induce an empathetic reflection on these urban icons of homelessness. But there is more: this narrative suggests that all happiness can be destroyed in a moment. Hopelessness is the tragic dimension that this micro-narrative ironically exploits, à la Samuel Beckett. This circus act conveys more meaning than meets the eyes. If a mainstream family were the heroes of this story, it would be perceived in the tragic mode. However, the victims are two clowns who symbolically represent an odd couple and thus doubly embody a liminal status with respect to the traditional norm. As we will see in Chapters 8 and 9, these ritualistic transgressors can be expected to expiate their antics.

A "normal" couple

In the 37th International Circus Festival of Monte Carlo (2013), one of the clown teams in competition was "Bella and Alex Cher." Their names as they appeared on the program clearly indicated that they form a traditional married couple both in life and on stage. Their act displays a visual narrative in which signs of gender and sex are redundantly foregrounded to the point of being the explicit objects of the action. They function semiotically as signals of parody. Alex wears a typical auguste costume: oversize trousers with large vertical black stripes, a single-button tight jacket over a white shirt with sleeves that are too long, a messy red tie that underlines his prominent belly, a dark cap that covers his ears, and large white sneakers. His makeup is rather crude, with some patches of red on the cheeks, blackened eyebrows, and a large zone of white around his mouth. Large-framed glasses add a touch of misplaced intellectualism to this uncharismatic profile. Bella's character is also of the auguste type. She projects the image of a homely woman whose natural curvatures are offset by the practical outfit she has donned to clean the house. She comes through as a wife obsessed with her domestic chores, wearing an apron and her hair covered by a conical hat. Her facial expression is dour and is not enlivened by touches of color. She wears spectacles, which further mask the feminine features of her eyes. When the act starts, Alex attempts to juggle some clubs, but she interferes with her dusting implement. His romantic approach with a flower is ignored as she runs through her cleaning chores with seemingly ferocious determination. Alex toys with a bundle, pretending that it is a baby, and asks a spectator to carry it in his arms, but Bella surges forward and grabs the bundle, showing that it is actually a mop, and defiantly fixes it at the end of her broom where it belongs. She embodies the killjoy of sexless domesticity. No wonder then that Alex notices an attractive young woman in the first row of the audience. With the permission of her boyfriend, Alex invites her to the ring. Alex is a grotesque, unlikely suitor, but he courts this lady with awkward gestures and a glass of wine. He then goes a step further and summons her boyfriend to the ring. He makes him do silly things like hold a candle and perform some ridiculous dance to entertain them while he pours wine in the glasses. Eventually, he decides to play it safe and tie up the man with a tape to a coat rack that stands in the ring. Bella comes in, oblivious to the situation, totally focused on her cleaning obsession, when she suddenly notices the young man glued to the pole. She marks a brief moment of hesitation. Then, in a flash, she discards her cleaning uniform and appears scantily dressed in some vivid-red apparel that reveals all her curves. She engages in a lascivious and seductive dance as she approaches the man. Confusion ensues. Alex intervenes. The young woman and her boyfriend are liberated and walk back to their seats. Bella accepts the flower Alex offers her. They kiss and leave the ring, apparently a happy couple again, ready for sex.

As we noted in previous chapters, clown acts always have a referential frame that may be an institution, a stereotypic situation, or a normative social behavior characteristic of the societies where they perform. Beyond these explicit themes it is possible to elucidate the deeper cultural constraints they address, which often pertain to the tacit rules governing cultures. Most Western societies traditionally consider that lovers must belong to the same age group and be compatible with respect to social ranking. Folktales and literary fictions feed on violations of these implicit requirements, which trigger the chain reactions that give form to plots. Countless crises and their resolutions gravitate around the issue of who can court and marry whom. Shakespeare's play *Romeo and Juliet* provides an iconic example of this in the tragic mode. Comedies offer another kind of sanction when courtships and marriages occur across the age divide: laughter aggressively mocks and mobs the transgressors. In many of Molière's plays, for instance, following the tradition of the Italian comedy, old men who want to marry young girls are heavily ridiculed and the eventual misfortunes of these inappropriate suitors are emphasized.

The circus exploited this vein by fostering a stereotype during the nineteenth century: the representation of the clown in love with the female equestrian. It may still be performed nowadays in the romantic mode as a nostalgic reference to the circus of the past and its artistic iconography, but in its initial form it was plainly meant to provide a comic instance while the equestrian was catching her breath between her strenuous exercises on the back of a horse. The social and age distance that stands between a gracious, attractive young female equestrian and a grotesquely attired old clown is maximal. The latter's pretense of courting her with a flower, and other stereotypical behavior, is considered ridiculous—that is, socially scandalous beyond imagination. There has always been an interface between circus equestrians and the local aristocracy. They share in common the knowledge and love of horses. The union of an old outcast such as an auguste with a beautiful equestrian falls so much outside the range of acceptability that it cannot even be conceived as a negotiable state of affairs. Laughter is the only possible response to what is culturally unthinkable.

Bella and Alex Cher, like a few other clowns of their generation, use what could be called the incompatibility formula, an algorithm that specifies the recipe, so to speak, for producing laughter by performing implicit or explicit transgressive sexual conjunctions. After giving evidence that the two form a dysfunctional couple, Bella leaves the ring, pursuing her dusting obsession. Alex turns toward the public and attentively scans the first rows of spectators until he identifies an attractive young woman sitting next to her husband or boyfriend. Whether these two persons are stooges or not is irrelevant. The appearance is that they are bona fide members of the audience. The woman is enticed to join the clown in the ring under the pretext of participating in a game. The auguste does not hide his interest in her body and engages in behavior that verges on the offensive. The woman giggles and looks incredulous before the advances of this grotesque character whose makeup and attire offer nothing endearing, let alone likable. Alex really looks like a scarecrow, and he wears spectacles with a heavy black frame, lending further aggressiveness to his face. Tempting the woman with a glass of wine is a step further in his ridiculous courtship. To add insult to injury, the boyfriend is summoned to move to the ring, where he is almost sadistically forced to hold a candle while the clown tries to seduce the woman, then to dance with erotic pelvic movements designed to entertain the "couple" as if they were sitting in a nightclub. The scene would be unbearable if the auguste were in the least attractive. It is his repulsive persona that emphasizes the unbridgeable distance between him and the woman, mainly in view of the handsomeness of the young man. When, for added security, Alex ties up the man to a pole, the situation reaches a climax in the anticipation that has been progressively built up. The audience may then anxiously wonder what will happen next. It is precisely at this moment that Bella reenters the ring and resumes her cleaning chores, wrapped in her functional, unsexy outfit, also wearing black-framed glasses. The tipping point is when she notices the young man, who has been tied to the pole like a prey ready for consumption. This unleashes her sexual desire, and she instantly transforms herself into a scantily dressed woman, all in red, ready to jump on the man's body. The confusion that ensues provides an opportunity for a return to square one, thus reversing the unbearable process that the crude transgressive behavior of the clowns has initiated.

The narrative was rather blunt and provocative, but it implemented the traditional pattern consisting of offering to the scorn of the public a prohibited union across the gap of age and social status. The eventual sexual reconciling of the clownish couple is obviously destined to make the whole performance ultimately acceptable to the audience. This act nevertheless pushes the limits of humor beyond the usual range of acceptability for the general audience of circus performances. Perhaps significantly, it did not receive any award at the festival in which it was featured. It was, however, important to consider it in detail in the context of this chapter, inasmuch as it lays bare the sexual paradigm in a category of clown acts well represented in the circus tradition and in its contemporary forms. This can be expected given that the notions of sex and gender, and the kind of social behavior they imply, are determined by cultural norms. Subtly bending these rules or brashly negating them are the two extreme positions on a scale of values allowing an observer to understand the mechanism of humor and the sort of meaning it produces. Bella and Alex, in their clown act, walk the fine line that separates teasing games, which remain inclusive, and harassment, if not bullying, which amounts to mobbing and exclusion. This ambiguity belongs to the nature of humor that targets others rather than the self. At no point in their act did the audience get the impression that the young woman and her friend had fun. They were victimized and looked more puzzled than anything else, even if they were putting up with the situation by displaying a social smile. The audience obviously believed they were genuine spectators, and everybody seemed relieved that the clown had not picked on them. There was no thunderous applause at the end of the act.

By contrast, the male trio from Ukraine that provided the other clown act in the competition included only tumbling, juggling, and slapstick comedy, with no hint of gender play or sexual innuendo. Their skilled acrobatics and humorous interactions earned them a prize in the competition.

In a trade that bills itself as family entertainment and performs under the sponsorship of princes and princesses and other social elites, the bawdiness of the earlier circus clowns is toned down but nevertheless proves to be resilient. Notwithstanding the unleashing of anarchic sexuality in some modern circuses such as Archaos or Cirque Lumière (Bouissac 2010: 183–184), mainstream circuses show more restraint than did the Bella and Alex act. Let us recall Rob Torres's allusive treatment (in Chapter 4) of the sexual theme when he suggested that a lady spectator could heal with a kiss his wounded private parts. Another example of the indirect sexual joke was provided by Peter Shub in the 1989 program of Circus Roncalli. This modern clown was toying with a camera and a tripod, which he anthropomorphized by fitting it with a hat and a jacket before attempting to photograph it. The tripod tipped over, and the clown set it up again, but upside down. The branches of the tripod then looked like legs, and the clown triggered laughter by peering attentively between the legs as if he were trying to determine the sex of this odd being.

A bird tale

We have so far examined some contemporary examples that clearly use sex and gender as the codes they manipulate symbolically to create humor by creating unexpected outcomes that nevertheless disclose hidden truths. We will now turn to a traditional clown act that lays bare the political economy of mating in its contextual culture and the conventional institution framing it. This act represents a scene of courtship that concludes with a wedding or, at least, a union. The narrative is expressed metaphorically in the language of the birds. It is called "the nightingales." It is a classic of the traditional clown repertory. The description provided below was completed in the early 1970s, following several observations of this act performed in France by the clowns Bocky (Roger Maslard) and Randel (André Tandel). This act had been observed many times in the previous two decades and was witnessed again in July 2013 as a part of the program of the Blackpool Tower Circus, where it was performed by the two resident clowns.

This narrative involves two characters who keep in their mouths a whistle through which they produce sounds mimicking the intonations of verbal utterances, from long ascending or descending acoustic curves to brief and abrupt outbursts or even staccato. The accompanying postures and gestures complement the whistled dialogue and ensure that the audience easily deciphers the meaning of the speechless statements. The staged stereotypical situations and interactions do not leave room for any ambiguity. Bocky, the whiteface, and Randel, the auguste, performed this act for many years, with great success.

Bocky, the male bird, appears in the spotlight perched on the top of the ring and walks around whistling seductively in all directions. He is smartly dressed in a cream-colored summer suit and wears an elegant straw hat with matching shirt and shoes. His face, however, identifies him as the whiteface who has played in his traditional glittering costume earlier in the program. This nightingale obviously broadcasts his readiness to mate. Suddenly, he notices Randel, who enters the ring in drag, carrying a handbag and wearing feathery headgear over his shaggy wig. His auguste makeup is unchanged, and a grotesque woman's dress lets his hairy legs and red socks show. He sports a prominent breast and a necklace. His shoes are, typically, big and gaudy. He walks in a manly manner and does not try to mimic a seductive demeanor. His mere appearance elicits laughter in the audience. A color photograph of the two clowns performing this act is available online at http://www.cirk75gmkg. fr/article-bocky-randel-cie-85041357.html.

Bocky falls in love at first sight and instantly starts to court the female bird by producing a passionate whistling. Randel makes a brief, dismissive sound and turns away in a sign of indifference.

Persisting in his pursuit, Bocky shows off his physical qualities by flexing his biceps with a cocky expression and resumes his amorous whistling. Randel mocks him through his whistle, which he blows in a descending staccato, and keeps walking away, albeit a bit more slowly than before. But he signals by his gestures that he is not so easily impressed and that he is not as easy a girl as Bocky's approach implies.

Bocky now holds a bunch of flowers that has been hidden on the side of the ring and, putting his right knee down in front of Randel, offers him the bouquet with what sounds like a long declaration of love. Randel looks suspicious, grabs the flowers, smells them, and throws them away with an expression of contempt and disgust.

Despondent, Bocky gives up and returns to his initial position, where he again broadcasts his call for a mate. He notices, though, that this time Randel shows signs of being jealous. Seizing this opportunity, he resumes his courtship, emitting desperate chirps. Randel grants him a brief kiss. Then, he presents Randel with a piece of jewelry he has extracted from his pocket. Randel closely examines this gift before accepting it. Emboldened by this positive sign, Bocky caresses Randel's throat. The latter makes a short, pleasurable sound. But enough is enough, and Randel moves away. Bocky, still whistling passionately, takes a handful of bills from his vest and waves them toward Randel, who signals his readiness to accept the money. Moved by this apparent willingness, Bocky makes an explicit proposal by mimicking copulation. "No way!" Randel replies by a dismissive whistling, and, at the same time, he outlines the large belly of a pregnant woman. He then extends his right hand on his side and gestures five or six levels of height, as if indicating children of different ages. He thus turns down the invitation by contrasting a brief moment of sexual pleasure with its long-term consequences for the female.

Bocky refutes the objection by emptying his pockets of all the money he has and giving the banknotes to Randel. He then extracts a red heart from his vest, as his whistling reaches new romantic highs. Randel signals his agreement to the invitation, and they leave the ring as a couple while the band plays a love song or a nuptial march.

There is more in this narrative than meets the eyes. Indeed, it does not represent a case of commercial sex but makes explicit the sociobiological process of mating and its relation to the institution of marriage. Using the birds as a metaphoric code, this act disentangles the knot of nature and culture occulted in the contextual culture. According to the traditional view of modern Western societies, reciprocal romantic love is the ground for the recognized union of a man and a woman. Moreover, the patriarchal overtone of this cultural norm assumes that the man chooses his mate and engages in courtship to prove his deep interest in establishing an official union based on true feelings rather than raw sexual desire. This ideology is forcefully deconstructed in the nightingales. This baring of the truth is made acceptable to statistically conservative popular audiences by using the pretense of impersonating birds and playing the story in the parody mode.

True to current evolutionary evidence, the choice of mating rests with the female, who assesses the fitness of the male before agreeing to mate. The male vies to attract the female's attention and seduce her, whereas the female pays attention to the hard evidence of fitness—both biological and economical—before capturing his resources to ensure the success of her progeny. This is the harsh biological subtext, so to speak, that is glossed over in the discourse of love and marriage. The clown act pulls down the veil hiding the mathematics of mating. The successive moves of the game are indeed significant. The male first shows off his singing and muscular abilities, but this does not add up to win him success. His gift of flowers, a beautiful but highly perishable good, is not a valid asset from the point of view of the female. She signals that for her "it stinks." However, the male is not rejected instantly. The first installments of the courtship motivate the female to stay around and fend off possible competition. But she wants to further test this male. The gift of a jewel, once she has determined its value, is a positive sign. However, this is not enough for bringing up children. The production of real money is what counts, and only then does she agree to mate. The male's final move, the symbolic presentation of his heart, is nothing but the cherry on top of the cake, as it occurs after her decision has been made. Then the institutional pomp of a honeymoon or a wedding can come into play.

Let us note that sociological research has also uncovered the actual factors that drive the mating process in societies that foster the delusional ideology of romantic love as the basis for marriage.

Gender play

Cross-dressing is a source of humor inasmuch as there is a marked discrepancy between the appearance of the male character and the result of his transvestism. No effort is made by the clown to blur the gender gap. Contrary to the case of the Kabuki Theater in Japan, in which some male performers master the local feminine code of makeup, garments, and social behavior in a manner that even exceeds their models in perfection, clowns in drag keep their typical makeup and emphasize the failure of credibly mimicking women's clothes and gestures. It is indeed only augustes that occasionally don female apparel and imitate feminine demeanor when the narrative they perform demands a female actor. But they do so in the mode of parody, which can be diversely construed as gross misogyny or homage to the high cultural standards of the feminine habitus that thus appears to be inimitable. At the same time, it is a way of foregrounding the artificiality of gender by dissociating the components of cultural demeanors from the individuals producing them. While transvestism consists for the Kabuki actor of creating a flawless image, an icon of an actress, the auguste exposes the cultural character of the signs of femininity in its contextual culture. The male clown's awkward attempt to recompose the opposite gender with artifacts and gestures lays bare the stereotypic nature of these components. The auguste thus dissociates culture from nature by emphasizing the arbitrariness of gendered behavior.

Examples are found in abundance in the iconography of the circus since the early nineteenth century. In France, prominent augustes such as Achilles Zavatta and André Gruss have been represented by artists in their parody of the female equestrian. They kept their typical makeup, with their bulbous red noses, but added a gauzy tutu around their waists. The mock bra they wore contrasted with their muscular arms and legs. During their acrobatic exercises on the back of a horse, they produced social gestures that did not convey an impression of effeminacy, but exactly copied some of the graceful movements typical of their female counterparts. They also indulged in behaving grotesquely, in a way quite unthinkable on the part of their models. Their act was a collage of dynamic patterns identifiable as typically feminine by their audience; these were superimposed upon their outstanding equestrian skills. There is iconographic evidence of these two augustes parodying female equestrians in photographs and in drawings dated from the 1940s (e.g., Foulc 1982: 102–103).

The ballerina, on horse or on stage, is an emblematic figure of femininity that augustes target on a regular basis. It is easier, though, to mimic fancy footwork and graceful arm movements on the ground than on horseback. The romantic mood is set by the music of popular ballets, which hardly matches the made-up face of the auguste and his caricatured wig. Swan Lake, for instance, is often interpreted by clowns, with the whiteface playing the dancer with some degree of credibility because of his cultivated elegance and the auguste sporting a tutu and oversized breasts. The man expresses some reluctance when he is confronted with the transfixed ballerina, who ogles him, and he eventually fails to catch her in time when she throws herself in his arms. In a Russian version of this parody, the auguste wears an inflated car tire under his tutu and bounces back when his partner lets him drop to the ground. Augustes in women's apparel form a rich paradigm in clowning. Parody cross-dressing and gesture mimicking objectify the social signs of gender, which are taken for granted in any culture.

Well-defined gestures or accessories are extracted from their usual context and recombined within different frames. This amounts to drastically subverting the gender distinctions that are naturalized in cultural codes. What first appears to be an essential property of a natural kind is suddenly revealed to actually be no more than a floating sign that can be appropriated by others. Culturally learned gender behaviors, as a whole, can be transferred across the sexes, as in the case of Kabuki actors or convincing drag-show artists. But the male clowns of the auguste sort do not pretend to be credible when they impersonate female characters or acrobats. By keeping their terrifying makeup intact, they explode the ideological pretense of these codes to express natural norms. By the same token, the laughter they elicit contributes to reinforcing these cultural norms by mobbing the transgressors. The ambiguity of the clowns' toying with the fundamentals of culture mirrors the incessant efforts of the tricksters to undermine the consistency of the rules as a way of transcending the norms and, at the same time, reasserting their binding power.

8

Clowns, Death, and Laughter

Death at the circus

Deadly accidents sometimes occur during circus performances, but they are extremely rare. However, the rhetoric of risk and the evocation of mortal danger are ever present in the discourse that frames acrobatic and wild animal acts. For example, expressions such as *salto mortale* [leap of death], the "globe of death" (a metallic sphere within which several motorcyclists simultaneously execute complex loops at high speed), and the "wheel of destiny" (a revolving circular apparatus on which daredevils run and jump at great height) explicitly construe some circus acts as potentially fatal. These are not mere metaphors, as some men and women have lost their lives while performing these feats. Other aspects contribute to reinforcing this theme: the "absolute silence" that is at times requested from the audience when, for instance, a funambulist is going to jump over an obstacle placed on his or her cable, high above the ring; the rolling of the drums accompanying some dangerous tricks, thus evoking the traditional execution of a criminal or, more anciently, the ascension of a shaman toward the upper regions of sacred space; the sign of the cross displayed by some wild animal trainers and trapeze artists before "attempting" a nerve-racking stunt such as putting one's head in a lion's jaws or launching oneself for a triple somersault; some musical themes such as Queen's "The Show Must Go On" when an equilibrist ascends an unstable tower of chairs (Bouissac 2012: 39–47). Indeed, the musical repertory performed to accompany circus acts is often in serious, even tragic modes. The multimodal combination of cultural signs such as the intonation of the presenter's delivery, the metaphors used in the introduction, the tunes played by the orchestra, the gestures the artists direct to the audience, and the discourse that provides a specific ideological context—all these contribute to foregrounding the assumption of maximal risk rather than the outstanding skills that characterize circus performances. The circus is indeed immersed in a symbolic universe of fiction, legends, films, and other popular forms of representation that play out the unique heroism of its folk, whose means of living is construed as a permanent, and usually triumphant, confrontation with deadly challenges.

This proximity to the tragic constitutes a large part of the ritualistic nature of circus spectacles and accounts for the intense attention and high level of empathy that can be observed in the audience. But how do the clowns fit in this context? Obviously, they bring comic relief and make people laugh— adults as well as children. Does this mean, though, that they stay clear of the theme of death in their gags and comedies? The ethnography of circus performances shows that this is not the case, as witnessed by recent as well as historical examples.

In the 2011 and 2012 programs of the German Circus Charles Knie, the Swiss clown André pretended that he was bothered by a mosquito. The illusion was created by combining a typical amplified sound produced by the orchestra with gestures that consisted of chasing the insect and making repeated but unsuccessful attempts to kill it. At last, a violent slap appeared to cause the sounds to stop. The clown mimed picking up the dead mosquito with an air of triumph and burying it under a little mound of sawdust after having performed a brief parody of a mortuary ritual. To conclude, he brought what seemed to be a heavy slab, which he placed on top of the mound. But as he started walking toward the exit, while directing the attention of the audience to the mosquito's tomb, the "stone" suddenly vibrated and appeared to be lifted from below. It was eventually overturned, and Woody Woodpecker's tune of triumph from Walt Disney's animation films resonated in the circus, apparently coming from the mosquito, which was again flying around. Whether it had not been fully killed or simply raised from the dead was left unresolved. Then, the clown resumed chasing the insect and left the ring.

In the 2010 program of the same circus, the Mexican clown Versace presented three small toy elephants, which he placed side by side on the ground. He started "winding up" the mechanism of one of them with an oversized key (so that everybody could understand the meaning of his gesture), while the orchestra provided the appropriate cranking sound. The wound-up toy walked a few meters and stopped, in need of being rewound. But after a while the little elephant fell on its side, and Versace kneeled down to listen to its heart and signaled to the audience that the elephant was dead. He performed some moving funeral rituals, accompanied by signs of the cross and mourning behavior while a sad tune was played. Sorrow and despair took hold of the ring for a few seconds, when suddenly, as a despondent Versace was leaving the ring, a faint beating (produced by the orchestra) was heard. It was the heart of the toy elephant, which was returning to life. Versace grabbed the elephant with ecstatic joy and unzipped its skin to reveal an exuberant little dog, which had performed all the tricks of walking, falling, being motionless, and jumping to life again, upon the cues of its trainer. The other two elephants were only inert dummies designed to confuse the audience and reinforce the illusion that they were in the presence of animated toys. Only one was constructed as a disguise for the dog.

These two acts can be analyzed from various points of view. In both cases, the multimodal text is generated by combining gestures that evoke common technical behavior (chasing mosquitoes, rewinding automatic toys) with acoustic information that redundantly makes these gestures meaningful. Of course, the high-frequency sound produced by a mosquito and the mechanical noise of a rewinding key could not actually be perceived by the audience. A mosquito could not be seen, either, at such a distance, and a mechanical toy does not have a beating heart. These are part of the circus conventions. The meaningfulness of the actions is entirely constructed with symbolic objects and behaviors that are organized in the form of micro-narratives. The goal of this chapter is not to discuss the technicalities of the gags that involve miming and interactions with the audience or the training of a dog in Versace's act. Let us simply point out two relevant features: the fact that death is represented as the focal node of the action and that both clowns belong to the category of the auguste. This may seem at first paradoxical, because the main role of this kind of clown consists of causing laughter though its antics. We are confronted here with an intriguing connection between the generic auguste and death, which, as we will see later, is much more common than could be expected—to the extent that one of the best chroniclers of the clown acts that could be observed in France in the twentieth century, Tristan Rémy (1945), voiced his irritation at the recurrence of this kind of thematic obsession.

In the two cases discussed above, however, the victims are not humans and death is only temporary. It is nevertheless represented realistically, with some of the paraphernalia and patterned behavior of the funeral rituals prevailing in the contextual culture. Let us focus now on some features of these two clown acts in order to better understand the meaning they produce for their audiences. Admittedly, both acts were designed primarily with children in mind, as they usually form a significant part of the public. The themes of these micro-narratives refer to the common occurrence of being harassed by an insect and playing with toys, respectively. These events and behaviors overlap with children's common experience. However, in all the performances of these acts that were repeatedly observed in several German cities, the attention and engagement of adult spectators were noticeable. Glimpses of André's act and his audience can be seen at http://www.clownandre.ch. In order to explore this experiential phenomenon, we will focus first on the characters, then on the narratives that constitute the multimodal texts of these two acts. It is also important to point out that their reception by the audience is not homogeneous, as there are several levels of understanding and appreciation, depending on the age, culture, and disposition of various subclasses of spectators, an aspect we will discuss at the end of this section.

Let us focus first on the actors' personalities as established by their respective facial features and demeanors. These clowns do not wear heavy makeup, but only slightly modify their natural faces, emphasizing playfulness and innocence. Versace blackens his eyebrows in a way that extends them laterally and interrupts them abruptly in the center of his forehead, above his nose. This gives a touch of artificiality to his face at a spot (the ocular area) that is always the main focus of the spectators' attention as in any face-to-face interaction. In addition, he paints a small red spot with a black outline on the tip of his nose, reddens his lips and his cheeks, and keeps his curly dark hair parted in the middle, thus exposing most of his forehead. These modifications of his natural features enhance the expressivity of his wide smiles, showing the bright whiteness of his upper teeth, which endow his face with engaging charisma.

André's makeup is slightly more pronounced, but remains on the light side compared to the stark chromatic contrasts found in some other augustes. His natural eyebrows are hardly visible under the base makeup that colors his whole face with a bright and light-peach-like hue. His eyebrows are subtly redrawn in sepia, following the original curve but forming a more defined half circle. His upper eyelids are whitened. His lower lids are underlined by a thin line of black mascara. The tip and sides of his nose are reddened. His lower lip is painted in white, with two black dots at each corner of the mouth and two additional black spots, one high on his right cheek and the other on his chin.

These two faces follow the biological canon of the infantile face, the neotenic morphology discussed in Chapter 1. The relative aggressiveness of the adult male face is artificially neutralized by the makeup. This allows the candid expression of emotions and facilitates empathetic feelings on the part of the younger members of the audience as well as protective reflexes from the mature adults. Children are no strangers to death. A common trauma in the life of a child is the loss of a pet, if not a family member. But in these two acts, not only are the objects that die—an insect and a toy—relatively remote from a child's emotional involvement, but also both acts represent a mock death. The two clowns tinker with funeral rituals until the punch line of the narrative reveals that the death was only apparent. The general public seemed equally engaged by these acts inasmuch as I could infer from the reactions of the spectators around me. The performed funeral rituals were salient, albeit brief moments in the narrative. In both cases, the outcome could not be anticipated because the two clowns appeared to actually walk out of the ring. This ending was certainly considered odd, but in conformity with the social experience of death, which is difficult to rationalize and which introduces a liminal feeling in the fabric of everyday life. In spite of their ludic overtones, these two acts address deep layers in the psyche of their audience. Can clowns joke with death and resurrection? This is an issue we will address in the next chapter.

Death of the auguste

The entry of November 15, 1929, in the diary of the Vesque sisters details an act performed by the celebrated Fratellini brothers, the trio of clowns we encountered earlier, in Chapter 4. The ringmaster is Mr. Lavata. Let us recall that the whiteface is François and the augustes are Paolo and Albert. Mr. Lavata arrives with a letter that, he declares, is addressed to Mr. Fratellini. Paolo steps up and says, "It is me." But François objects, "No, it is me." Then Mr. Lavata adds: "Wait a minute. It is addressed to Mr. Fratellini, the idiot." François steps back and declares contemptuously, "Oh! It is him." Paolo is handed the letter, with which he fiddles, puts on his glasses, acts as if he cannot see well because of the poor light, moves closer to the area of the ring that is better lit by the spotlight, and suddenly starts crying loudly. Tears run down his face—some water is discreetly released from his hat—and the audience can see the drops falling to the ground. He promptly collects the liquid in his top hat and instantly drinks its contents. Out of apparent sympathy, François also cries noisily. Mr. Lavata returns to inquire about the cause of this crying. François answers, "I don't know." Paolo tries to speak while crying, "I can't…I can't…I can't read!" François scolds him: "At your age! Aren't you ashamed? Truly, you embarrass me." Mr. Lavata: "You don't know how to read either!" François: "Yes, but I can write!" Mr. Lavata reads the letter, which announces that a big surprise box has been shipped to the clowns. At this precise moment, a huge decorated cube is brought to the center of the ring. Mr. Lavata opens it. A large dummy pops up and oscillates as an effect of the spring that has been released to propel it up. Paolo is scared but soon imitates its mechanical movements and eventually hits it, then gets his head caught under the cover. The dummy is an effigy of the second auguste, Albert. François, Paolo, and Mr. Lavata leave the ring as Albert enters, holding a bottle and acting as if he is inebriated. He is surprised and moved when he realizes that this dummy looks exactly like him and, apparently transfixed by this encounter, lets the contents of the bottle run to the ground. Albert mimes a range of emotions in response to this unexpected confrontation with his double: stupor, worried curiosity, inquisitive attention to detail, playful interest, and mischievousness. He then starts pulling and punching at the dummy, until the springs come undone and it jumps out of the box and collapses on the ground. Mr. Lavata enters the ring at this very moment and, taking in the catastrophic destruction of the gift, convinces Albert to simply take its place so that his partners will not notice that the toy has been wrecked. As François and Paolo rush to the ring with wooden swords and cardboard canons, with the intention of attacking the dummy toy for fun, Mr. Lavata tries to hold them back, but to no avail. Albert, standing in the box where the dummy used to be, is hit again and again, and tries to take the blows, acting as if he actually is the dummy. In the end, it is too much, and he collapses.

With a deadly serious tone, Mr. Lavata declares, "You have killed your brother!" They all proceed with the funeral. A long box is brought in to serve as a coffin, and the bottle is placed at the side of the corpse according to the will of the deceased. A crown of straw is put on top of the coffin, and they start the funeral procession by carrying the box around the ring on a stretcher. But soon the audience discovers that Albert, who has sneaked out of the box, follows his own funeral procession, with the crown of straw around his neck and the bottle in his hand. All is well that ends well. Another scene of this clown act begins immediately, with no transition, as the props have been promptly discarded and the same characters are available for a new game.

Two remarks are in order. First, it is the auguste who "dies," as in all the other examples we will review in this chapter. There is no instance of the whiteface suffering such a mock fate. Secondly, the death that is performed is a temporary one, as if the auguste is always destined to rebound to the kind of life that is his lot. The whiteface briefly plays the role of the undertaker and presides over the ceremony, often helped by his sidekicks until the "dead" auguste rejoins his partners. A further interesting aspect of this act as it was performed by the Fratellini is that it involved a double of the auguste, which was destroyed by the auguste himself. The theme of the double recurs in clown acts, as we saw earlier when we examined the clowns' play with the notion of identity, notably in "the broken mirror" (Chapter 5). In the Fratellini act, Albert destroys his own image before being killed by his brothers, as if the murder of a simulacrum necessarily led to the destruction of the genuine article. What, indeed, is the persona of the auguste if not a mere image that can be substituted for other similar images? On the one hand, it is extremely fragile and can be easily shattered; but, on the other hand, it is indestructible, as it can always rise again as a phoenix from its ashes. This is precisely what the conclusion of this act achieves. The auguste is by essence both dead and undead. Charlie Cairoli Jr., who adopted the same persona as his deceased father, reported that when he was performing, some spectators came to him and said, "I am glad to see you again. I thought you were dead!"

Realm of the macabre:
Ghosts, corpses, and skeletons

Tristan Rémy, the French circus historiographer and novelist who we have encountered earlier in this volume, published in 1962 a set of clown comedies that he had collected from archives and through personal observation. The dialogues and staging of sixty clown acts are recorded in his book and provide invaluable information about the content and dramatic structures of the acts that were performed in circuses for over 100 years, between the mid-nineteenth and the mid-twentieth centuries. Of course, many of these acts can be traced back much further in the past in the comic repertory of ancient popular entertainment. This collection is all the more important as most of the acts that are documented in it can still be observed in today's circuses, with minor modifications and adjustments to contemporary culture.

"Dead and alive" is the working title given to an act that was performed in the 1870s but can be observed nowadays in various versions. In the documented slapstick comedy, the whiteface clown was Whytoine, and he was performing with two augustes—Secchi and Alfano. The act unfolded as follows: Secchi asks Whytoine to allow him and his friend Alfano to play in the ring. This is the type of request that would be expected from children. They are granted 5 minutes. Whytoine checks his watch and leaves the ring. The augustes decide to compete to find out which one has the harder head. As a measure of toughness, they will test their capacity to balance on their heads with their feet up. The one who is able to stand the longest in this position will win the bet. This assumes that both will play fair; they are back to back and cannot verify each other's position, but it turns out that Secchi is a honest player and Alfano is a cheater who takes frequent rests, standing on his feet behind Secchi. Every time the latter manages to check his friend's resistance from his upside-down stand, Alfano quickly returns to his headstand. Eventually, the trick is uncovered and the two start arguing and fighting until Alfano gets a blow on the head and collapses in the ring. As he lies there motionless, Secchi assumes that he is just pretending to be dead and begs him to stop joking and rise to his feet. He seizes his partner's hand to pull him up, but the arm falls back, inert on the ground. Successive attempts to make him stand up convince Secchi that his partner is indeed dead, because he shows all the symptoms of a cadaver whose limbs and body are stiff.

Because the 5 minutes are now past, Whytoine comes back and discovers the dramatic scene: there is a corpse in the ring, and the one who is alive must be the murderer. He declares that he has no choice but to go and call the police. Secchi panics and tries to pretend that he too is dead by lying down next to Alfano. He pleads with Whytoine, and they come to an agreement that if he quickly takes the corpse out of the ring, this crime will not be a matter of concern for Whytoine. Secchi is given 5 minutes to transport the body of his partner out of the circus. Then a series of maneuvers, during which Alfano maintains absolute stiffness, provides grounds for gag after gag on the theme of "how to get rid of a corpse that does not cooperate."

Whytoine comes back and shows displeasure at the situation. Secchi begs for a little more time and requires some planks for a coffin. But he is given only "half a coffin," in the form of a single plank. Various strategies are attempted to place Alfano on the plank. In the end, the body slides back and Alfano now stands straight up on his head in the middle of the ring, while Secchi thinks that he is carrying him away on his back. Whytoine protests that the corpse is still there. But Secchi concludes that now Alfano has won by standing in this position on his head. He requests a wheel with two handles, puts them in Alfano's hands, and rolls him out of the ring by pushing him by the feet as if he were a wheelbarrow.

Many secondary gags are inserted as the act proceeds. They are allusions to the treatment of the dead in traditional European culture—for instance, the farts produced by the body during the wake and the problems that may be encountered in making a stiff corpse fit into a coffin.

The sudden appearance of a "ghost" (usually a sidekick covered with a white sheet), a mummy (a partner wrapped in rags), or a skeleton (which dangles at the end of a long rod held by a helper) is a common occurrence in performances that stage a frightening contact with death framed as a gag. This relates to a long tradition. For instance, in the "Harlequin and Mother Goose" pantomime of Grimaldi fame, whose script was preserved and has been published by Andrew McConnell Stott as an appendix to his masterful biography of the illustrious clown (2009: 325–343), the use of a skeleton appears to be a common occurrence in this type of performance. Let us put this sinister prop in its narrative context and reflect on the transformations of identities that the story illustrates.

Mother Goose, a mythical figure originating in folktales, has raised a storm in a village in which a rich old man in his hunter's attire is going to marry a girl (Colinette) who is in love with a young man (Colin). The girl is led by her guardian (Avaro), who hands her over to the old man. But she resists. Mother Goose now raises the skeleton of the old man's dead wife from her tomb as an attempt to discourage him from going ahead with the wedding. But the man takes this lightly and sings:

> *First wife's dead*
> *There let her lie*
> *She's at rest*
> *And so am I*

Mother Goose is arrested as a witch and is threatened with being condemned when the young man (Colin) frees her and she escapes to her domain. She thanks the young man by giving him a golden egg as well as the goose that lays such eggs every day, and she promises him that he will be reunited with the girl he loves. The young man comes and shows his gift to the guardian in the hope of claiming the girl and marrying her. The guardian falls for the deal but wants to kill the goose in order to get all the golden eggs immediately. The young man prevents him from doing so, but the arrival of the old man prompts him to agree to the killing for fear of losing the girl. The goose disappears, and Mother Goose returns. In retaliation, she throws the egg in the sea, changes the actors into characters of the Commedia dell'Arte, and sends them on a quest to retrieve the egg in the depths of the ocean. Now Colin appears as Harlequin and Colinette as Columbine. The guardian is transformed into Pantaloon (as a servant of Mother Goose) and the old man into Pantaloon's servant, the Clown.

In these new guises, the characters form two teams of adversaries: on the one side, Harlequin and Columbine; on the other, Pantaloon and Clown. But if we were to list all the actions that occur in fast succession throughout the fourteen scenes, it would be obvious that Harlequin and Clown are the main protagonists. Harlequin is the hero on his quest for the golden egg. He is helped by the magic wand (a sword), which was the second gift from Mother Goose. Clown is the pursuer who tries unsuccessfully to prevent him from acquiring the golden egg. Eventually, Mother Goose returns to restore everybody to their former identities and reconcile their differences once Harlequin has retrieved the holy grail of the story.

Of course, such sinister displays are not restricted to pantomimes and modern clown acts. They are found in old folk festivals in the European tradition, a contemporary manifestation of which is prominent at Halloween. But this latter spectacular treatment of death through ghastly imagery and behavior greatly transcends the European cultural area in which these festivals can still be observed nowadays. As Lee Siegel has masterfully shown in his account of laughter in India, death is ever present at the heart of comedy: "The skull, the face of death, eternally laughs with a shrieking silence at the living. The conceit of the laughing skull in Sanskrit poetry followed naturally from the common usage of the phrase, 'showing the whiteness of one's teeth,' as an expression for laughter" (Siegel 1987: 398).

In 2010, the resident clowns of the Blackpool Tower Circus performed a classic of the repertory: the haunted house. As the auguste and his partner were lying in their bed after they had blown out the candle (the circus spotlights were simply dimmed), an Egyptian mummy entered the ring and approached the bed while the clowns were supposed to be asleep. Suddenly, they awoke in terror, and the auguste was told it was a mummy. Playing on the homophony of the word, the auguste rushed toward the intruder as a child would toward his mother, while calling with tender intonation, "Mommy, Mommy!"

What does make clowns, more particularly the auguste, so prone to deal with death? We know that periodic rituals in many cultures evoke the dead and their continuous or episodic presence. Masks are always an essential part of these celebrations. They bracket together individuals out of their civil identities. Masks in the form of makeup are essential to clowns. One of their properties is that the textures, patterns, and colors of their makeup do not vary with time. In this respect, clowns are out of time. But constant change is what defines life. Therefore, the relation between permanence and changeability can be considered commensurate with the opposition between death and life. Furthermore, the changing of patterns and colors in the natural faces is what grounds an identity in the social web. Even if the makeup artificially freezes the hues and outlines of caricatured cheerfulness, there remains in the interactions with clowns' faces a haunting sense of weirdness and uncanniness. By the same token, as we saw in the previous chapter, their faces and general demeanors disqualify clowns for love. The well-known stereotype of the "ugly" clown courting the young equestrian girl who makes fun of him constitutes an impossible couple in the popular and artistic imagination. It juxtaposes life and death with the force of a German expressionist painting.

Clowns and death in the arts: Laughter at the edge

In the Leopold Museum in Vienna, a painting by Austrian expressionist Egon Schiele (1890–1918) represents two small children on the lap of an emaciated woman who could have been, if the German word (der Tod) were of the same grammatical gender as in Latin languages (e.g., la Mort, la Muerte), the personification of death itself. It is a pictorial motif that the artist has treated at least three times toward the end of his short life. Mutter mit zwei kindern II [Mother with Two Children II] (1915) is devoid of any suggestion of maternal nurturing. The colorful costumes of the children contrast with the drab hues of the woman, whose grayish face evokes a skull. The same situation is repeated in the third version of this painting, Mutter mit zwei kindern III (1915), which appears to be a more colorful rendering of the first painting bearing this title. The three oil canvasses exploit the same configuration, with modifications to the positions of the children on the woman's lap and to the chromatic intensity of their costumes. Their contrasted attires bear unmistakable resemblance to those of the two typical clowns who, at the turn of the century, dominated the circus rings of Europe. The child on the right looks like a miniature whiteface clown; the one on the left is a diminutive auguste. Both children wear the respective makeup of these roles. Chromatic and pattern variations between versions II and III belong to the same paradigm. In the second version, the auguste is lying on his back and his upper body is half raised. In the three versions, the mother is expressionless, emaciated, and livid. Decay and death are obsessively present in Schiele's works, including for instance *Der Tod und die Frau* [Death and the Maiden] (1915), in which death is personified as an old man. But the theme of the dead mother also recurs during the same period. Schiele appears to suggest in his *Mutter mit zwei kindern II* that clowns are the children of Death.

Another artist of the same period, Georges Rouault (1871–1958) fully exploited the theme of death and decay associated with clowns. Paintings such as "Tragic Clown" (1911), "Clown with White Stockings" (1912), "Three Clowns" (1928), "The Old Clown" (1930), and the color etchings with aquatint that compose the portfolio titled *Cirque de l'étoile filante* [Circus of the Shooting Star] (1934) orchestrate the notion of the clown as a crucified being, crushed by destiny. This topic has been discussed by historian of literature Wallace Fowlie in *Jacob's Night* (1947).

Why is the figure of the auguste so consistently associated with death while it is at the same time equated with laughter? The meaning of laughter remains one of the most intractable problems encountered by humans when they reflect in earnest upon their own behavior. Countless books have been written whose authors' claims of providing a definitive answer have usually been met with doubting smiles. At most, their theories can apply to a small set of occurrences and fail to reach the holy grail they had embarked to capture. In his fascinating quest for the truth of laughter, Lee Siegel endeavored to get to the very source of wisdom in the sacred texts of the immemorial Vedic tradition. His book *Laughing Matters* (1987), quoted above, recounts his frustrating quest in search of the roots of the comic tradition of India. The character of the Vidushaka, a generic comic character in the Sanskrit drama, shares in common some remarkable features with our modern circus clowns and even more broadly with numerous other traditions (Siegel 1987: 19, 28, 199–200, 285–290). But documenting over a long period of time a type whose historical origins are obscure and pointing out some similarities in other later characters obtained by descent from a common ancestral type or by convergence determined by comparable cultural constraints does not amount to explaining laughter. We are confronted with the laborious cogitations of philosophers and rhetoricians who have for millennia speculated on how many sorts of laughter there are and how many categories of comic effects can be found in oral and written literary traditions. The rational explanations they offer are certainly clever and appear exhaustive, but laughter transcends the whole enterprise, which itself is laughable (Bouissac 1992).

There are indeed extreme circumstances and situations in which laughter is the only humanely possible response. It appears, in fact, that laughing is the ultimate gesture that both sanctions and liberates the pure information that cannot produce any meaning from the raw confrontation with the absurd. Lee Siegel (1987: 145–147) tells us an enlightening story from the *Kathasaritsagara*, which can be summarized as follows:

> *A royal couple was proceeding through a forest when they encountered a ghastly and all-powerful sacred demon, which threatened to devour them unless they provided him a 7-year-old boy to be sacrificed. The gory requirement was that the boy should be brought to the forest by his own parents, who would have to hold his arms and legs while the king slaughtered him and extracted from his chest the heart, to be eaten by the monster. Only on this condition would the royal couple be saved. Hearing this, a devout boy volunteered, and the king promised his parents that they would receive a life-size gold statue of the boy if they consented to the sacrifice. They agreed, and the victim was taken to the forest. As the boy's parents were holding his limbs, the king drew his sword. Suddenly, the child smiled and then burst into loud and hearty laughter. Stunned by this unexpected behavior, all present—including the demon—bowed reverentially to the boy, with their hands joined to express their awe and devotion to the divine child.*

This narrative may shed some light on the ultimate philosophical significance of laughter, if not on its very nature, as we will suggest in the conclusion of this volume. It evokes Nietzsche's laughter in *Also Sprach Zarathustra* (1973 [1884]), the bursting into laughter of "Der Wanderer" that echoes the laughing skulls of Shiva.

9

Profaning the Sacred: The Saga of the Clown

The avatars of *Clown*

Before becoming a generic in contemporary English, *Clown* was the name of a character in the British pantomime of the eighteenth century. But, originally, it was a common word referring to the class of uneducated peasants. Similarly, the *augustes* that appeared a century later in the European circus drew their name from the antiphrastic use of the noble name August as a way of ridiculing a person as slow-witted, clumsy, and possibly inebriated—somewhat like calling Einstein someone unable to add and subtract correctly. The Latin adjective *augustus*, which philologists relate to the idea of being blessed by the gods (Ernout and Meillet 1967: 56–57), was added to the name Octavius when this adoptive son of Cesar became the first Roman emperor, henceforth known as Augustus. The most plausible anecdote proposed to explain the sarcastic application of this name to a clown is that, during a circus performance in Berlin in 1864, the grotesque attire and behavior of an equestrian performer or a circus hand triggered laughter and jeers from the popular audience, which shouted the word "August," a common insult in the local slang (Towsen 1976: 206–223, 371). There are, however, other theories that date the birth of the auguste under this name much earlier in the nineteenth century, but the mockery implied in the name remains valid (Rémy 1945: 64–82). Antiphrastic expressions, which consist of sarcastically denoting something by its opposite, is a common phenomenon in the pragmatics of any language.

What "clown" and "auguste" have in common in the language of the circus is that these names were initially used as terms of abuse. Those who are designated by these monikers are excluded from social groups that foster a sense of normalcy and decency. It is a form of semantic mobbing. Nowadays, "clown," "auguste" (or "gugusse" in French), as well as "circus," are often used as derogatory references to individuals or institutions that appear to be at odds with the rules whose respect defines law and order in civil society. These terms imply some degree of chaos and convey a negative connotation.

Historians of the European circus have documented the stages in the evolution of comic characters, from Joseph Grimaldi to the present. But they have focused on a limited number of individuals and their comparative merits. They have marshaled anecdotes, biographical data, and iconographies to form a variegated mosaic from which some high-profile figures emerge. However, the vast majority of the clowns who have performed for centuries in seasonal fairs and nomadic circuses rather than in permanent buildings in the major cities of Europe have largely escaped the attention of these chroniclers. The history of the circus and the evolution of the skills it displays are truly elusive. Regarding the repertoire of the clowns, the temporal development of these narratives can be captured only sporadically by probing whatever information has survived in the writings of chroniclers, and their origins are lost in the deep past of European cultures.

It is possible, of course, to retrace the broad changes that took place during the past two and a half centuries (Levy 1991: 22–30). The British-style clown was heir of the Commedia dell'Arte and excelled in humorous acrobatics like his early embodiment in Joseph Grimaldi. This clown became a whiteface when he started performing with a partner, an auguste whose makeup and behavior were markedly different, and who was mocked and victimized in the ring or on stage. Subsequent stylizations crystalized the opposition between a dominant character and an underdog, to create the iconic pair that has been, and still is to a large extent, a focal point of circus performances. But, as was noted in previous chapters, the auguste tended to acquire some autonomy, play tricks of his own on the whiteface, and eventually perform alone in the last quarter of the twentieth century. The auguste thus came to forge a new identity independently of the whiteface partner. Various factors are involved in such changes. These include the particular talent of individual augustes who gained celebrity status and did not need the support of a whiteface, the fact that the role of the modern whiteface needed an auguste, while the reverse was not a given because interacting with the ringmaster was always a possibility, and the economic considerations regarding the sharing of the fees that circuses were prepared to pay when they hired clowns. As to the final point, the early model was indeed that circuses contracted a whiteface, and the whiteface, in turn, hired an auguste, who was poorly compensated for being slapped and ridiculed. Then, cases in which it was the auguste who started employing a poorly paid whiteface occurred more frequently, until the role of the whiteface became largely redundant and expandable.

In previous chapters we have examined particular clown acts belonging to the repertoire of a long tradition of micro-narratives that constitute the backbone of the art of professional clowning. But it was always necessary to emphasize that each of these acts was only a variation of a hypothetical prototype whose origin is impossible to pinpoint in historical time. Comparing these acts shows that the kernel narratives function like scores that clowns interpret without much concern for authorship or fidelity to a model. Variations are introduced within the limits allowed by the narrative constraints of particular scenarios. Each clown brings to bear the marks of his or her personality and creativity upon the details. Some innovations happen to be assimilated into the tradition, but their origin quickly becomes blurred. The dynamic inherent in the narratives themselves is the force that drives clown acts down from generation to generation, or horizontally from clown to clown, who are prone to imitate each other while claiming that the invention of any successful novelty rests with him or her. But despite occasional variations originating with the interpreters, the narratives transcend individual performers.

Therefore, it is possible to consider the particular artists who interpret these narratives as mere variables. Clowns under whatever name they choose to be known are truly interchangeable, without altering the structure of the score they perform. Of course, some may be more effective than others, but the chronicle of the circus offers many examples of the shuffling of individual performers. Some whitefaces have teamed up with a succession of augustes, and the same phenomenon has played out with augustes when they have tended to be more prominent. However, there have been some perfect fits between two complementary artists that have left their mark in the history of the circus. Throughout these changes, narratives have proved to be extremely resilient over as long a period of time as clown acts have been remembered and sometimes recorded.

A grand narrative and its fractal performances

All clown acts are characterized by a small number of recurring narrative patterns. First, the number of protagonists is limited to two, whether the act involves the typical pair formed by the whiteface and the auguste or actualizes the duality of roles by pitching the auguste against either the ringmaster or the public. Occasionally, the role of the auguste is duplicated or even triplicated in order to enrich the dramatic texture of the act. In the latter case, though, the basic pair of opposite agencies remains the dialogic core of the act.

Secondly, a clown act always starts with a disruption of the expected order. An announcement by the ringmaster or a musical performance by the whiteface is interrupted by the auguste, who triggers a cascade of unexpected events. Solo augustes often enter the ring unannounced, without using the artists' entrance, emerging from the public and crossing the border that delimits the ritual space of the ring or mingling in the audience and causing some brouhaha requiring the intervention of the ringmaster.

Thirdly, a clown act always hinges on a transformation of situation or status such as the breaking of an object or a rule, the loss of a game, a punishment, a reversal of fortune, or a surprising development. This syntax articulates content that is of interest to the audience either because it refers to issues that are alive in the contextual culture or because it addresses the very foundations upon which that particular culture rests—foundations that must remain unquestioned if the culture is to stand as an absolute source of meaning. The best guarantee of this ontological anchorage is that those who participate in this culture remain unaware of the fragility and vulnerability of its basis. As we have seen again and again in the course of this book, clowns disclose the conventionality of the laws and the taboos that sustain them. But the virtual chaos they unleash during a performance is quickly brought under control. This outcome is generally symbolized by the performers playing music while marching together, thus restoring the harmony that they disrupted at the inception of their act.

Indeed, a clown act always concludes with the reconciliation of the two (or more) antagonists so that the narrative in one form or another can start a new cycle of disruption, transformation, and reconciliation in the next show. A clown act does not reach a final state that would represent a narrative dead end, as is the case in tragedy and melodrama through the death of one or several characters, and in comedy usually through the triumph of the protagonist with whom the audience identifies. The end of a clown act is not the end of an episode, to be followed by another episode, but instead makes possible a new beginning of the same series of events from a clean slate.

However, if all the narratives are brought together, a general pattern emerges. The narrative structure reproduces in many respects the micro-narratives of the gags that are embedded in its multimodal fabric. This theoretical perspective obviously requires a high degree of abstraction, but it is sufficiently explicit to be operational—that is, to effectively map through to the development of the concrete acts themselves. A few examples are now in order.

Among the acts that have been described in the preceding chapters, let us recall, for example, the breaking of a mirror (Pipo and Zavatta), the destroying of a puppet (the Fratellini), flouting the social contract (the honey), and the spilling of a pail of paint (Charlie Cairoli). Under whatever name and particular appearance, the antagonists of these episodes have constant qualities and functions, like the heroes of myths and folktales. Therefore, we can assume that a great proportion of these micro-narratives are fragments of a grand narrative or, rather, that the clown acts coming from the traditional repertory are narrative fractals rather than individual stories independent of each other. They replay the same drama, involving the same roles. Naturally, new stories can be invented following the same structure as long as it involves a transgression and the punishment of the transgressor followed by the restoration of order. At least there seems to be good evidence that this pattern holds true for the core body of clown acts. Of course, this interpretation is not absolutely limiting. Cultural evolution is unpredictable, and new forms can always emerge from instigators of chaos, such as clowns whose subversive behavior systematically undermines the tacit rules that govern the norms of their time.

The sacred and the profane

The two complementary notions of sacred and profane overlap, in part, with the opposition of secular and religious. Etymology and archaeology can shed some light on the practical realities that account for these related concepts. The Latin *sacer* designated in high antiquity a place, object, or person that could not be touched, that had to be kept separate because it could either contaminate—or be contaminated by—the human who would break the taboo and get into contact with its power. The inherent ambiguity of the "sacred," a term that has inherited some of the semantic values of its ancient meaning, conveys the idea that its nature cannot be reduced to categories such as good or evil. To define the sacred would be to make relative something that must remain absolute. There can only be definitions by extension of the sacred, in the form of an open list of forbidden behaviors. But even making such prohibitions explicit would constitute a step toward transgression, because articulating such a possibility would make it thinkable. This is why the most fundamental laws grounding human cultures in their tacit principles can be revealed only when they are broken.

The Latin word *sacrum* pertains to what belongs to divine agencies, notably the space of the *templum* [temple] and the sacrifices that are performed to connect with, and hopefully please, the gods. Both *templum* and *profanum* are words that apply to a well-defined consecrated space. The Latin prefix *pro-* meant "before," "in front of." Thus, the word *profanum* refers to what is outside the boundaries, both physical and conceptual, of the sacred realm. Profaning ultimately means bringing out into the open what was secluded and protected by taboos in the temple. By extension, it signifies refusing to accept the limits that determine normalcy and decency in the culture in which it occurs. The concepts of sacred and profane relate to—but do not exactly coincide with—the opposition of religious to secular. Religions are threatened by sacrilege and blasphemy because these behaviors generally do not trigger naturally negative consequences. This is why punishment can only be generated by society itself, or a dominant group, on the behalf of the favored system of belief. *Secular* refers to societies that dismiss the ontological and moral distinctions between sacred and profane by relativizing these notions. Nevertheless, even in a secular culture, revealing, exposing, and disclosing what should remain secret, untold, and hidden jeopardizes the power of what is taken for granted—the peg from which the consistency and legitimacy of civil society hangs (McCoy 2013; Shilling and Mellor 2013).

As we saw in Chapters 7 and 8, clowns by profession break a wide range of rules. They toy with the code of civil interactions. Usually these infringements are not such that they could qualify as violations or crimes requiring police intervention and legal redress. There is, however, a culture-dependent scale of toleration of humor. A sociological investigation of the degree to which a sample of thirty-three national cultures can accommodate irony and parody—that is, can foster individuals and institutions that mock the status quo and lampoon celebrities or values—shows a great variability of the threshold beyond which a clown or comedian may venture (Gelfand et al. 2011: 1100–1104). In 2013, the press reported that eight humorists were condemned to jail for defaming the image of the United Arab Emirates. The twenty-first century already has its own chronicle of death threats issued against cartoonists and comedians. But accepting that some individuals may enjoy the freedom of limitless joking does not necessarily means total impunity. Transgressions have a cost because they need to be framed by constraints lest they lead to anomie through the generalization of their counterprinciples. In contemporary Western secular societies, legal systems provide means of prosecuting humorists if it can be shown that defamation, apology of crime, or political subversion is involved in their writings or performances. Most circus clowns stay clear of explicitly loaded issues, but they can nevertheless go quite far because their status of outcast makes them immune to some legal retaliation. However, even when they are celebrated by the media, journalists feel compelled to crack some stale jokes about clowns and to laugh at them, because clowns are supposed to stand in the margin of cultural normalcy and decency. They are excluded from civil society due to their appearance, personae, and performed behavior. Their performing identities transcend the rules of propriety; they are improper by essence. As we will see in the next section, their cultural profanation is so radical that society prefers to stigmatize them as "clowns" rather than explicitly confront their insolent unpacking of the tacit principles that must be left unquestioned if social life is to continue to run its course unchallenged despite its fundamental discontents (e.g., Bouissac 1990; Marshall 2010).

Putting things inside out and upside down

The metaphors "inside out" and "upside down" approximate the way in which clowns toy with the norms grounding the personal and social lives of their audience. However, the ludic mode implied by the notion of toying wrongly conveys the impression that their contrived playfulness has no serious consequences. Deviant behavior can always become normative, for the simple reason that merely demonstrating the possibility of such actions can lead to their generalization and usher in chaos. On a very basic level, if everybody wore a clown's makeup and transmogrified their face beyond recognition whenever they wanted, individuals would escape the gaze of others and could follow their desires without restraint. Nothing could compel them to stick to the same makeup forever, or, equally disturbing, a large number of people could adopt the same facial makeup. A completely different kind of society would result from such a generalization. Flouting the principle of social identity is a major transgression that can defeat the control upon which law and order rest. On occasions, gangsters have used clown makeup and costumes to rob banks. Carnival parties in which men and women wear masks open the way to sexual license. Recent activist social movements have resorted to the use of such a device to panic the establishment they intended to subvert. Anonymous and anomie are dangerously close.

Another pillar of society is language. It is based on conventions that must be considered binding if society is to serve its functions. Language is extremely vulnerable, however—so much so that it constantly evolves and needs to be put in the straitjacket of arbitrary rules that are taught and enforced by their appointed guardians. The whiteface's hypercorrect eloquence expresses its lawful competence. The auguste, on the contrary, commonly mispronounces words, makes grammatical mistakes, and ignores the pragmatic norms. Thus, the auguste undermines the very possibility of the power of discourse that spells out the laws. A famous example in English is a clown who pretended to confuse "address" and "undress" when told by the ringmaster to "address the audience." Any such possible phonetic proximity is fodder for the clowns, mainly if it allows the breaking of social propriety.

Indexical forms also open the way to ambiguities that are often exploited in clowns' dialogue. A frequently performed act unfolds as follows: Two augustes arrive in the tent from the public's entrance and wander among the audience until they find their way to the ring. They carry oversized suitcases that are covered with stickers indicating the cities to which they have traveled. They are musicians looking for a place to perform. They sit down on the border of the ring and start unpacking their instruments. The ringmaster rushes from the artists' entrance and angrily tells them that they cannot play "here" and that they should move on. He then leaves the ring. The clowns put back their instruments in the suitcases, which they load on their backs, and walk a few meters along the border of the ring. Then they settle in this new location and resume their unpacking. But the ringmaster appears again and repeats that they cannot play here. One of the augustes asks for confirmation of the order: "So, we cannot play here either?" "That is right!" shouts the ringmaster. The augustes start again their packing and unpacking routine much further along the ring. They are now sitting at a spot diametrically opposed to their initial position. This triggers an argument with the ringmaster about what "here" means. Eventually, they are allowed to play, and their next skit can start now that they have successfully exposed one of the main liabilities of language. Indexicality is indeed a tricky aspect of language, which the augustes lay bare. This is why written laws are linguistically so complex, spelling out all the possibilities legislators can think of. Even then, enough ambiguities remain in the texts for lawyers to argue endlessly on whether or not a law applies to a particular case. In everyday life, the disrespect of the indexical pragmatic conventions could easily usher in social chaos.

But clowns go further in their symbolic subversions. We have encountered in the course of this volume numerous instances of disrespect for the social hierarchy as it is embodied in the whiteface and the ringmaster. Contemporary clowns have even been emboldened to cross the fence between performers and audience, who are no longer immune to being dragged into the ring for the amusement of the other spectators—as we saw in the acts of David Larible and Kenneth Huesca. Through this blurring of roles, subversion can spill over. Immersive performance includes the germ of contagion, the implicit threat of spreading a clown culture whose slogan could be "nothing is sacred."

Throughout this book we have encountered perhaps more drastic transgressions than the ones mentioned above. We have witnessed funeral rituals being mimicked to bury a toy and a mosquito. Clowns have mocked corpses and ghosts. Death has been treated as an object of laughter. Romantic love symbolized by the nightingale's song has been deflated to reveal the brash economic nature of mating. Sexual license has been represented more or less directly in Rob Torres's request for a healing kiss from a lady spectator. Peter Shub's tripod has been anthropomorphized to allow racy behavior. Genders have been blended. In contemporary circuses, however, bawdiness is toned down compared to the more salient presence of phallic jokes in earlier shows before the circus became marketed as family entertainment. But it is a resilient component of clown performances, and glimpses of the past resurface from time to time either as allusions or, more crudely, like the cuckoo clock bird that briefly emerged from the zipper of the trousers of an auguste in the Rastelli troupe. Some modern circuses produced for adult audiences have unleashed unrestrained transgressive performances (Bouissac 2010: 182–183, 2012: 178–179, 193–194). Modern secular urban cultures have integrated ludic dimensions far beyond the traditionally restricted time and place of ritualistic carnivals. A relative anomie festers in the social media. But the clowning that happens under the magnifying glass of the circus ring articulates with blinding clarity the questioning of what audiences take for granted. The clowns' performances deliver information that is so difficult to stomach that we have to laugh it off. Not everybody in the public of a circus show can indulge in the kind of reflexivity that this volume has proposed. But subversive information is processed all the same. Societies are haunted by their clowns, who bang on the ground upon which we rest and make it sound hollow. It resonates with their sarcastic laughter.

Their ritualistic violations of cultural norms covertly bear upon imperatives of lesser or greater prominence. From breaking plates to breaking taboos, there is a scale of transgressions that generates mirth and laughter of variable intensity. Let us return to the case of the plates to which we alluded in Chapter 3. Why should the breaking of plates be such a big deal? China plates are a staple of the modern household that are the object of special care, as they are essentially fragile. Children receive constant injunctions to handle them gently. When a plate is accidentally shattered, this event triggers a crisis of variable intensity, because, ultimately, plates are indices of harmonious commensality and civilized eating. Breaking a plate jeopardizes the integrity of the household. Disputes between spouses often end up with a symbolic shattering of plates and other china implements, to signify the breaking up of the sacred bond. Anybody familiar with the performance of circus clowns has probably witnessed a version of the act that will now be described.

The whiteface demonstrates his juggling skill by climbing on a chair and throwing a china plate high above his head. As the plate falls, he catches it in his hand just before it reaches the ground. Then he balances the plate on one of his shoulders and lets it slide down his arm until he grasps it before it can crash. The auguste wants to imitate him, but the plate hits the ground and breaks into many pieces. For this kind of act, a portable wooden floor has been quickly installed on top of the sawdust or the carpet that covers the ring, in order to provide a hard surface. The auguste is given another plate, which is also shattered. He breaks several plates as he tries various methods of catching them. At long last he succeeds, but in a gesture of triumph, the plate he holds in his hand hits the back of the chair. More plates are brought to the ring. Now the auguste stands in the middle of a heap of shattered plates. Eventually, he throws a last plate high in the air and surprises the contemptuous whiteface and the audience by catching it with his hand behind his back. But again his victory does not last, because the plate is crushed into pieces when he mindlessly sits down on the chair upon which he has delicately placed the plate. In all the versions of this act, the clowns display exuberant fireworks of noisy smashing, shattering, and disintegrating of fragile objects, which always elicits mirth and irresistible laughter.

But beyond its literal significance, the ritualistic breaking of plates can be considered an effective visual and resounding metaphor for the breaking of more powerful taboos. To illustrate this point, let us now revisit Rob Torres's act, which was described in Chapter 4. After hurting his thumb with his juggling implements, he behaves like a child and requests a healing kiss from a woman in the audience. He thus construes her as a maternal figure. Then he hurts his nose and comes back to the same person, with a hint that the accident might be intentional, in order to receive more attention from her as a loving mother. But when he apparently hurts his testes and walks toward that lady, this move suggests potential incest—all the more because his horrified gesture of refusal as a second thought seems to signify that the "mother" was ready to comply. This symbolic breaking of the taboo of incest rests on the recategorization of body parts and female roles. On the one hand, the clown ignores the cultural divide of the upper and lower regions of the body by treating the forehead, the nose, and the testes as parts of equal natural status—which indeed they are, because the face and the sexual organs are mere areas on a continuum. On the other hand, he denies another powerful cultural disjunction between the female as mother and the female as lover. But, of course, this semiotic distinction is not grounded in nature. Furthermore, by acting as a child but trying to implement a sexual agenda, he transgresses the cultural status of the child, which is considered to be asexual or, rather, whose sexuality is taboo. Clowns symbolically straddle a dangerous line between the permitted and the forbidden, the moral and the immoral, the legal and the illegal, and the profane and the sacred.

10

Clowns without Borders

Mapping clowns around the world

Although there has been no systematic research of clowning on a global scale, sporadic studies indicate that clowns, or their equivalents under any other names, are found in almost all cultures in the world. Some ethnographers, anthropologists, sociologists, historians of popular entertainments, and performance theorists have documented religious and secular institutions that foster actors whose public behaviors are more or less transgressive and who often cause a mixture of fear and laughter among those who witness their antics. Such displays are usually contained within boundaries of time and space and possess a ritualistic character. This volume has selectively probed traditional European clowns acts over some three centuries of documented circus and stage performances, including today's spectacles, which can be construed as secular rituals (Bouissac 2012: 23–27). Expanding the scope of this ethnographic inquiry beyond the domain of professional clowns in the European cultural context is not a part of this book's agenda. However, two further paths should be explored in order to provide the reader a broader appreciation of the phenomenon of clowning. First, we will briefly examine the performances of traditional clowns in distant cultural areas. Secondly, we will discuss the contemporary spread of clowning as a form of social service and activism. In this latter case, clowns break away from the confines of the traditional ritual space and time, and selectively penetrate the texture of their society and its institutions. These clowns, however, are markedly different from the professionals we have documented so far in this volume. Clowning is thus democratized in the sense that anybody with minimal training can wear a red nose and indulge in his or her own interpretation of the genre for a variety of purposes.

But before addressing the issues raised by the quasi universality of clowns and the contemporary trivialization of clowning in the name of commendable concerns for the well-being of communities, let us point out that the art of clowning is context-sensitive. Clown acts of the sort we have examined in the previous chapters of this book are very rarely portable from one country to another, even if necessary language adjustments are made. Purely visual narratives and gags are not independent from the complex semiotic context within which they produce meaning, because the gestures and artifacts they use do not stand alone, but implicitly refer to the more or less tacit rules governing the particular cultural norms of their social milieu. Audiences are immersed in a virtual web of values, habits, and moral constraints that they take for granted and that allow them to make sense of events. As we emphasized when we analyzed the nature of gags in Chapter 4, cultural relevance is the key to understanding why jokes and gags make the public laugh. When this condition is overlooked—as occasionally happens in this age of cultural exchange and global mobility—clowns fail to elicit the reactions they anticipate. Such an example is now in order.

Clowns without borders?

Tokyo, February 15, 2011. The conference on manga in which I participated is now over. One of the issues the speakers addressed was the reason for which this typically Japanese genre of comics is received with enduring popularity worldwide. It appears that for manga there are no borders. Its visual and narrative appeal is quasi universal (Bouissac 2011). During the past 3 days, I have been pondering its striking difference with circus clowns. Manga is a medium that, from my limited experience, appears to stand clear of humor.

Today, I am free to spend my time as I want. It just happened that, the day I arrived, I was lucky to come across an advertisement for a Russian circus performing in Tokyo. I could not miss this opportunity of probing the reception of a foreign circus in Japan. How are the people going to handle the clowning part of the program? Circus Nikulin is well known. It performs in its own building in Moscow and occasionally goes on international tours. Typically in Japan, performing space is not where Westerners expect it to be. I went once to a theater that was on the fifth floor of a high-rise. This time, I have to struggle with the map until I discover that the circus is located three floors below street level. The huge, cavernous space has been fitted with bleachers in front of an elevated circular arena, and the pictures featured on the printed program announce a traditional circus show with acrobats, dogs, bears, horses, and clowns. It is early in the day. The audience is mostly made of Japanese families.

After a spectacular opening, the public is treated to a colorful hodgepodge. A dozen acrobats in medieval attire perform a range of jumps at a fast pace, while the female ballet dancers who have graced the beginning of the show handle the props such as hoops, ribbons, and flags. The space is cleared, and the clowns appear. A man and a woman with no distinctive makeup walk to the center of the ring. They evoke a domestic scene. Lev Zaitcev and Olga Zaitceva are actually husband and wife. The woman has curlers in her hair and wears a kind of ordinary housedress. The man's white shirt and brown trousers create a casual look. They seem to be an ordinary Russian couple with a hint of the usual bickering in their relationship. Ironically, the accompanying music is the march from Rossini's Wilhelm Tell opera. The man performs magic directed to his wife and makes an American dollar appear from thin air. The woman immediately wants to grab the bill, while whistling aggressively with her police-type whistle. This means of expressing a range of emotions and thoughts is often used by clowns in countries whose language they do not speak, as they assume that intonation will suffice to convey meaning. But this holds only within certain limits, because not all languages foster the same range of intonation patterns. However, it seems obvious that the woman wants more money, and the man complies by producing another dollar, which he instantly makes disappear. She protests and signals that she believes he is hiding it in his clothes. He shows that his pockets are empty. But she insists and forces him to strip until he wears only his underwear, baggy striped boxers. The woman plunges her hands in the front of the underwear and forages for a few seconds until she extracts an oversized dollar bill. Thus ends this interlude, without eliciting anything more than a brief, polite applause. A quick look at the audience indicates that they seem somewhat puzzled, if not appalled. Probably this clown act makes people laugh in Russia because of the misogynist depiction of a bossy and greedy wife, and the not-so-subtle sexual innuendo of the concluding action. The Russian producers of this program have obviously overlooked the fact that they were going to perform in the country of the powerful Yen, where the green bill is not worshipped as it is, or used to be, in Russia and other Eastern European countries. Moreover, the economic balance in Asian couples is markedly different from that of their Western counterparts. Finally, the underwear episode was more shocking than funny in the context of a family show. There were other aspects in this act, such as the curlers in the woman's hair and the sloppiness of her attire, which were problematic for a Japanese audience that could not relate spontaneously to the cultural codes this clown act was symbolically manipulating.

Four acts later, the same clown couple returns to the ring, while the circus attendants install the requisites for a trained bear display. The music is Rossini's The Barber of Seville. *The woman cracks a whip and gives orders to the man while pointing an imperative finger with her free hand. She makes him balance on a plank placed on a cylinder. The props are icons of an ordinary domestic setting: pails (cylinders), pots, and pans placed on top of each other to form an unstable construction on which the man demonstrates his balancing skill. But his wife is not satisfied, and she orders him to perform ever more difficult exercises. Eventually, she pushes forward a huge steaming pot full of hot potatoes that the man has to juggle, apparently to avoid burning his fingers. He must now balance this hot pot at the top of a perch that rests on his forehead. As he moves closer to the first row of the audience, the smoking pot tips over, but the potatoes hang from strings and do not fall on people, who nevertheless recoil in fear in their seats. Once again, polite applause greets their bowing to the spectators.*

Russian and European audiences in general undoubtedly have no problem identifying boiled potatoes, a staple of their most common diet. They are also familiar with the experience of burning one's fingers when holding hot potatoes before they cool down. We can assume that this experience is only marginally shared among the members of a rice culture such as Japan. But this is not all. The caricatured reversal of gender roles represented in this act and purported to provocatively reveal who is the real boss in a married couple was at odds with the Japanese preference for more subtle, implicit verbal or visual statements.

It would be a mistake to conclude from the tepid reception of these two clown acts that Japanese audiences lack a sense of humor. Visits to the popular Mokuba Theater in Asakusa, or storytellers and Manzai performances in Tokyo and Osaka, show that Japanese audiences enjoy humor and laugh at jokes and gags that are pertinent to their cultural context. The Russian clowns of the Nikulin Circus wrongly assumed that their antics were portable across cultural borders.

This does not mean that all clowning is a prisoner of its cultural context. There is a scale of dependency whose parameters can be measured. The most common ground for sharing humor is probably the form and functions of the human body.

The famed Russian clown Karandash never failed to elicit unrestrained laughter with his act involving a copy of the marble statue of the Venus of Milo. Even for an audience unfamiliar with the cannons of ancient Greek art, the female body is spontaneously identified despite the absence of the arms that characterizes this particular icon of highbrow museum culture. The statue had been placed on a pedestal in the center of the arena when Karandash appeared and was asked by the ringmaster to clean it with a feather duster. The clown's mime conveyed a sense of embarrassment in front of this nude body whose intimate parts he had to dust along with the rest of the statue. An awkward gesture suddenly caused the statue to tip over, fall to the ground, and break into pieces. This prop was actually built with separate horizontal sections piled on top of each other in order to construct an apparently seamless body. Karandash then endeavored to reconstitute the statue, but kept making mistakes, putting the parts in the wrong order and orientation such as placing the breasts where the buttocks should be. Naturally, at the end, he was desperately looking for the missing arms. This humorous end depended, of course, on the premise that the audience had identified the statue and its cultural significance, although this act could work even in the absence of this layer of reference in the mind of some spectators.

But the body itself cannot be considered an absolute common ground for the universal interpretation of gags focusing on its parts and functions. In some societies, strong taboos and rules of propriety would interfere with the humorous acceptance of Karandash's transgressive manipulations. There are also limits of another kind. For instance, even the small, rounded red nose that Western auguste clowns usually consider a universal recipe for appearing funny or innocent, as we saw in Chapter 1, is not such a valid transformative, minimal mask once ethnic borders are crossed. A small, round nose is a common feature of the facial morphology of many Asian populations. "Long-noses" is a slur that some eastern Asians use to mock Caucasians whose comparatively huge nasal appendages are found quite hilarious in countries in which rounded, neotenic faces are the norm.

Clowning beyond the cultural fences

The ethnography of clowning should not in principle limit itself to a single cultural area, however broad it may be, as we have chosen to do in this volume. The examples presented in the previous section show how difficult it is to bridge cultural gaps through clowning as compared with sports, acrobatics, dance, and, to a large extent, music. Even when clown acts do not involve language as the medium of communication, the reliance on visual means such as dynamic interaction, gestures, and artifacts is not a guarantee that spectators will be able to construct the intended meaning and appreciate the humor it is purported to create. This is simply because nonverbal communication is ruled by culture-specific codes. Having explored clown performances in various Asian countries, I would now like to discuss examples of the incommunicability of humor in the absence of a cultural exegesis.

A case in point is a clown act I discussed earlier (Bouissac 2012: 184–187) but which deserves further attention in the context of this chapter. This kind of act is known in European circuses as "The taxi," sometimes qualified as "The crazy taxi." It involves a taxi that constantly breaks down when the clowns board it and try to drive. This generates plenty of opportunities for efficient slapstick. The prototype of this act can be found in earlier times in the form of a horse-drawn carriage with an uncooperative animal and various mishaps such as the breaking of a wheel or the bucking of the horse. The "taxi" exploits other possibilities provided by the mechanics of automobiles. Many traditional European clowns have interpreted this scenario with variations in the design of the car, the narrative, the gags, and the actors' characterization. The first time I saw this act in an Indian circus, in the southern state of Kerala, I thought I was in known clowning territory. But my blasé attitude was soon replaced by utter puzzlement. The narrative involved five actors. At first, a woman dressed in a blouse and a short skirt was sitting with a clownish dwarf on the side of the ring, obviously waiting to be picked up by a car. A taxi arrived, but there were already two men sitting in it, in addition to the driver—one in the front seat, the other in the back. The former was elegantly dressed in a suit. The latter was wrapped in a traditional Hindu white fabric, leaving most of his upper torso uncovered. The dwarf stopped the taxi and indicated that the woman wanted a ride. This created some commotion, as it seemed that the simple solution of using the vacant seat at the back was not obvious. There were excited gestures and arguments in Malayalam, the local language. Eventually the two men sat side by side in the back seat and the woman took the front seat next to the driver. The dwarf was standing on the running board of the vehicle. The taxi was ready to go. After a few meters, the car broke down. Everybody had to get out while the driver tried to fix the problem. Then, everybody boarded the vehicle again. But successive mishaps such as a flat tire, a motor explosion, and a falling part of the car forced the passengers to wait in the ring until the repair was made. There were some arguments between the two men while they were waiting. Both tried to capture the attention of the woman and get closer to her, in spite of the distance the dwarf and the driver endeavored to enforce for her protection. At some point, I recognized a classic gag of European clowns when one grabs the shirt of another and pulls it from the top, but it is an extremely long shirt that is folded inside his trousers, and the end of it is reached only when the clown has arrived at the other side of the ring. In this case, the suited man (the one who grabbed the shirt) had to pull laterally because of the way the Hindu priest (the one being pulled) was dressed. As a result, the latter was spinning while his cloth was pulled. Eventually, everybody was back in their seats, but as the taxi left the ring, an explosion caused the taxi's back seats to tip over, and the two men find themselves upside down with their legs sticking out from the car.

Apparently unlike the audience, which often burst into laughter during this act, I had the feeling of having seen it all before. The gags were worn-out slapsticks for me, because I interpreted this performance in the context of my past experience of European clowns. My research assistant was a student at the local university, and, after the show, I conveyed to him my disappointment concerning the lack of originality of this act as well as my surprise at the obvious enjoyment of the public. He strongly disagreed and quickly showed me that I had not understood the point made by this narrative, which he found brilliant. The woman, a clown in drag, was not, as I had thought, a prostitute, but instead an iconic Anglo-Indian lady, the daughter of a mixed couple from the times of the British Empire. The dwarf was her servant. The man in the suit was a Muslim from northern India. His hat was typical, and he was holding a little book indicating that he was well educated. The other man was a traditional Hindu priest wearing all the customary attire and the paraphernalia of a Brahman.

Suddenly, the narrative came alive in my mind when I realized what I had missed. I had indeed forgotten in my hasty dismissal that slapsticks are only syntactic structures that articulate semantic contents. It is not because a person slips on a banana peel and falls to the ground that the witnesses of this accident will necessarily laugh. It entirely depends on the qualities of the victim whether he/she is a pretentious character whose arrogance implies that he/she is above such an accidental humiliation or a vulnerable elderly person whose mishap will immediately trigger empathy.

The visual statements that formed the multimodal discourse of this clown act pertained to the very social fabric of modern India. Each of the actors represented a religious community whose harmonious cohabitation with the others traditionally depended on the respect of rank and the proper political economy of space. The initial seating in the taxi respected this order. Everybody was in his proper place, and the taxi was running without problem. The intrusion of the Anglo-Indian woman disrupted this balance and forced the reshuffling of spatial distribution. Now let us note that this act was observed in Kerala, a state that is nearly 100 percent literate and whose citizens consider themselves more intellectually mature than the rest of the country. My assistant pointed out to me that it would be risky to perform such an act in any of the other states, which are prone to communal riots. He also emphasized that the gentleman in a suit could clearly be identified by his costume and demeanor as an intellectual Muslim from the northern part of India, whereas the Hindu priest was typical of traditionalist Tamil Nadu, another, more religious southern state. All this was obvious to the audience, which could enjoy some degree of feeling of superiority with respect to the antics of the clowns who were representing and mocking others of their culture.

But there was more in this act. As we saw in the case of Karandash's handling of the Venus statue, intertextuality effects are at play in clown acts. The spinning of the Hindu priest as he was endlessly unwrapped from his cloth could only evoke a famous episode of the Mahabharata in which Draupadi, the wife of Arjuna, is saved from being raped when the god Krishna renders her sari infinite. The fact that a caricatured priest embodied the same situation was found hilarious by the educated audience that attended the spectacle.

Clowning in Java

In the 1990s, circumstances brought me to Indonesia to participate in conferences and give seminars. My first experience of the traditional Javanese shadow puppet theater was somewhat puzzling. Local colleagues fed me with the basic information I was lacking. I soon learned to distinguish the angular profiles of the heroes that were made to reenact on the screen episodes of Indian epics the Ramayana and the Mahabharata. The subtle signs both verbal and visual that allowed the audience to tell one character from the other, and appreciate the particular skill of the puppet master in lending them his voice and gestures, at first escaped my discriminatory capabilities. However, I could not miss the occasional presence of more rounded figures whose dialogue and movements were strikingly different from those of the other silhouettes. I was intrigued by the fact that these distinctive shadows were consistently eliciting smiles or laughter from the audience. I soon noticed that the gamelan orchestra was playing a special tune whenever they appeared and that the puppet master was making them speak with a particular voice and intonation. My Indonesian colleagues explained that these four comic characters were called the Punakawans and that their function was to interrupt the thread of the grand narrative that was represented by making ironical comments and cracking jokes. I could not fail, of course, to relate such a dramatic pattern to the role of clowns in a circus program, but in subsequent conversations with them I discovered that my suggestion that the Punakawans were clowns of sorts was for them totally irrelevant, if not scandalous. They had a low opinion of Western clowns, which, as I found out later, they knew only through popular movies and advertising, including the icon of the McDonald's hamburger chain of which red and yellow plastic embodiments were found in several prominent places in Jakarta.

In the following days, I was told that there are several traditional media for Wayang performances. What I had seen that evening is called Wayang Kulit, a show for which figures are cut out from thin leather and fixed on wooden frames. These puppets have movable parts, and their shadows are projected onto a screen while the puppeteer tells the narrative and impersonates the voices of the heroes. The same stories are performed with three-dimensional wooden puppets in the Wayang Golek. The dramas can also be represented by dancers wearing masks. But, sensing my deep interest in these performances, one of my colleagues suggested that I should see the Wayang Orang, in which real actors play episodes of the Indian epics on a stage and the Punakawans appear several times during the evening. He kindly invited me to the Bharata Theater. I would often return there on each of my visits to Jakarta, as well to other venues in Semarang, Surakarta, and Yogyakarta where Wayang Orang was performed on a regular basis.

Although the actors of the Wayang Orang speak in Javanese, an idiom more ancient and complex than the current official Indonesian language, the narratives are somewhat easier to follow visually on stage than on a dim screen if a native speaker provides minimal explanations and occasional translations. Between 1992 and 1998, several research grants allowed me to hire competent students to assist me in documenting the looks, words, and deeds of the Punakawan in their stage performances. They wear distinctive makeup similar to that of Western clowns, and they are dressed like traditional peasants, with checkered black-and-white aprons. They play the role of servants to the gods and heroes of the Hindu epics, which became a staple of Javanese culture after these eastern islands were colonized by invaders from the Asian subcontinent and entered a period of some 10 centuries marked by a succession of warring Hindu and Buddhist kingdoms until these started to be displaced by Islamic sultanates in the thirteenth century. Typically, after a first installment of an epic drama from the repertory—which can deal, for instance, with Draupadi's misfortune when her husband loses her in a game of chance and the god Krishna intervenes to save her integrity—the action stops, the gamelan music changes its rhythm and melody, and the four Punakawans enter the stage walking like tired farmers coming from toiling in the fields. Sometimes they sit down on the floor and start telling stories, commenting on the plot, or bickering. The leader is Somar (or Semar), a portentous older man who distills plain common sense and wisdom. He is accompanied by his three sons: Petruk, a tall, strong, and straight man who sports a long nose; Gareng, a witty character with a slim, twisted body that is slightly deformed; and Bagong, a persona who embodies many of the features we have identified in the auguste. Bagong, indeed, has much heavier makeup, behaves awkwardly, and makes dumb remarks that actually point to the arbitrariness of social and language rules. He is prone to transgress conventional behavior and is often scolded by his brothers, with whom he argues. He consistently elicits laughter from the audience.

The Punakawans are interpreted by several troupes of actors. But, in spite of personal variations in the makeup, voices, and demeanors, their performing persona is immediately identifiable, and their distinctive roles are consistent. No two Somar's makeup is exactly alike, but all are recognized as being the face of Somar. This goes as well for the others—Petruk, Gareng, and

Bagong. Each categorical makeup is generated by an algorithm that allows for some pattern variations, as is the case for the makeup of the whiteface and the auguste in the European circus. As for the whiteface, Somar's facial expression is serious and severe, and the three sons show some resemblance with the auguste through the more salient use of red and black painted on the white background of their faces. Bagong in particular is characterized by heavy red designs around his eyes and mouth. Although the Punakawans cause laughter mostly through their dialogue and songs, they occasionally engage in some slapstick comedy. A poster photographed in a theater in Semarang provides evidence that they also perform on musical instruments: Petruk, Gareng, and Bagong play, respectively, a bass, a violin, and a guitar. It is worth noting that these three instruments are appropriate with respect to their performing personas. The Punakawans are central characters in the Wayang. In fact, Somar is endowed with sacred status.

As a local anthropologist explained to me, the Punakawans represent ancient Javanese gods, a resilient survival of pre-Hindu religions. They became servants of the heroes and deities of the colonizers but they transcend them. Their low status allows them to pass blunt, irreverent judgments on the values and icons of the new order. According to the tradition, Somar is indeed a deity who was born from a primordial egg. While his twin brother decided to dwell in heaven, he chose to marry an earthly woman. Now he toils with his handicapped sons in the service of their masters, but they maintain their freedom of judgment and cast a critical eye on them and their actions. The public loves the Punakawans and at regular intervals during their performances throws gifts to them in the form of cash, packages of cigarettes, and other valuable items.

Surakarta, July 23, 1993. I am travelling in search of Wayang Orang performances with my assistant, Mr. Eko Setyo Utomo, who studies English and semiotics at the University of Indonesia in Jakarta. He is a native speaker of Javanese, the language used by the Punakawans, which is markedly different from Bahasa Indonesia, the official language of the country. We are lucky to find that there will be a performance later in the day. We take our seats in good time in front of the stage, which is built under a light wooden construction with open sides to let breezes cool the tropical atmosphere. Dusk is coming. Some gamelan is being played nonchalantly by the musicians as they take their places in front of the stage. They will accompany the performance. As is usual in traditional performances in Asia, there is no formal announcement. The audience is slowly eased into the action. I ask Eko if it has started yet. He laughs. Night has fallen suddenly. Some brilliantly dressed actors are arguing at the side of the stage. Eko is not sure what their problem is. The plot will progressively emerge. They are characters from the Mahabharata. Eko follows attentively. He will explain all this later. Some tourists take photos or record the music on bulky tape recorders. We will do the same when the Punakawans appear. Here they are, walking awkwardly to the music of the leitmotiv that signals their entrance. They greet a very tall character who stayed on the stage when the others left. Eko whispers in my ear, "This is Narada."

The divine hero declares that his current incarnation is as a giant. The Punakawans greet him. Petruk asks him if it is the rainy season now in heaven and if there is lots of mud. Bagong intervenes: "Probably. This is why you wear these strange shoes, because of the mud." They make fun of Narada's costume. Narada protests that it never rains in heaven. Petruk remarks that the god's shoes resemble Aladdin's Arabic shoes. Narada replies that thanks to these shoes he can fly, walk on water, and step on fire, although, he adds, "This is not because of the shoes, but because I am a god." They keep discussing the strange costume Narada wears. "Well, you have to wear this kind of dress if you are a Narada. If I do not wear it, the Dalang will be angry." The Dalang is the puppet master. I note that this refers to the shadow version of the play rather than its stage implementation and that, in addition, it is a metadiscursive remark because Narada now expresses himself as an actor rather than the god he represents. The brothers pity him because his giant costume forces him to stand uncomfortably straight, with his head facing upward. Gareng says that he worries because Narada cannot look down to the floor. Bagong decides to test if this is the case and shouts, "Uncle, there are ten thousands rupiahs on the ground!" Narada bends his torso, but his head is still facing upward. The movement nevertheless suggests that this lofty god is greedy. Gareng exclaims, in reaction to Bagong's words, "Ah! We also can lie to the gods!" thus implying that they must not be omniscient if Narada did not know that there was no money on the ground. Narada replies, "Yes, I also need some money." Whether he is speaking as an actor or a god is ambiguous. Bagong asks, "When will you retire from your duty as Narada?" Narada: "There is no retirement if you are a god!" The brothers make further jokes about the gods. They point out that Somar is also a god but that they are different in heaven. Petruk gives his opinion about what they eat in heaven: "Smoke (incense) and flowers. But Somar likes to eat lots of substantial food. He prefers human cooking." "Of course," says Narada, "we have separate duties. Somar lives on earth and I have to do my job in heaven." Eko points out that Narada at times uses the low-level language of a common man instead of the noble style that would be appropriate for the divine nature of the character he represents. This is what makes people laugh.

In spite of the cultural gap and the incommensurability of the references that stand between the European clowns and the Punakawans, we can notice some striking similarities in their treatment of social status and rules of propriety. The Javanese "clowns" are down-to-earth and are spokesmen for the natural order as opposed to the ideological pretense of the theological or political icons they mock. Although Somar is supposed to be a god, he is an autochthonous deity who has taken the side of the earthly nature. The corrosive humor of his sons reveals the vanity, and ultimately the unreality, of the pompous heroes and deities of the Hindu traditions that Javanese people have inherited. Specialists in Hinduism might point out that Narada is not, properly speaking, a god but instead a sage who attained a quasi-divine status through his merits. The Wayang takes some liberties with such details. But there is more. We can recognize in the above rendering of a Punakawans performance the clowns' typical drive toward metadiscursive strategies in the form of self-reference and disclosure of the artificiality of their very art. Narada deflates his own godly status through speaking at times like a poor actor in need of money. This implies that the Punakawans are no different. They are also actors, but it is important to note that they are endowed with the power of ritual agents. Their role in society might cast a revealing light on the European clowns, who are not strangers to the sacred, as we saw in Chapters 8 and 9. We will discover in the next account of a Punakawans performance that the resemblance extends to the deconstruction of the language and social rules that govern their cultural context.

Jakarta, September 15, 1993. The performance has already started when we arrive at the Bharata Theater. Beating the late afternoon traffic in the center of Jakarta is quite challenging even in a motor rickshaw that dangerously meanders through lines of speeding cars and trucks. The stage is brightly lit, and three heroes declaim their misfortunes in front of an Indian palace painted on the canvas that hangs at the back. Eko quickly informs me that these are two of the Pandawa brothers, Bima and Arjuna, and the son of the latter, Abhimanyu, who has just been entrusted with some task and then left alone. At the end of his anguished soliloquy, the Punakawans enter the stage from the right and greet their master. As the audience laughs, I turn to Eko with an inquisitive look. He refers me to a previous conversation we had about the complex system of address in Javanese, which depends on the relative status of those who interact. Bagong just ignored these rules and informally addressed the hero. Although the Punakawans try to use the proper words to express their greetings, they occasionally fall back on the language they would use with their equals, thus ignoring the hierarchical order. This code of social behavior is so strict that transgressing it in the situation depicted on the stage is found hilarious by the spectators. But the clowns, notably Bagong, can get away with murdering politeness, so to speak, and they introduce an irreverent casual mood. As Abhimanyu looks despondent, they decide to entertain him with some songs they believe will make him happy. This provides them with an opportunity to interact with the members of the gamelan orchestra as they discuss which songs to play. They crack jokes with them and make fun of their reputation of promiscuity. Gareng shouts, "What kind of music is this? It is too hectic. Calm down, man." The musicians promptly reply by producing funny sounds and melodies that transgress the musical cannon, thus mimicking the Punakawans' flouting of the pragmatic rules of the Javanese language.

The musicians suddenly play a faster rhythm, and Bagong starts quaking convulsively, as if he were in a trance. Gareng asks, "Hey, Bagong! Is that a dance or an attack of epilepsy?" Bagong claims that he does not care and dances to any kind of music, thus showing a lack of cultural discrimination. He takes his pleasure where he finds it. Petruk dismisses this attitude and tells him that he does not have good taste. To this reproach Bagong replies, "Yes, I have good taste, but I don't use it." In the meantime, Somar and the others have started singing for Abhimanyu to try to cheer him up. Each one has a different song; some are well known, but they change the words in a way that makes people laugh. Then they reproach the musicians, claiming that their music is getting worse because there is a new Dalang. All Wayang performances are presided over by a Dalang, the puppeteer, storyteller, and master of ceremonies, who is endowed with a kind of priesthood status. This is not the kind of person to whom one would normally show disrespect, if only because Dalangs are credited with magical power. But Gareng takes aim at his inexperience, and Somar pleads for clemency: "Everybody has to learn." As Eko remarks, this one is actually a new, younger one. This is a real-life situation, which adds to the transgressive dimension of the performance. The Dalang becomes the butt of Somar's jokes. I scribble "metadiscourse" in my notebook, because it is obviously an instance of relativizing the sacred by associating it to a skill, if not a trade. Like the clowns of the circus, the Punakawans contextualize their performance, taking advantage of unexpected events and circumstances and turning them into fodder for their jokes.

The Punakawans resume their songs, whose tune and words they mangle, or simply hum when they have forgotten a line, as Petruk notes. From time to time, they also reverse the order of syllables and make outrageous puns, or they vary the regular intonations, or add phonemes to produce unexpected meanings. Eko comments that the laughter we hear just then was caused by Bagong addressing Abhimanyu as Abhimanyu-k. "Manyuk" happens to refer to impolite people. Petruk scolds Bagong: "Why did you use that word? It is a bad word!" "What do I have to say?" asks Bagong. Petruk: "Please give me your order, my Lord; this is enough." Bagong turns toward Abhimanyu and repeats the sentence verbatim, including "this is enough." Gareng tries to improve the teaching of Petruk by telling Bagong where to put commas between words. The result is still worse, because Bagong adds the word "comma" in the sentence.

Later during this interlude, Somar undertakes to educate Bagong: "You should say, 'My Lord Abhimanyu, please kill me.' Now repeat that sentence." Bagong: "My Lord Abhimanyu, please kill Somar." The ambiguities of the *indexical use of the pronouns trigger a quarrel. Somar had indeed said "kill me," meaning Bagong. But because Somar himself uttered the sentence, "me" was referring to Somar, in Bagong's opinion. The dispute escalates, and Bagong blames his father for having neglected him: "Even my circumcision, I had to do it myself." Eko explains that in Java the tradition is to circumcise the boys around the age of 9 to 11. Petruk intervenes: "It is easy to do that with a door." Bagong protests: "No! This is horrible. My penis would be cut off." After this sexual joke, which elicits laughter, Bagong moves toward Abhimanyu and sits down close to him. Somar takes exception to this: "Don't sit so close to your master." Bagong claims that he and his master are like the two sides of a leaf, but he adds, "Of course, I am on the other side of the leaf." This breaking of proxemic rules does not fail to cause the audience to laugh.*

Interested readers can get a glimpse of the Wayang Orang performances by visiting two YouTube videos that offer two successive installments of a play involving both Hindu heroes (including Abhimanyu) and the Punakawans. In the latter's interlude, first the three sons of Somar sing funny songs before performing slapstick comedy in which Bagong, whose persona is similar to the auguste of the Western circus, is the butt of his brothers' jokes. He is, however, the one who triggers the loudest laughter from the audience. His heavier makeup makes him stand apart from the others. With the father's arrival, the dynamics of the interaction is transformed. The resemblance of Somar's makeup with the whiteface is noticeable. Although the scene represented with Abhimanyu toward the end of the second video is not the one I have described, it conveys a sense of the staging of these plays and the appearance of the characters. Note that the makeup patterns that can be observed on the Punakawans' faces are specific to these particular actors but implement combinations that are governed by the same algorithm for each role. No two Bagongs look exactly alike, but the audience always identifies Bagong as well as the others. As we have seen in Chapter 1, the same applies to the auguste and whiteface of the traditional European circus.

http://www.youtube.com/watch?=o6rZ5UFkAFQ

http://www.youtube.com/watch?v=nmodU5tg2cc

In the gags described above, we can easily recognize the logical structure that was elucidated in Chapter 4. At the beginning of the Punakawans' episode, the Mahabharata hero Abhimanyu is addressed by Bagong. The collocation of two characters who are maximally distant on the social scale—all the more so as Bagong is the lowest of the Punakawans—entails some definite expectations in the representation of a society obsessed with status ranking.

In many respects, the stage reflects the cultural landscape of its context but also provides the possibility of symbolically manipulating the system that regulates social interactions.

First, there is no symmetry in the norm: the master addresses the servant to give him orders or to scold him. The latter role is to reply either with appropriate words or gestures. As Eko pointed out to me, the Javanese lexicon is a powerful tool for signifying dominance and subservience, respect for the elders, and equality among peers. He gives an example: if he wants to refer to "water" in a conversation with his grandmother, he must use a word that is different from the one he commonly uses with his siblings and classmates. The premise is thus posited by juxtaposing Abhimanyu and Bagong. The expected argument is the production of appropriate language and gestures. Bagong's behavior is not only deviant but amounts to a systematic denial of the constraints to which individuals are expected to submit. This is expressed linguistically and, at the end of the above episode, in terms of the management of space. In fact, Bagong's latest remark about being so close to Abhimanyu that they are like the two sides of a leaf evokes the dialectic of complementary concepts: master and slave presuppose each other, like father and son. Neither of the two words has any meaning without the other. This mutual logical or semantic necessity can easily lead to the subversive notion that the master depends on the slave for his very existence. From the semiotic point of view, the formulation provided by Bagong is the same as the one through which Saussure attempted to define metaphorically the relationship between the signifier and the signified to convey the idea that the two must be thought inseparable and cannot exist alone. The information delivered by Bagong is maximal, because it aims at the very heart of the sociocultural system within which the performance is taking place.

Secondly, we can note that until we reach this latter blow, the Punakawans have mounted their subversive attack in a staggered manner. They applied their corrosive humor to the language, spatial, and musical orders. Moreover, their mocking of the Dalang showed that the performance order itself was not immune to their critical discourse. They used a dialogic method to make their subversion efficient. Through the guise of the bickering among them, mostly scolding Bagong by reminding him what the rules were, they gave enhanced visibility to the subversive behavior they displayed with impunity.

The gentrification of clowning

Probing clowning beyond the cultural borders of European clowns has shown that, on the one hand, "exotic" performances require an exegesis because linguistic and cultural barriers are not permeable to humor. On the other hand, this excursus has demonstrated that the syntax of clowning is probably grounded in a universal human ability to question the tacit constitutive rules of the socioeconomic systems that define cultures. Such virtual deconstructions, however, are achieved in the form of ritual performances by individuals whose status within their society is marked, downgraded, or otherwise stigmatized. These performers can even be considered as outcasts or scapegoats, as we saw in Chapters 8 and 9, while remaining objects of fascination that are both feared and admired. Of course, the examples presented in this chapter are far from doing justice to the full scope of clowning on a global scale. Others have more fully documented this quasi-universal phenomenon. For instance, to name only a few, William Mitchell (1992) edited a collection of articles covering performance humor in the South Pacific; Lee Siegel (1987) has fully documented the comic tradition in India; Amin Sweeney (1972) has provided a detailed account of the Malay shadow-play, including the role of clowns in the narratives derived from the Hindu epic tradition. But informal clowning is also abundantly present outside the specialized institutions described in the ethnographic literature. See also Scott-Kemball (1970).

Clowning behavior indeed seems attractive to many who try to emulate the jesters in family and social settings. Telling jokes or acting funny makes some individuals popular among their relatives and friends. But there is a wide gap between making the company laugh and entertaining large audiences as a professional on a daily basis. However, amateur or professional clowning deceptively appears to be within the reach of anybody. All the other circus skills require long training and constant practice, and involve serious risks. During the twentieth century, some large circus corporations or state-sponsored circuses offered training in the art of clowning. Running off to the circus by registering in a clown college was appealing, and many youngsters learned the basic tricks of the trade under the tutelage of retired artists. They were schooled in how to create clown makeup, how to dress, how to manipulate props such as balloons and magic flowers, how to fall without breaking one's neck, and how to slap another clown without actually touching him or her. All this know-how allowed the graduates of these "colleges" to play a part in some shows. Only a few, however, achieved artistic excellence through personal development and challenging experience in the real business world of the circus. Professionals usually cast a critical eye on these newcomers to the traditional arena.

Whether this phenomenon can be characterized as the gentrification or the democratization of clowning is debatable. However, it is a fact that there now exists in the Western world a large population of semiprofessional and amateur clowns, both male and female, who engage in entertaining specific audiences at particular occasions such as birthday parties, charity performances, marketing campaigns, parades, and other public events. By necessity, their acting is brief and mostly solitary. They play a few tricks to cheer the party and add extravagant sounds and colors to the setting. They can take advantage of their makeup to behave obnoxiously at times toward some individuals, just for fun, to make people laugh. For instance, they may produce grotesque imitations of some of the guests' ways of walking or talking. They may steal a hat or a handbag and pretend to extract unexpected objects from them. But they are drastically limited in their antics by the rules of proper social behavior, which they can transgress only to some extent. What is permissible is, of course, determined by the culture within which they perform. It could be claimed that rather than actually clowning, they symbolically represent the world of clowns we have documented in this book. Their stunts are not clown acts, either traditional or novel, which require a longer span of attention and can capture the interest of adult audiences. These amateur clowns cannot be considered on a par with the professional circus artists we have encountered in the chapters of this volume. Party clowns, though, lend an air of exceptionality and freedom to family and social celebrations because they evoke the festive atmosphere of the circus. They carry with them some of the symbolic capital of the imaginary circus and the fantasies it generates in many people. We cannot forget, however, that some individuals have a kind of psychological allergy to clowns, whose persona and behavior they resent and fear, as we pointed out in Chapter 1.

It is not enough to sport a red nose and a green wig to sustain the attention of an audience, as restricted and familiar as it may be. The effect of surprise quickly wears off. It takes some skill to create a consistently comic persona and elicit some genuine laughter. The institutional teaching we mentioned above definitely provides students of clowning with some competence, even if it does not lead all of them to a full-fledged professional career. In some instances, this training has provided a credible alternative to the traditional circus way of becoming a clown through the family transmission of the tricks of the trade. In fact, it has been a fertile ground for stimulating creativity and the spreading of innovations in the art of clowning.

Clowns with a mission

Smiling and laughing are generally considered signs of joy and pleasure. It suffices to attend a circus show and to observe the facial expressions of the members of the audience, in particular the children, during a clown act to be convinced that clowning indeed causes most people to feel carefree and happy when they watch such performances. Laughing is contagious, and it often happens that gags generate waves of irrepressible laughter and create collective euphoria.

However, there are many places in the world where joy and pleasure are in short supply and where children suffer the worst hardships of life. Hospitals, refugee camps, war-devastated regions, and factories that thrive on cheap labor are such places. International agencies, private foundations, and charity organizations strive to bring some relief to these children deprived of the amenities of life because of their social conditions or poor health. There are many national and international associations whose goal is to provide food and medical care to those who need it most. But some people with clowning abilities and experience believe that once the basic necessities are fulfilled, something might still be missing: being able to enjoy happy moments and to laugh within a congenial context. This is why volunteer clowns are called upon to help cheer up those who have no opportunity to smile. Professional clowns often pay visits to children's hospitals as a part of their circuses' endeavor to show concern for the communities they visit. Physically challenged children are often given free access to the shows. But volunteers provide the bulk of clowns on a mission.

The best-known organization in North America to provide such a service is the International Shrine Clown Association, which sponsors circus shows in exchange for a percentage of their profits being donated to hospitals with an emphasis on children's medical care. The association's website encapsulates its members' commitment to the welfare of children in the following sentence: "No man stands so tall as when he stoops to help a child." This group holds regular conventions at state, national, and international levels, and organizes competitions on makeup, balloons, and skits. Group photos taken on the occasion of these congresses show all the participating members dressed as clowns, with individual makeup and costumes whose diversity nevertheless reflects the same basic principles we have discussed in this volume with respect to the auguste. The European whiteface clown type, though, is conspicuously absent for the obvious reason that its authoritarian persona would not fit into the jovial informality conveyed by these amateur clowns, who may be civil servants, businessmen, or professionals in real life but fully engage in their redemptive mission when they don their jester mask and garb.

The interface between clowning and children in the hospital context goes a step further when the rationale for these interactions is therapeutic rather than simply ludic. Some claim that cheering up sick children can contribute to curing them. This controversial approach has given rise to theories and experiments. The First International Conference on Pediatric Hospital Clowns: Reflections on Research and Training was held on October 17–18, 2014, in the Meyer Children's Hospital of Florence, Italy (http://www.meyer.it/clownconference/).

Its rationale clearly spells out the philosophy of the clowns' therapeutic mission: "Amongst the different approaches that, since the late 1980s, have been pursuing the growing quality of pediatric hospitalization or the minimization of its negative impact on the child's welfare and development, those that combine art, playfulness, and humor—more specifically the hospital clowns' interventions—have been revealing very promising benefits. Concomitantly, many hospital clowning organizations have been flourishing all over the world, as well as training and research in the field." The issues addressed in the proceedings of this program included "the clowns' initial and continuous training, coaching and supervision; the boundaries between the artistic and therapeutic role of hospital clowns; the clown's place in the ward." Information on research and events on this topic can be found on the website of the Healthcare Clowning Research International Network, a scholarly association based in the Netherlands that is dedicated to the study of healthcare clowning (http://humorlab.nl/herin). A detailed account of the humor movement in health institutions can be found in *The Primer of Humor Research* (Raskin 2008). In *The Humor Code*, Peter McGraw and Joel Warner devote a full chapter to this issue and document among other efforts the Gesundheit Global Outreach, another humanitarian enterprise that endeavors to alleviate children's misery, in this case by exporting American humor to the Amazon (2014: 175–196).

The purpose of these ventures is certainly commendable, but the enthusiasm of its proponents and practitioners is not based on hard evidence. It is indeed unthinkable that such therapeutic interventions would be tested following the same rigorous protocols as those that are conducted for medical treatments. In spite of an abundant literature, so little is understood about the relationship between the physiology of laughter and its meaning (Gervais and Wilson 2005) that attempting to generate humorous or hilarious situations in hospitals in order to alleviate or even cure some diseases is at the very least risky. Some specialists of laughter research tend to cautiously dismiss therapeutic claims in this regard in the absence of hard proof, but agree that the social setting created by these clowns could indeed prove to be conducive to improving patients' moods, at least for some individuals (e.g., Provine 2012: 63–64).

Not everybody, indeed, reacts positively to the appearance and antics of clowns. We discussed in the first chapter the well-documented phobias clowns may cause. Handing over balloons, toys, and candies or doing instant gags and skits requires minimal skills that cannot compare with the demands and sophistication of true clown performances. Projects such as "Clowns without Borders" are paved with good intentions in their emulation of "Doctors without Borders," but they are largely utopian and rest upon a superficial understanding of clowning. There is also a pervasive misconception about laughter as the unqualified expression of joy and happiness. Hospitalized children as well as adults generally suffer from ailments that can make laughing painful, and they are often under medications that alter their mood and make them insensitive to humor. For all these reasons, many health institutions ban clowns from their wards.

From the point of view of this book, it is interesting to witness the contemporary therapeutic application of clowning. It is an obvious extension of the ritualistic nature of clown performances, albeit in a toned-down, almost-homeopathic, formula. No substance is involved, though, in the assumed cure provided by hospital clowns. They simply behave in an odd manner and manipulate special artifacts. Their impact is purely psychological, similar to the mode of action of traditional shamans. It is tempting to consider that circus clowns engage in mass therapeutic sessions when they bring down the house with the antics and gags they perform in the ring. There is no doubt that most people in the audience feel better after the clowns make them laugh. But what is this mysterious laughter that everybody experiences and nobody truly understands?

Conclusion: Contribution to the Theory of Laughter

What is laughter?

As our exploration of the world of clowns comes to a close, a discussion of the nature and meaning of laughter is in order. Laughter is indeed the lifeline of professional clowning. This is the currency of the trade. Clowns who fail to elicit laughter simply disappear. The narratives, skits, and gags that have been described in the chapters of this book were selected because they caused their audiences to laugh every time I attended their performances, with the exception of the failed Russian act discussed in Chapter 10, which offered telling evidence of the cultural sensitivity of clowning. But laughing is not a behavior easy to understand, despite being experienced by most humans worldwide. All who have tried to come to grips with this familiar phenomenon have voiced frustration and proposed theories that were merely tentative. A thorough review of the abundant literature on this topic led its authors to define this field of research as a theoretical quagmire: "In spite of 30 years of intense research the scientific study of laughter and humor is still in its infancy relative to other comparable subjects in emotions and communication research" (Gervais and Wilson 2005: 397). This domain of inquiry is characterized, in their own words, by "empirical neglect and theoretical incompleteness" (397). The following decade witnessed more publications, but laughter is still a conundrum that proves very hard to crack (e.g., Parvizi et al. 2009; Provine 2012). This concluding chapter does not claim to provide a final answer to the many questions raised by laughter, but simply to bring to this field the benefits of an ethnographic research into the social contexts in which laughter is the main commodity. From this point of view, a circus tent under which clowns make an audience laugh can be construed as a quasi laboratory in which reasonably controlled observations can be made, although truly scientific knowledge can only be reached with investigative means unavailable to me during these largely impressionistic, albeit methodical, investigations. A brief review of contemporary research into laughter and the earlier philosophical speculations that are still quoted in the literature will help outline the epistemological landscape to which this chapter endeavors to make a small contribution.

Physiologists describe laughter as a syndrome of neuromuscular events that broadly correspond to the account provided by Charles Darwin: "The sound of laughter is produced by a deep inspiration followed by short, interrupted spasmodic contractions of the chest, and especially of the diaphragm. [...] From the shaking of the body, the head nods to and fro. The lower jaw often quivers up and down [...] During laughter the mouth is open more or less widely, with the corners drawn much backwards, as well as a little upwards; and the upper lip is somewhat raised" (Darwin 1872: 199). Chapter 8 in Darwin's *Expression of Emotions in Man and Animals*, from which this brief quotation is excerpted, addresses a range of emotions from joy to devotion. Laughter is assessed from a phenomenological point of view on a continuum from smiling to extreme laughing. Darwin provides an account of these observable dynamic facial patterns in terms of the muscles that are contracted to create them. He points out that although laughter is associated with high spirits, expressions of joy, and ludicrous ideas, laughing is also produced by mechanical means such as tickling. Moreover, mentally impaired humans are prone to outbursts of senseless laughter. Darwin also refers to ethnographic evidence showing that this puzzling behavior can be triggered, among some other "races," by situations and events that can hardly be construed as joyful or comical. Darwin's discussion of laughter is inconclusive because it lacks any kind of explanation, evolutionary or otherwise. He simply quotes Herbert Spencer, who considers in his *Physiology of Laughter* that laughter is a discharge of nervous energy when the mind is excited by pleasurable feelings or events and thoughts that are unexpected: "[...] a large amount of nervous energy, instead of being allowed to expend itself in producing an equivalent amount of the new thoughts and emotion which were nascent, is suddenly checked in its flow [...]. The excess must discharge itself in some other direction, and there results an efflux through the motor nerves to various classes of muscles, producing the half-convulsive actions we term laughter" (Spencer 1863: 114).

We find the same kind of hydraulic metaphor in Sigmund Freud's attempt to come to grips with the problem of laughter in relation to jokes (Freud 1991 [1905]). In fact, Freud quotes Spencer in support of his argument, although the gist of his explanation is markedly different. Because the constraints of the social order block the free expression of the sexual and aggressive drives of individuals, humor is the outlet that makes it possible to articulate these natural pulsions. It is a socially acceptable way to rebel against oppressive norms. Like dreams, jokes condense meanings and swap categories. Jokes are disguised ways of expressing deep repressed desires even if they are perceived as mere ludic wordplays. This, according to Freud, explains the gratification caused by jokes. Let us note, however, that in Freud's theory, laughter is taken for granted and jokes are analyzed as texts that come alive in social interactions. He uses phonology, syntax, and semantics to show how jokes are constructed and deliver the relief of revolt without exposing oneself to retaliations (Billig 2002).

Henri Bergson's three essays on laughter, later published as a book, endeavor to uncover the meaning of the comic (1911 [1900]). He successively addresses the comic in general, the comedy of forms and the comedy of movements, and the expansive force of the comic. For him, laughter is a human characteristic that is essentially social and results from the cognitive assessment of situations and events. Bergson has in mind comedy that represents human behavior in fictive situations on the stage. He finds it difficult to understand how the mere perception of absurd acts or illogical reasoning could elicit by itself the noisy reaction of laughter. Therefore, the explanation of its meaning must be found in its social function. Laughter is a social gesture, an aggressive way of controlling asocial deviance that could jeopardize the harmony of civilized life. It intimidates the transgressors through humiliating them. Correcting wrongs through laughter is an old classical principle that Bergson endorses. An anomaly to which he pays special attention is the contrast between the adaptive spontaneity of life and the rigidity of mechanisms: the comic arises when something mechanical appears in something living. There is for him a significant analogy between the conception of a comedy scene and the crafting of a toy such as a jack-in-the-box. This theory also applies to verbal jokes, which he considers kernels of comedies. In brief, laughter is the guardian of commonsensical norms that maintains social harmony and controls deviance.

The meaning of laughter

"What does laughter mean?" Thus starts Bergson's essay. But, as we saw in the previous section, he merely proposed an assumed social function based on speculations rather similar to those developed by Freud, who, incidentally, mentioned Bergson's theory in his own book. Freud, though, was concerned with psychological explanations, whereas Bergson mostly dwelled on sociological considerations. Drawing from his own experience, Freud used an abundant corpus of Jewish jokes to proceed with his demonstration. Bergson relied on ad hoc examples and thought experiments cast in light of his hypotheses. His often-quoted example of someone slipping on a banana peel suggests that we laugh because "something mechanical" invades "something living." But this hypothesis glosses over the fact that our reaction depends on who this person is. It is certain that the fall of a pompous man who slips without seriously hurting himself can be comical, but if this is a frail elderly person or a pregnant woman, we are more likely to feel empathy and rush to rescue the victim of this accident. Darwin himself referred only to anecdotal evidence and commonsense knowledge in the brief chapter he devoted to laughter among other positive emotions.

These three beacons of early speculation on the nature of laughter stand out because they are the first attempts in modern times to take this common human behavior seriously and elevate it to a serious topic of philosophical discussion, to the point, for the latter two, of devoting a full book to this topic. It is noticeable, however, that their opinions on the meaning of laughter were not grounded on actual research but developed hypotheses on the basis of scant evidence and commonsensical assumptions. It is symptomatic that Freud alludes to clowns in a single sentence in the third part of his book, to note that we laugh because of their exaggerated and pointless gesticulations. This certainly does not do justice to the rich repertory of skits and slapstick comedy we have described in this volume, as the readers will undoubtedly agree. Circus clowns were immensely popular in Vienna and Paris at the time when these books were written, but paying scholarly attention to lowbrow entertainers was still considered demeaning. Furthermore, the idea that ethnographic evidence should be an essential part of such inquiries on laughter was alien to the philosophical culture of the time. Dealing with laughter was provocative enough for high-profile philosophers or psychologists. Stooping to the systematic observation of circus performances with the same attention as that granted to Molière's comedies or to witty jokes was well beyond the pale of their intellectual commitments.

The purpose of this book is to document in detail the abundant productions of professional clowns and to show that their performances are more complex and sophisticated than is usually thought. As we have repeatedly pointed out, clowns exist only inasmuch as they create pleasure through causing people to laugh. But the mere correlation of laughter with some crucial moments during a clown performance does not necessarily provide an explanation of why the audience laughs and, more generally, feels euphoric. Darwin's declaration that we laugh when we find something hilarious is a tautology. Similarly, both Bergson and Freud take laughter for granted and search for its function either as a release of nervous or mental energy or as an aggressive behavior designed to correct social deviance; but such reasoning is circular. They ignore altogether the fact that laughter also occurs in the absence of the contexts in which they chose to study this universal human behavior. Laughter does not exactly map onto the situations with which they associate it in order to define its meaning. It is a much broader neuromuscular and social phenomenon that just happens to be triggered by jokes and the antics of clowns, among many other individual and collective circumstances. There is no one-to-one correspondence between humor and laughter, but there is strong evidence that humor triggers laughter. Rather than reducing laughter to an appreciation of the comic and dismissing other occurrences of laughter as irrelevant, we should ask what humor and the other causes of laughter have in common. Instead of asking, like Bergson and others, "What does laughter mean?" perhaps we should wonder whether laughter has any meaning besides being a symptom of some brain processes that transcend the particular instances in which it is observed and can be triggered by a great variety of causes. If indeed, as Robert Provine (2000, 2012) has discovered through empirical research, most laughter is not in response to jokes or humor, laughter is dissociable from gags. In semiotic terms, laughter and jokes are not in a relationship similar to the signifier and signified in language, nor can laughter be considered as the necessary immediate index of jokes. We must hypothesize a middle term, a process that is not exclusive to humor but is triggered by some properties of humor. Perhaps broadening the scope of the inquiry to include pathologies, epidemics of laughter, and social signaling will help pinpoint the actual cause of the laughing usually elicited by circus clowns.

Senseless laughing

If we understand humor as the necessary complement of laughter to the point of constituting its meaning, the occurrence of laughter in the absence of humorous acts or situations is a paradox that is not easy to solve but cannot be ignored, all the more so because most laughter is produced outside humorous contexts (Provine 2000). In such cases, laughter appears to be senseless. Let us consider, for example, two kinds of laughter that do not correlate with humor: pathological laughter and social laughter. During the past two decades, empirical researchers have provided evidence that laughter is a far more complex physiological, psychological, and social phenomenon than was suggested in the pioneering work of Darwin, Freud, and Bergson. Their numerous followers have not added much to their early theoretical views. Gervais and Wilson (2005) have provided the best account of several decades of research on humor and laughter but eventually acknowledged that the results remain inconclusive. Parvizi et al. (2009) reviewed the medical literature of the previous decades that probed the correlations of uncontrollable laughter and tears with lesions in particular parts of the brain. As they point out, the early evidence came from the autopsies of patients who had suffered strokes, and the results were rather imprecise and tentative. But with the advent of neuroimaging methods, the localization of infarcts that correlated with unmotivated laughter became more precise, albeit still inconclusive.

Nevertheless, a better understanding now seems within reach mainly because it is possible to elicit laughter by stimulation of precise regions of the brain. The natural complement of these investigations is obviously to identify individuals who have lost the capacity of laughing as a consequence of lesions, as this would be as significant from the point of view of neuroanatomy as the effect of the destruction of inhibitory circuits. What is most relevant in this kind of research is to determine what other behaviors besides laughing are correlated with the parts of the brain whose impairment has an impact on laughing, either to trigger it without apparent reason or prevent it when it should be expected to occur. Some of these pathologies are linked with outbursts of mirthless laughter, crying without a corresponding mood of sadness, or with both laughing and crying at the same time. These two behaviors are indeed associated even in normal subjects who shed tears when they are shaken by irrepressible laughs. The difficulty of probing the neuroanatomy and physiology of laughter is compounded by the lack of convenient animal models, which restricts empirical research to noninvasive observations because only humans can laugh. There is, however, pathological evidence that make possible some progress in the understanding of laughter.

On June 18, 2014, the Advanced Medical Image Center in La Paz, Bolivia, reported that a six-year-old girl who had uncontrollable and inappropriate fits of laughter was diagnosed to have a hamartoma, a small, benign tumor-like growth, pressing on the temporal lobe of her brain. Her *gelastic* seizures (from ancient Greek *gelos* for laughter) stopped after the tumor was surgically removed. Normal laughter is an emotional reflex and its accompanying motor action involves the hypothalamus, the temporal cortex, and several regions of the brain stem. Gelastic nervous breakdowns occur mostly in the temporal lobe, a condition more frequently observed in children who traditionally were considered to be possessed by the demon and were beaten and exorcised (Téllez-Zenteno et al. 2008). Let us note in passing that in traditional Christian cultures, laughter, whether pathological or associated with humor, was attributed to the influence of the devil, whose profile is comparable to the trickster in other cultures. Naturally, the clowns—as transgressors whose business is, as we saw in the successive chapters of this volume, to violate the fundamentals of social constructs and by the same token reveal their fragility and abusive power—were persecuted.

Social laughter is another important behavior that must be taken into consideration. A great deal of laughter, indeed, occurs when people interact in dyads or larger gatherings, quite independently from any forms of humor (Provine 2012). In this context, laughter appears to act as an affiliative signal or a social facilitator (Amoss 2013). Some individuals are prone to burst into laughter under any pretext without displaying any symptom of the pathologies mentioned above. But there are some idiosyncratic ways of laughing that irresistibly evoke asinine or turkey-like signaling as a kind of unaccountable reflex to social stimuli such as stereotypical greetings or remarks about the weather. Moreover, children laugh before they can speak and before their cognitive development could allow them to understand puns and jokes. Finally, it is everyone's experience that, from an early age, tickling elicits laughter. Primatologists have provided evidence that young apes, notably chimpanzees, react to tickling in a way similar to human infants by displaying a half-open mouth and emitting brief and successive panting evocative of the staccato of human laughter. Jaak Panksepp (2007) claimed to have identified similar playful vocalizations in rodents. All this has led some researchers to consider laughter as a signal that bonds people together and also makes possible the noisy mobbing and bullying of scapegoats, two functions that are intimately related.

The social significance of laughter is neurologically grounded in its contagiousness. Bergson noted that laughter always has an echo in groups in which it occurs. This characteristic can easily be observed in the circus when laughter spreads as a wave among the audience, often starting with an individual who bursts into shrieking laughter and creates an instant amplification throughout the public. Provine (2000, 2012) has run experiments among his students that show that even a mechanically caused laughter is contagious. In television sitcoms, canned laughter is a well-known means to prime laughter among the spectators. This fundamental contagiousness accounts for the many cases of epidemics of laughing that have been documented both in the past and more recently (Provine 2012: 39–43) that are not related to humor.

Laughter is also an important communication tool to convey a variety of feelings and attitudes. As a wired-in behavior, it is found in courtship, erotic play, ludic activities, and submissive signaling toward dominant individuals. It also can be produced deliberately under a range of vocal versions to signify sarcasm, irony, or self-deprecation. Social media make great use of hehehe, hahaha, and lol (laughing out loud), most of the time to indicate that what has just been written was not really funny at all.

Laughing as an addiction: A hypothesis and an agenda

The theories of laughter that we have briefly reviewed so far attempt to provide a functionalist rationale for this universal phenomenon. Because it is exclusively human, the general assumption is that laughter is an evolved behavior that is adaptive. Then the next step is to find out what it is good for:

relieving pressure, controlling deviance, bonding with a group, etc. But the belief that whatever natural behavior is found in humans must be adaptive is an evolutionist delusion. Archaeologist Robert Bednarik (2011) has developed a cogent argument to demonstrate that anatomically modern humans carry a heavy baggage of genetic liabilities. It is sufficient that these maladaptive traits happen to be outsmarted or simply balanced by adaptive ones. Natural selection does favor adaptive traits with respect to particular natural and social environments. No adaptation is absolute, and there is always a trade-off. It is not difficult to imagine situations in which the natural contagiousness of laughter can lead to catastrophic consequences. Nevertheless, laughing is generally considered by most humans as a gratifying experience.

Indeed, it is not so much the physical production of laughter by itself that motivates us to seek the stimulation provided by clowns and comedy, but rather the euphoria that accompanies laughter. We now know that this feeling of satisfaction, like any kind of high, is caused by the influx of the neurotransmitter dopamine, which stimulates the reward centers of the brain. The dopaminergic neurons produce this hormone when a vital function such as nutrition or sex has been satisfied.

Heuristically, we can develop the following argument: if it takes a brain event to trigger laughter, we can make a list of the kind of events that have been empirically demonstrated to qualify as physical causes of laughter. These include pathological modifications such as pseudobulbar palsy, tumors, electrical stimulations, neuromuscular stimulations such as tickling, and psychotropic substances such as cannabis (because the smokers of marijuana are known to be prone to bouts of laughter). Where do humor and social laughter fit in this picture? Let us assume that both have to create similar brain events stimulating the same neuromuscular apparatus as the known causes listed above. A plausible hypothesis is that information is involved. While the brain on average processes redundant information that consolidates the status quo or modifies the quantity of information within expectable limits—for instance, whether it rains or snows in winter, whether the appointment is today or tomorrow, whether you take milk or cream in your coffee, and the like—information that reaches levels beyond the thresholds of the expectable are bound to trigger brain changes whose magnitude can potentially be measured. Could these changes be the cause of the stimulation of the brain regions responsible for the neuromuscular production of laughter and the concomitant stimulation of the dopaminergic neuronal systems?

But can the mere quantity of information, irrespective of its nature, suffice to explain laughter in the circumstances in which we can observe this behavior? It can be objected that an explosion, the collapse of a building, an earthquake, and the diagnosis of a fatal disease, for instance, constitute information of great magnitude, inasmuch as they are totally unexpected. These events do not usually trigger laughter. They instantly call upon brain resources more closely related to the fight-or-flee reflex than laughter, or they cause chaotic panic. But if we pay attention to the nature of the information whose quantity may create the conditions for laughter, a brain event that some specialists have associated with a brief epileptic crisis (gelastic epilepsy), we will notice that it concerns exclusively cultural information. Acrobats or wild animal trainers who create information by apparently violating physical or biological laws create anxiety rather than laughter because they evoke primal survival reflexes and empathy. The clowns, by contrast, specialize in transgressing cultural norms.

Are there limits to the range of transgressions they can symbolically represent? In their deliberately humorous but at times insightful book on humor, McGraw and Warner (2014) rightly describe humor in terms of the violation of the norms, but they feel the need to make the distinction between violation and benign violation. They represent these domains as a Venn diagram in which two circles partially overlap to define a region they label "benign violation," which corresponds to humor. Their definition of what is benign, however, is rather fuzzy and impressionistic. All value judgments are relative, and it seems that they refer to the limits of acceptability within a particular culture and within a particular social context as far as jokes are concerned. The same criticism can be addressed to Thomas Veatch (1998), who based his theory of humor on the violation of a "subjective moral principle." These reflections on humor are indeed biased by the fact that the subject of their inquiry is the verbal performance of stand-up comedians, with no consideration for the type of multimodal representation enacted by clowns. This is unfortunately a characteristic of humor research to date. Victor Raskin, for instance, both in his theoretical work on the *Semantic Mechanisms of Humor* (1985) and as editor of the *Primer of Humor Research* does not devote any significant space to circus clowns, their narratives, and their gags.

Keeping this caveat in mind, there is obviously a general agreement that humor of any kind is related to some form or another of transgression. However, these theories do not explain why transgressions that are represented semiotically through language, gestures, and actions trigger laughter and cause euphoria. As we have noted when we analyzed gags as arguments in Chapter 4, humorous behavior produces information that both qualitatively and quantitatively forces the brain to restructure the neuronal connections supporting the cognitive habits that define our cultural norms and constantly generate anticipations. Unexpected outcomes following a familiar premise necessarily create a shock that suddenly blocks the prediction processes upon which our mental life is based. The more information a joke or a gag delivers, the more intense is the upsetting of the preset connections. An approximate metaphor could be that, like a projectile that misses its soft target and hits beside it a hard surface creates vibrations, information that does not perfectly fit expectations similarly disturbs the neuronal networks. This might be the trigger that causes the brief gelastic epilepsy we call laughter. The advantage of this hypothesis is that it complies with the other natural causes of laughter that have been empirically studied, all of which incriminate neuronal disturbances.

The next question to answer is: Why is laughing pleasurable? The hormonal stimulation of the reward centers of the brain could then be a side effect of the mechanical processes of laughter that would activate the production of neurotransmitters such as dopamine. Of course, this hypothesis is counterintuitive, like any scientific discovery usually is. We think we know what laughter is because we experience it intimately. However, phenomenological evidence must be handled with suspicion, because there is no evolutionary necessity that it could yield true knowledge beyond what is required for making decisions on the fly. We can describe humorous laughter, but we cannot yet explain it. Scientific knowledge is always mediated by discovery protocols that lead us to some truths through a temporary cognitive night by blindly sticking to a method. The accidental correlation of laughter and pleasure as a possible explanation of humor is merely a hypothesis, but it is a falsifiable one given the investigative means that are now at the disposal of neuroscientists.

This approach could also account for social laughter, notably in gatherings in which there is necessarily an overload of information caused by the density of interactions. We can also note that laughter always involves at least some amount of sociality and that the latter is a universal source of positive feelings when laughing together helps reinforce ancient bonds and create new ones. This cannot be totally separated from the collective gratification derived from laughing at outsiders, outcasts, or scapegoats.

The interface between laughter and the stimulation of the reward centers by dopamine is well documented in the literature, although the full consequences of this process for the theory of laughter does not seem to have been fully exploited (Iversen et al. 2010). In his discussion of mirthful laughter, Panksepp notes that "[a] subcortical locus of control for affect generation has been long supported by animal studies. Thus, it would seem that in order for cognitive stimuli to provoke laughter, they must interact with critical subcortical circuits, where homologies across mammalian species are more abundant than in cortical regions, especially the association cortices such as the massive frontal and parietal cortical expansions of humans. [...] this does not mean that there will not also be non-affective motor areas for laughter subcortically" (2007: 238). Panksepp points out that this brain region also elaborates some strictly motor components of laughter. "However, these inter-digitate with nearby circuitry that also promotes mirth, as seems evident from the use of deep brain stimulation to alleviate Parkinsonian symptoms" (2007: 238).

Panksepp notes that the regions of the brain implicated in laughter are richly innervated by dopamine circuits. "Since burst firing in brain dopamine neurons is a critically important aspect of anticipatory eagerness and seeking-exploratory urges in the pursuit of pleasures/reward, one could suggest that the anticipatory pleasure and eventual gratifications of funny punch-lines of jokes may reflect sudden engagement of this circuit" (238–239). Panksepp further refers to empirical results in the current literature up to 2007, which link the mechanisms of laughter to the stimulation of dopaminergic neurons.

This perspective raises the interesting issue of the addictive power of humor and laughter that seems to be relentlessly pursued by humans both individually and collectively. After all, we should not forget that cocaine is addictive because it mimics the chemical structure of dopamine. Whether laughter itself is an adaptive behavior or not is irrelevant to a theory of humor. Addictions are run by their own biological logic, and laughter might be attractive only because it generates dopamine, among other neurotransmitters, which creates a sought-for euphoria. It could be contended that laughter is a double-edged behavior, as it can disable someone both socially and physically as well as enhance the popularity and attractiveness of an individual, and the bonding of a group toward a common goal. Many of those who have endeavored to reflect on laughter have been obsessed by its evolutionary significance and have inconclusively struggled to find a function either biological, cognitive, or social that could account for its assumed natural selection (e.g., Hurley et al. 2011). But in spite of the determination of those who want to justify all organs and behaviors through their adaptive advantage, many aspects of living organisms are flukes that just happen to be neutral or to constitute nonlethal liabilities. At the core of any theory of laughter we find an intractable paradox: why some sophisticated cognitive and cultural constructions such as jokes, gags, and clown acts that we can describe with semantic and semiotic precision should trigger gelastic seizures of various intensities that happen to stimulate the dopaminergic systems of the brain. The information shock that their transgressive qualities cause primes brain processes, which trickle down to stimulate some neuronal secretions that certainly did not evolve for signaling an appreciation of humor but instead to indicate satiation pertaining to nutrition and reproduction. This approach might explain why laughter appears to be a jack of all trades, a bundle of side effects, some of which are so irresistible that humans have been defined by philosophers as the animal that can laugh. But they arbitrarily chose only one particular circumstance when laughter occurs. The laughing capacity may be an accident of the entanglement of the brain's circuitries. This view might be considered to be a laughable theory of laughter, but at least it suggests the possibility of being expressed as a set of testable hypotheses.

References

Adolphs, R., 2008. Fear, faces, and the human amygdala. *Current Opinion in Neurobiology* 18 (2): 166–172.

Amoss, R., 2013. *The Good, the Bad, and the Funny: A Neurocognitive Study of Laughter as a Meaningful Socioemotional Cue*. Psychology Dissertations. Paper 123, http://scholarworks.gsu.edu/psych_diss.

Bakhtin, M., 1968. *Rabelais and His World*. Bloomington: Indiana University Press.

Bednarik, R. G., 2011. *The Human Condition*. New York, NY: Springer.

Bergson, H., 1911 [1900]. *Laughter*. London: Macmillan.

Billig, M., 2002. Freud and the language of humor. *The Psychologist* 15 (9): 452–455.

Bolognesi, M. F., 2003. *Palhaços*. São Paulo: Editora UNESP.

Bouissac, P., 1977. From Joseph Grimaldi to Charlie Cairoli: a semiotic approach to humor. In *A Funny Thing, Humour*. A. Chapman and H. Foot (Eds.). London: Pergamon Press, 115–118.

———, 1978. A semiotic approach to nonsense: clowns and limericks. In *Sight, Sound, and Sense*. T. A. Sebeok (Ed.). Bloomington: Indiana University Press, 244–263.

———, 1982. The meaning of nonsense: structural analysis of clown performances and limericks. In *The Logic of Culture: Advances in Structural Theories and Methods*. I. Rossi (Ed.). South Hadley, MA: Bergin, 199–213.

———, 1990. The profanation of the sacred in circus clown performances. In *By Means of Performance: Intercultural Studies of Theater and Ritual*. R. Schechner and W. Appel (Eds.). Cambridge: Cambridge University Press, 194–207.

———, 1992. A laughable theory of laughter. *High Quality* 22: 8–11.

———, 2010. *Semiotics at the Circus*. Berlin: De Gruyter.

———, 2011. Mangas unbound: understanding the cross-cultural diffusion of complex signs. In *The Locality and Universality of Media Geijutsu: Beyond "Cool Japan"*. Hiroshi Yoshioka (Ed.). Tokyo: Fujitsu Research Institute, 43–49.

———, 2012. *Circus as Multimodal Discourse*. London: Bloomsbury Academic.

Bourdieu, P., 1987. *Distinction: A Social Critique of the Judgement of Taste*. Translated by Richard Nice. Cambridge: Harvard University Press.

Bratton, J. and Featherstone, A., 2006. *The Victorian Clown*. Cambridge: Cambridge University Press.

Breton, A., 1924. *Manifestoes of Surrealism*. Translated by Richard Seaver and Helen R. Lane. Ann Arbor: University of Michigan Press.

Bruce, V., A. Cowey, A. W. Ellis and D. I. Perrett (Eds.), 1992. *Processing the Facial Image*. Oxford: Clarendon Press.

Burke, P., 1978. *Popular Culture in Early Modern Europe*. New York: New York University Press.

Carroll, M. P., 1984. The trickster as selfish-buffoon and cultural hero. *Ethos* 12 (2): 105–131.

Cawley, F. S., 1939. The figure of Loki in Germanic mythology. *The Harvard Theological Review* 32 (4): 309–326.

Chevillard, A., 2013. Dans la dynastie des Sosman: Pipo de père en fils pour le meilleur et pour le rire. *Le cirque dans l'univers*. Vol. 251: 28–31.

Darwin, C., 1872. *The Expression of Emotions in Man and Animals*. New York, NY: D. Appleton.

Davison, J., 2013. *Clown: Readings in Theater Practice*. Basingstoke: Palgrave Macmillan.

Diamond, S., 1972. Introductory essay: job and the trickster. In *The Trickster*. P. Radin (Ed.). New York: Schocken Books, xi–xxii.

Duchenne, G. B., 1876. *Mécanisme de la Physiologie Humaine*, 2nd edition. Paris: J. B. Bailière.

Dumézil, G., 1948. *Loki*. Paris: Maisonneuve.

Ekman, P., 1979. *Darwin and Facial Expression: A Century of Research in Review*. New York, NY: Academic Press.

———, 1982. Methods for measuring facial actions. In *Human Ethology*. J. Aschoff, M. von Cranach, K. Koppa, W. Lepennies and D. Plog (Eds.). Cambridge: Cambridge University Press, 169–202.

Ekman, P., W. Friesen and P. Ellesworth, 1972. *Emotion in the Human Face*. New York, NY: Pergamon Press.

Ernout, A. and A. Meillet, 1967. *Dictionnaire Étymologique de la Langue Latine*. Paris: Klincksieck.

Foulc, T. (Ed.), 1982. *Clowns et Farceurs*. Paris: Bordas.

Fowlie, W., 1947. *Jacob's Night*. Lanham: Sheed and Ward.

Fréjaville, G., 1922. *Au Music-Hall*. Paris: Monde Nouveau.

Freud, S., 1991[1905]. *Jokes and Their Relation to the Unconscious*. Harmondsworth: Penguin.

Fridlund, A., 1994. *Human Facial Expression: An Evolutionary View*. San Diego, CA: Academic Press.

Gelfand, M. J. et al., 2011. Differences between tight and loose cultures: a 33-nation study. *Science* 332: 1100–1104.

Gervais, M. and D. S. Wilson, 2005. The evolution and function of laughter and humor: a synthetic approach. *The Quarterly Review of Biology* 80 (4): 395–430.

Hoche, K., T. Meissner and B. F. Sinhuber, 1982. *Die Grossen Clowns*. Königstein: Athenäum.

Hurley, M. M., D. C. Dennett and R. B. Adams Jr., 2011. *Using Humor to Reverse-Engineer the Mind*. Cambridge: Massachusetts Institute of Technology Press.

Hynes, W. J. and W. G. Doty, 1993. *Mythical Trickster Figures: Contours, Contexts, and Criticisms*. Tuscaloosa: University of Alabama Press.

Iversen, L., S. D. Iversen, S. B. Dunnett and A. Bjorklund (Eds.), 2010. *Dopamine Handbook*. Oxford: Oxford University Press.

Izard, C., 1971. *The Face of Emotion*. New York, NY: Appleton Century Crofts.

Kervinio, Y., 2005. *Le Clown*. Etel: L'Aventure Carto.

Lévy, P. R., 1982. Le répertoire clownesque. In T. Foulc (Ed.), *Clowns et Farceurs*. Paris: Bordas. 98–120.

————, 1991. *Les Clowns et la Tradition Clownesque*. Sorvilier: Editions de la Gardine.

Lévi-Strauss, C., 1983. *From Honey to Ashes: Introduction to a Science of Mythology*. Translated by Doreen Weightman and John Weightman. Chicago: University of Chicago Press.

Lipovsky, A., 1967. *The Soviet Circus*. Translated from the Russian by F. Glagoleva. Moskow: Progress Publishers.

Little, K., 1993. Masochism, spectacle, and the "broken mirror" clown entrée: a note on the anthropology of performance in postmodern culture. *Cultural Anthropology* 8 (1): 117–129.

Lutz, S., 1979. *De Circusclown*. Nieuwkoop: Heureka.

Marshall, D. A., 2010. Temptation, tradition, and taboo: a theory of sacralization. *Sociological Theory* 28 (1): 64–90.

McConnell-Stott, A., 2009. *The Pantomime Life of Joseph Grimaldi: Laughter, Madness, and the Story of Britain's Greatest Comedian*. Edinburgh: Canongate.

McCoy, D., 2013. *The Love of Destiny: The Sacred and the Profane in Germanic Polytheism*. Lexington, KY: McCoy.

McGraw, P. and J. Warner, 2014. *The Humor Code*. New York, NY: Simon and Schuster.

McManus, D., 2003. *No Kidding! Clown as Protagonist in Twentieth-Century Theater*. Newark, NJ: University of Delaware Press.

Mitchell, W. E. (Ed.), 1992. *Clowning as Critical Practice: Performance Humor in the* South Pacific. Pittsburgh, PA: University of Pittsburgh Press.

Niedenthal, P. M., M. Mermillod, M. Maringer and U. Hess, 2010. The simulation of smiles (SIMS) model: embodied simulation and the meaning of facial expression. *Behavioral and Brain Sciences* 33: 417–480.

Nietzsche, F., 1973 [1884]. *Thus Spoke Zarathustra [Also Sprach Zarathustra*. Translated by R. J. Hollingdale. New York: Penguin.

Oreglia, G., 1968. *The Commedia dell'Arte*. London: Methuen.

Panksepp, J., 2007. Neuroevolutionary sources of laughter and social joy: modelling primal human laughter in laboratory rats. *Behavioral Brain Research* 182 (2) 231–244.

Parvizi, J., K. L. Coburn, S. D. Shillcutt, C. E. Coffey, E. C. Lauterbach and M. F. Mendez, 2009. Neuroanatomy of pathological laughing and crying: a report of the american neuropsychiatric association committee on research. *Journal of Neuropsychiatry and Clinical Neurosciences* 21: 75–87. http://neuro.psychiatryonline.org/article.aspx?articleid=103630

Pelton, R. D., 1980. *The Trickster in West Africa: A Study of Mythic Irony and Sacred Delight*. Berkeley: University of California Press.

Provine, R. R., 2000. *Laughter: A Scientific Investigation*. London: Viking/Penguin.

————, 2012. *Curious Behavior: Yawning, Laughing, Hiccupping, and Beyond*. Cambridge: Harvard University Press.

Radin, P., 1972. *The Trickster: A Study in American Indian Mythology*. New York: Schocken Books.

Raskin, V., 1985. *Semantic Mechanisms of Humor*. Dordrecht: D. Reidel.

————, (Ed.), 2008. *The Primer of Humor Research*. Berlin: Mouton de Gruyter.

Rausser, F. and H.-P. Platz, 1975. *Cirque, Zirkus, Circo*. Lausanne: Mondo.

Rémy, T., 1945. *Les Clowns*. Paris: Grasset.

————, 1962. *Entrées Clownesques*. Paris: L'Arche.

Renevey, M., 1977. *Le Grand Livre du Cirque*, Vol. II. Genève: Edito-Service.

Riggins, S. H., 2003. *The Pleasures of Time: Two Men, A Life*. Toronto: Insomniac Press.

Rooth, A. B., 1961. *Loki in Scandinavian Mythology*. Lund: Christian Wilhelm Kyhl Gleerups Förlag.

Schillbach, L., S. B. Eickhoff, A. Mojzisch and K. Vogeley, 2008. What's in a smile? Neural correlates of facial embodiment during social interaction. *Social Neuroscience* 3: 37–50.

Scott-Kemball, J., 1970. *Javanese Shadow Puppets*. London: Shenval Press.

Semprini, A., 1991. Old Regnas et le droit chemin: analyse sémiotique et opérateurs topologiques. *Semiotica* 85: 319–333.

Shilling, C. and P. A. Mellor, 2013. "Making things sacred": re-theorizing the nature and function of sacrifice in modernity. *Journal of Classical Sociology* 13 (3): 319–337.

Siegel, L., 1987. *Laughing Matters: Comic Tradition in India*. Chicago: University of Chicago Press.

Singer, T., 2006. The neuronal basis and ontogeny of empathy and mind reading: review of the literature and implications for future research. *Neuroscience and Biobehavioral Reviews* 30: 855–863.

Spencer, H., 1863. The physiology of laughter. *Essays on Education, etc.* London: Dent.

Stacey, D., 2013. Chicky. *King Pole* Vol. 193: 30–32.

Sweeney, P. L. A., 1972. *The Ramayana and the Malay Shadow-Play*. Kuala Lumpur: The National University of Malaysia Press.

Téllez-Zenteno, J. F., C. Serrano-Almeida and F. Moien-Afshan, 2008. Gelastic seizures associated with hypothalamus harmatomas: an update in clinical presentation, diagnosis, and treatment. *Neuropsychiatric Disease and Treatment* 6 (6): 1021–1031.

Towsen, J. H., 1976. *Clowns*. New York, NY: Hawthorn.

Toynton, G. (Ed.), 2011. *Northern Traditions*. Australia: Numen Books.

Veatch, T. C., 1998. A theory of humor. *Humor: International Journal of Humor Research* 11 (2): 161–215.

Verne, M., 1930. *Musées de Voluptés*. Paris: Editions des portiques.

Williams, D., 2012. *The Trickster Brain: Neuroscience, Evolution, and Narrative*. Lanham, MD: Lexington Books.

Index